"Full of life, light and languor, but also of brooding memories . . . his portrait is created out of fragmented reflections, in the same way that an artist might create a mosaic out of colourful mirrored stones"   ANTHONY SATTIN, *Sunday Times*

". . . written with softly spoken elegance, delighting in the simple distillation of his own experience into prose. Part travelogue, part memoir, part discourse on a whole host of other literary wanderers, his writing does not strive for effect, but comes to echo the languor of his subject – the islands of the south-western coast of Italy . . . It includes the pickings of a lifetime's enthusiasms and paradoxes, the windfalls of its reading"

     PHILIP MARSDEN, *Sunday Telegraph*

"Like a conversation with an erudite and entertaining companion . . . a book to be savoured"   RON CLARK, *Herald*

"Ross carries a full cup which overspills with information of a literary kind all along the way . . .[this is] writing of an intelligence through whose searchlit territory an unaccountable multitude of books have passed, each one paying the tribute levied from it by sharp analysis and a retentive memory . . . he quarters every island, views every mountain, visits every beach, and everywhere he is at pains to forge a key of words which makes places his captive territory"   PHILIP GLAZEBROOK, *Spectator*

"It is a relief and a pleasure to read a travel book written in an attractive prose style, one observed with a poet's eye, and, behind the author, a well-stocked, well-thumbed library of all the right books . . . 'If we are travellers at all, we are literary travellers,' Bruce Chatwin claimed of himself and Paul Theroux, at a symposium in London in the 1970s. With this deeply engaging book Alan Ross proves himself to be of that same ilk"

     ROBERT CARVER, *Times Literary Supplement*

"Ross creates a web of old-fashioned charm, mixing reminiscence, literary allusion, digression, straightforward travel diary and belle-lettrism. He swoops in and out of the books and poems he is reading, has read, once read, or is reminded of by the place, until their texts and textures become enmeshed with the reality of his travels. It all works with ease and elegance . . . throughout this unusually enjoyable, learned, good-natured book"

JAN DALLEY, *Financial Times*

"Lyrical and funny by turns"   *Condé Nast Traveller*

"As a distinguished poet and the editor of the *London Magazine*, Ross is superbly well placed to share his experiences with the likes of Neruda, Rilke, Edward Lear, Norman Douglas and Lawrence Durrell, for whom 'Ischia became The Spot'. The fragmentary nature of his writing – in which poetry sits alongside more prosaic observations, and informal connections make for serendipitous revelations – mirrors the ever-changing seascape that confronts him as he drifts through the isles"

LILIAN PIZZICHINI, *Independent on Sunday*

ALAN ROSS was born in Calcutta and spent his childhood in Bengal, arriving in England at the age of seven. He went to Oxford, serving in the Royal Navy during WWII. For 40 years he was a consistently fine editor of the *London Magazine*. Authors whose work has appeared under the London Magazine Editions imprint include: Roy Fuller, Paul Theroux, Tony Harrison, Gavin Ewart, Graham Swift and Hugo Williams. Alan Ross's own books include five poetry collections; three travel books, including *Time Was Away* (illustrated by John Minton) and two volumes of autobiography, *Blindfold Games* and *Coastwise Lights*. *After Pusan* and *Winter Sea*, published by Harvill in 1995 and 1997 are part travel, part memoir, part poetry. Alan Ross died on Valentine's Day, 2001. His selected poems will be published by Harvill in 2002.

Also by Alan Ross

Poetry

POEMS 1942–67
THE TAJ EXPRESS
OPEN SEA
DEATH VALLEY

General

COLOURS OF WAR
A STUDY OF WAR ART 1939–45
THE TURF (EDITOR)
THE EMISSARY
G.D.BIRLA, GHANDI AND INDEPENDENCE

Travel

TIME WAS AWAY (WITH JOHN MINTON)
A JOURNEY THROUGH CORSICA
THE GULF OF PLEASURE
THE BANDIT ON THE BILLIARD TABLE
A JOURNEY THROUGH SARDINIA

Autobiography

BLINDFOLD GAMES
COASTWISE LIGHTS
WINTER SEA
AFTER PUSAN

Cricket

AUSTRALIA 55
CAPE SUMMER
THROUGH THE CARIBBEAN
AUSTRALIA 63
WEST INDIES AT LORD'S
THE CRICKETER'S COMPANION (EDITOR)
RANJI
THE LIFE OF THE INDIAN CRICKETER-PRINCE
GREEN FADING INTO BLUE

Alan Ross

REFLECTIONS ON BLUE WATER

JOURNEYS IN THE GULF OF NAPLES & THE AEOLIAN ISLANDS

With illustrations by

Jane Rye

THE HARVILL PRESS
LONDON

First published in 1999 by The Harvill Press

This paperback edition first published in 2001 by The Harvill Press
2 Aztec Row, Berners Road, London N1 0PW

1 3 5 7 9 8 6 4 2

www.harvill.com

© Alan Ross, 1999
Illustrations © Jane Rye, 1999

Maps by Reginald Piggot

A CIP catalogue record for this book is available from the British Library

ISBN 1 86046 893 4

Designed and typeset in Baskerville at
Libanus Press, Marlborough, Wiltshire

Printed and bound in Great Britain by Mackays of Chatham

CONDITIONS OF SALE

All rights reserved. No part of this publication may be reproduced, stored in a retrieval system, or
transmitted in any form or by any means, electronic, mechanical, photocopying, recording or otherwise,
without the prior permission of the publisher

This book is sold subject to the condition that it shall not, by way of trade or otherwise, be lent, re-sold,
hired out or otherwise circulated without the publisher's prior consent in any form of binding or cover
other than that in which it is published and without a similar condition including this condition being
imposed on the subsequent purchaser

CONTENTS

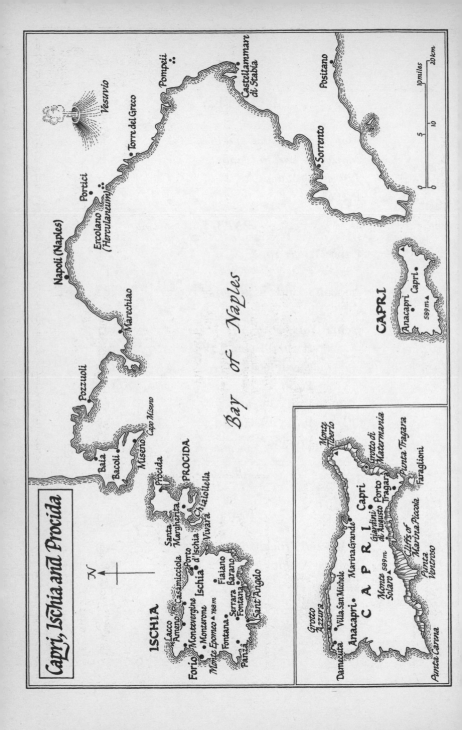

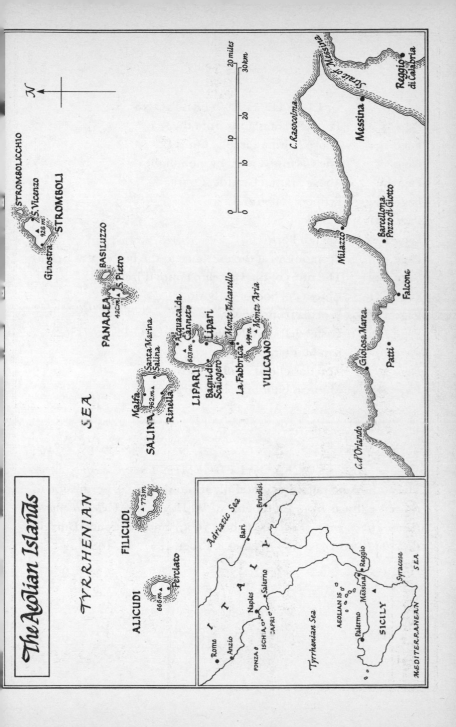

The Aeolian Islands

TYRRHENIAN SEA

STROMBOLI
STROMBOLICCHIO
S. Vicenzo
926 m ▲
Ginostra

PANAREA
BASILUZZO
420 m ▲
S. Pietro

ALICUDI
665 m ▲
Perciato

FILICUDI
773 m ▲

SALINA
Malfa
962 m ▲
Santa Marina
Salina
Rinella

LIPARI
Acquacalda
Canneto
603 m ▲
Lipari
Bagni di
Scalogero
La Fabbrica
Monte Vulcanello
Monte Aria
499 m ▲

VULCANO

Milazzo
Barcellona
Pozzo di Giotto
Falcone
C. Rasocolma
Strait of Messina

Gioiosa Marea
C. d'Orlando
Patti
Messina
Reggio di Calabria

20 miles
30 km
0   10   20
0   10   20

N

Inset map

Rome
Anzio
PONZA
ISCHIA
CAPRI
Naples
Salerno
Tyrrhenian Sea
I T A L Y
Adriatic Sea
Bari
Brindisi
AEOLIAN IS
Reggio
Messina
Palermo
SICILY
Syracuse
MEDITERRANEAN
SEA

LIST OF ILLUSTRATIONS

ACKNOWLEDGEMENTS

The author and publisher gratefully acknowledge the permission to reprint extracts from the poems of W. H. Auden, *Collected Shorter Poems 1927–1957* (Faber & Faber, 1969) and Lawrence Durrell, *Collected Poems 1931–1974* (Faber & Faber, 1957, rev. 1980).

PART I

Preface

ON THE RECOMMENDATION of a brother naval officer, who had long had Italian connections, I first came to Ischia and Procida in 1947. The war was not long over; I had only recently returned from Germany, where memories of Belsen, of ruins and refugees were still too close for comfort. Naples and the islands of the gulf seemed in comparison something akin to paradise.

On my first visit I walked over most of the two islands with a beautiful Polish girl, no stranger to deportations and concentration camps. She died long ago, but the journal I kept – a kind of anatomy of landscape – was an attempt to make sense of the peace and of my own feelings. It is reproduced here with all its limitations and inhibitions of emotion for which topographical description became a substitute.

In the succeeding years I returned many times, with my family and friends, generally to Forio, where villas were cheap. In the 1950s and 1960s Forio became a centre for writers, painters and musicians. We avoided Capri, its days of high fashion in decline.

Eventually, I had my fill of the gulf, such excursions as I could manage taking me to Greece, Yugoslavia, Turkey. In the late 1990s I became curious again about these half-forgotten islands: how much had they changed, been spoiled?

Most especially, Capri, for nearly a century an island of legendary beauty, of scintillating conversation, in which the idle rich, political exiles and others on the wrong side of the law took refuge. The inhabitants had little part in the history of their time except as spectators, hard put to eke out a living from the inhospitable soil.

Their ghosts roam these pages. Deliberately, I returned out of season, when summer islands are once again private, almost unrecognisable in their emptiness. As well as to Capri, I went back to Ischia and the Aeolian islands. You are never out of sight of the sea and its heady presence. Even in winter, this is where blue water properly begins.

Capri: *Winter 1998*

A STRIKE, NOTHING unusual, of the comely, white ferry steamers; so instead of the leisurely, fresh air approach to the island, the gulf fanned out and to be appraised under benevolent sun, there was nothing for it but the *aliscafo*, enclosed, urgent, pressing, its windows so salt-stained that nothing was to be seen beyond the foamy moustaches at the bow. The sea was flat, slightly ridged, the sky a cool blue.

On the port side, growing closer, the scaly extremity of the Sorrentine peninsula; to starboard, receding, the outlines of Ischia and Procida, smoothed out as if under clingfilm.

Few passengers in mid-January, a Japanese couple, a handful of commercial travellers. We cross the seventeen sea miles unescorted, our wake a straight line as if we had been invisibly pulled on a tautening string. In forty minutes we are stopped short by the vertiginous cliffs rising sheer ahead of us. We sidle into the harbour, almost apologetically for our sparse cargo of passengers. In winter this is an island far from its famed image, spectral.

It was not at all the atmosphere that Bunin's Gentleman from San Francisco envisaged, travelling with his wife and daughter in November to live it up in the Old World, the pay-off for years of exploiting thousands of Chinamen in his factories. He had crossed the Atlantic in luxury, the weather foul, but the passengers, rich and extravagantly dressed, soothed, dined, massaged and generally cradled, were mostly immune to the world outside the *Atlantis*. At Gibraltar it cheered up, an Asian prince joined the ship, then, once in the Mediterranean, winter returned. "Waves, large and florid as the tail of a peacock, waves with snow-white crests heaved in the bright lustre of a perfectly clear sky . . . Ischia, Capri, could be seen through the glasses, then Naples herself, looking like pieces of sugar strewn at the foot of some dove-coloured mass; whilst beyond, vague and deadly white with snow, a range of distant mountains."

Naples did not appeal, dirty, wet and dull, "the cigar ends of the fat cab-men, whose rubber rain-capes flapped like wings in the wind, seemed insufferably stinking", the women were disgustingly short-legged and the fish on the quays smelled horrible. The Gentleman from San Francisco, to whom Bunin allots no name, and his wife begin to bicker; they are told on all sides that in Capri it will be different, "there it was warmer, sunnier, the lemon trees were in bloom."

There are few hotels open but we learn the name of one and haul our bags on to the funicular. On the way up branches of lemon trees brush the side of the car, we climb through orange trees, the fruit hanging like light bulbs, then into the silver glimmer of olives. In the piazzetta – Piazza Umberto I – at the top only a handful of people, coat collars turned up, loiter in the space between the three outdoor cafés, a similar number of dogs trotting purposefully among the cane chairs. There is a weak sun, but the air sharp, the sky cloudless.

In summer, this is where everyone hangs out, a perfect stage set, town hall, *campanile*, church – with oriental-style dome and baroque façade – fourteenth-century palace, all whitish or pale biscuit, tiny alleyways running off it and a flight of steps leading up to the terrace below which the gulf is spread out, Ischia, Procida, Vivara all visible. Alberto Sarinio called this terrace, terminus of the funicular, "the anteroom of Capri, a sampling room open to the four winds."

We don't for the moment dawdle up here, but make our way down the steep little Via Vittorio Emanuele, past the Hotel La Palma with its autocratic palms, and then turn sharply in front of the Quisisana, last of the truly grand hotels from Capri's heyday, down the short Via Camerelle with its line of boutiques, Gucci, Hermès, Ferragamo, Grey Flannel, and finally into the lush Via Tragara, which is our destination. This part of the Via Tragara, balancing villas with exotic gardens on one side and a kind of meadow with yellow flowers on the other, is one of the few non-precipitous streets in the island, though where it twists down towards the sea above the Faraglioni it reverts to type.

We find our hotel perched among various layers of terrace; potted plants, orange trees and oleanders at all levels. From our balcony we look through a frieze of palms at sea and sky merging, their different blues barely detectable. We are the only guests.

The Gentleman from San Francisco had no such luck in his passage to the island. Vesuvius was obliterated by fog, the sea was leaden and heaving, Capri was invisible. "The little steamer . . . tossed so violently from side to side that the family from San Francisco lay like stones on the sofas in the miserable saloon of the tiny boat, their feet wrapped in plaids, and their eyes closed."

The Gentleman from San Francisco, unlike his wife and daughter, was not actually sick, but, lying flat on his back, in cloth cap and overcoat, had a ferocious headache. His activities restricted by the bad weather, he had taken to the bottle and become addicted to the *tableaux vivants* on offer in the shadier parts of Naples.

Once on shore, though all were badly shaken, spirits revived. They were greeted with great ceremony by the elegant and frock-coated young proprietor of the hotel, which must have been the Quisisana, his exact double curiously seen in a dream the previous night by the Gentleman from San Francisco, and installed in a suite lately occupied by royalty. The French *maître d'hôtel* introduces himself and announces that lobster, pheasant, roast beef, asparagus etc. along with various other delicacies are on the evening menu. Although the floor is still rocking under his feet, the Gentleman from San Francisco confirms that they will be taking dinner, ordering a local wine and champagne "moderately dry and slightly cooled". Carmela and Giuseppe, celebrated dancers, would perform the tarantella after dinner.

In preparation for the banquet ahead of him the Gentleman from San Francisco shaves and washes carefully, rearranges his artificial teeth and steps into silk underwear, black silk socks and patent leather slippers. Recovered from his seasickness he is by now very hungry, anticipating eagerly his first spoonful of soup, the first sip of wine. Shirt, trousers and cuff-links safely installed, there only remains the exhausting obstacle of the collar studs and stiff collar.

Justice done to his appearance the Gentleman from San Francisco, alerted by the dinner gong, sets off for the reading room to await the appearance of his wife and daughter. "From the darkness came a waft of soft air, and there loomed the top of an old palm tree that spread its boughs over the stars."

In the reading room, having collected a large Manilla cigar from a tray, the Gentleman from San Francisco settles himself into a leather armchair. Casting a cold eye at a grey, untidy German "looking rather like Ibsen in his round silver-rimmed spectacles and with mad astonished eyes", the Gentleman from San Francisco opens a newspaper, begins to glance at headlines about the never-ending Balkan war, when suddenly "the lines blazed up before him in a glassy sheen, his neck swelled, his eyes bulged, and the pince-nez came flying off his nose . . . He lunged forward, wanted to breathe – and rattled wildly."

It is the end of the Gentleman from San Francisco, deprived at the last of all the pleasures and sensual delights for which he had made others slave for so long. The hotel staff, anxious to spirit the body away to avoid upsetting other guests, are foiled by the German, who runs into the dining room yelling in alarm. Meanwhile, attended by fumbling porters and waiters tearing off his clothes, the Gentleman from San Francisco is only too plainly writhing in his death throes. The proprietor's nervous assurance that it is only a fainting fit are to no avail. The diners watch horrified and fascinated as he rolls his head, "rattles like one throttled, and turns up the whites of his eyes as if he were drunk."

The still writhing body is hastily removed to a poky little room, a far cry from the fine suite from which the Gentleman from San Francisco had emerged only minutes earlier. Watched over in silence by his wife, daughter, doctor and various servants, the Gentleman from San Francisco suddenly expires: "his features begin to grow thinner, more transparent . . . with a beauty which might have suited him long ago."

No sooner is death pronounced than the proprietor – does Bunin really mean the manager? – orders the corpse's removal from the hotel, coldly rebuking the wife of the Gentleman from San Francisco, who starts to protest at such callous haste. "If Madame does not like the ways of the hotel, he dare not detain her."

That, more or less, is the end of the Gentleman from San Francisco and of Bunin's gently created moralistic story. The corpse, accompanied by wife and daughter, is borne away to the mainland on the morning steamer, while on the island a party, of which the Gentleman from San Francisco had planned to be a member, is preparing to make the steep ascent of Monte Tiberio, alongside them old beggar-women with sticks and mouse-coloured donkeys with red saddles.

Bunin is not quite finished, however, for he returns to the *Atlantis*, homeward bound to the New World, but this time with the tar-coated coffin of the Gentleman from San Francisco in its hold. The liner passes Capri close to "and to those who were looking out from the island, sad seemed the lights of the ship slowly hiding themselves in the sea's darkness."

On board, despite a snowstorm "booming like a funeral service, rolling up mountains of mourning darkness silvered with foam", there is dancing, and the same handsome young couple, hired for the occasion to provide some romance for mostly ageing passengers, go wearily through their routine, bored with the ship and bored with each other.

I have the book with me, in a translation from the Russian by D. H. Lawrence and S. S. Koteliansky. Published by Leonard and Virginia Woolf at the Hogarth Press, Paradise Road, Richmond, in 1922, the title page bears a pasted-in correction slip. "Owing to a mistake, Mr Lawrence's name has been omitted." There are three other stories in this elegantly produced volume, with a cover whose orange, blue and green chevrons suggest Vanessa Bell, and for these Leonard Woolf adds his own name as translator to that of Koteliansky, Lawrence dropping out.

On our balcony, a solitary gardener busying himself below us, and the boatless sea like a blue cummerbund behind a rigging of sea-pines, I return to Bunin, whose book was a wedding present to me from his publisher in 1949 and has long ceased to exist.

Did Ivan Alekseyevich Bunin ever set foot in Capri? He left Russia in 1920, at the age of fifty, settling in the South of France. A member of a declining noble family, a natural sceptic, he had kept clear of pre-revolutionary activity, though in general sympathy with the views of the movement led by Maxim Gorky, whose publishing house Znariye produced Bunin's first five volumes. Acclaimed initially as a poet, awarded the Pushkin medal three times, Bunin took time to discover that it was in prose that he really wanted to write. He was over forty when stories such as "The Premier of Love" and "Chang's Dreams" began to make a reputation for him. The 1917 Revolution led him to emigrate and he never returned to Russia. None of his later books was published there until after his death.

As a result, the marvellous stories of his middle and late years, most still set in Russia, gained him only a modest number of readers and little money. He was unlucky in his translators and though the Nobel Prize in 1933 helped him financially the outbreak of war in 1939 left him isolated in Grasse.

Bunin has the same skill as Turgenev and Chekhov in immediately establishing a sense of place and arousing curiosity. "Visiting Cards" begins: "It was the beginning of autumn and the steamer *Goncharov* was making her way along the deserted reaches of the Volga." The opening sentence of "At Sea, At Night", "During the night, the ship which was on its way from Odessa to the Crimea dropped anchor outside Eupatoria", rouses similar expectations. The first line of "The Caucasus" is: "Arriving in Moscow I took rooms, furtively, in an obscure lodging house tucked away in an alley close to the Arbat." "Roosya"'s beginning is typical: "At eleven o'clock at night the fast train from Moscow to Sevastopol stopped at a little station beyond Podolsk."

You are in the story straight away. Many of Bunin's stories, whether set in Russia or elsewhere, involve journeys and illicit assignations, snatched moments of love in existences denied it. He was a master of compression, a few pages enough to squeeze the juice out of situations.

Looking out over the orange trees on this crisp January morning I imagine him beginning a story "They left Naples in a hydrofoil that was nearly empty. They had never been here before together and when she first saw the saddle-shaped, indigo outline of Capri she caught her breath. Their problems seemed to drop away." There is no spare flesh in a Bunin story, every detail, in the setting of scene, the description of clothing even, tells. He plays games sometimes with titles. "The Steamer *Saratov*" describes a late-night meeting between an army officer and his mistress. When she tells him she has decided to go back to her husband he shoots her. The ship of the title makes no appearance until the final paragraph: "In December of that same year the steamer *Saratov* of the volunteer fleet was sailing from the Indian Ocean to Vladivostock." On board, sweltering in the heat, are a number of convicts, half-naked and with iron fetters round their ankles. There is no linking passage but simply this: "He, like all the others, was naked to the waist, and his thin body was tanned from exposure . . . Leaning on the handrail, he gazed fixedly at the dark blue water below, lapping the high sides of the ship, and from time to time he spat down into its depths."

"The Gentleman from San Francisco", both in and outside the hotel, suggests high society of a kind, a fashionable meeting place, a general air of bustle. Trans-Atlantic liner-travel, on which the winter season in Europe must have to an extent depended, was at its height at the time of which Bunin was writing. Flying put an end to that long ago, and now from

November to March practically all the hotels are closed. We were lucky to find this one, amongst the most perfectly situated, even half-open. The bar and restaurant are shut. Along the Via Tragara the smart shops are undergoing repair, there is a smell of sawdust, three-ply wood leaning against open doorways, a racket of hammering, planing, sawing.

Every morning, when we get up, we become aware of the angostura light on the cliffs of the Marina Piccola below us, the first delicate, rather hesitant intimation of a new day. This could be a northern island at this time of year, the colours pastel, the air clear, with no suggestion yet of heat.

We called in on our way here at San Remo, to see an Edward Lear exhibition at the Palazzo Borea d'Olmo. It is curious that Lear, who lived in Italy for so long and travelled extensively in Calabria, never seems to have got to Capri. One would have thought that this most dramatic of islands would have been irresistible to him.

On 25 January 1848 – 150 years ago to this day – Lear was in Rome, on his way to Albania and Greece. He writes to Ann Lear: "Sicily is utterly revolted and gone; and we wait daily for certain news . . . Every day brings ugly tidings from Naples, the English are fast leaving it and flooding here. The foolish King will not take warning, and worse events must follow. At Naples all the shops are shut."

In April, however, we find him writing from Malta: "My journey down to Naples by diligence was most extremely pleasant . . . One of my fellow passengers was a Neapolitan noble, exiled for 16 years; when he saw Vesuvius first, he sobbed so that I thought he would break his heart. Naples I found yet more unsettled and excited than I had left Rome. No-one could tell what would happen from one hour to the next . . . As usual, I found numbers of friends at Naples and had dinner invitations for the 6 days I

was to stay. The English fleet being there made a deal of gaiety.
We left the harbour at noon and truly glad was I to be out of
Italy." Malta, from a drawing point of view, had no appeal for
Lear and he was soon on his way to Corfu. But he appears to have
spent six days in Naples and although hypochondriacal and
nervous of seasickness, was not a timid traveller. Perhaps social
distractions were too many or boats too few or the sea too rough.
Whatever, from our point of view, it seems a missed opportunity.

The San Remo exhibition contained several of Lear's most
nourishing watercolours – views of Ain Howara, with its group
of camels in the desert foreground and mere suggestions of
mountains in the distance, Villefranche, La Spezia, an almost
unknown 1878 *View of the Campagna* – but an equal number
of dully grey engravings and stolid oils. Here, though, he would
have loved Capri's ferocious cliffs and rocks, the luxuriant
Giardini di Augusto, the donkeys and honeycomb white houses
packed into hillsides among olives and pines, the distant silhouettes of other islands.

In San Remo, on a Sunday, there was altogether more an air of
people and parade than in Capri's piazzetta. Along the marbled
Corso Imperatrice with its magnificent palms that runs parallel
to the single track railway and the Ligurian sea for two miles,
elegant fur-coated women of all ages and shapes walk their dogs
and menfolk. The marble shines like ice, the sea glitters, the
dogs are jacketed, muzzles dangling loose on their chests like
surgeons' masks after operating.

The air was voluptuously soft and it is not hard to imagine
why Lear favoured this green and pampered sea-city sand-
wiched between mountains and water. It was in 1870 that he
settled here, after considering the claims of Cannes and Nice. "I
have never met people as accommodating and pleasant as the

people of San Remo" he wrote to Lady Waldegrave. He bought a plot of land, built himself a sumptuous villa and studio among semi-tropical trees and with a view of the sea – the villa, Villa Emily, seems to have gone up with astonishing rapidity – and was soon joined by his cat Foss. Giorgio, his faithful servant, was in charge of arrangements. "I realise that I have not lived so well for twenty years."

Lear had only been installed a few years when, on his return from abroad, he found a five-storey hotel under construction between his house and the sea. His paradisal existence ruined, he was forced to find a new plot, his grand friends Lords Derby and Northbrook rescuing him with loans. With their help he was able to build a new house identical to the Villa Emily so that Foss would not get lost, which he called Villa Tennyson. "My new property," Lear wrote, "has only the street and the railway between the house and the sea, and unless even the fish begin to build I would not suffer further inconvenience."

Lear lived another eight years, dying in Villa Tennyson in late January 1888, exactly this time of year. He did a lot of his best work in San Remo: his Corsican book, several collections of Nonsense, illustrations to Tennyson.

On a mild, windless day we sought out his grave in the beautiful La Foce cemetery overlooking the sea. At the foot of cypresses, umbrella pines and palms his tombstone, newly scrubbed probably for the benefit of visitors to the exhibition, gleamed in the pearly light. "In memory of Edward Lear, landscape painter in many lands," it was inscribed. "Born at Highgate, May 12, 1812, Died at San Remo January 29, 1888, Dear for his many gifts to many souls." Alongside Lear's grave is another inscribed with the names of Lear's Albanian servant Giorgio, actually buried in Mendrisio, and Giorgio's son Nicola, buried in La Foce.

Although San Remo has a delectable situation – like those other places on the Nice–Genoa railway line Lear liked to paint: Eze, Bordighera, Menton – and a striking Chirico-like *città vecchia* high above its twin harbours, it is the parallel of single railway line and marble promenade under the tall palms, the sea on one side, the mountains on the other, that graces the city. Edward Lear's two villas shared the view and he lies buried only a hundred yards to the west of it. Dogs and cats equally appear to find the promenade congenial, among them perhaps Foss's descendants.

It is curious how the memory of San Remo and Lear lingers with us here in Capri, the light similar, the air slightly scented, the sea briefly inviting. D. H. Lawrence when he was here one January felt tempted to bathe and indeed when we took the steep winding path one morning to the Marina Piccola there were a few children frolicking on the edges and a lone swimmer far out in the bay. It reminded me of that other indomitable swimmer, my friend Charles Sprawson, and his magical book *Haunts of the Black Masseur.*

The quickest way for us to get to the Marina Piccola would normally be down the Via Matteotti, past the Carthusian monastery, and along the Via Krupp, which snakes down under the Giardini di Augusto to the sea far below. But a landslide under the Villa Krupp, now a hotel, had sealed off the road. The name Krupp does not ring kindly to English ears but the German industrialist, a voluntary exile for one reason or another – sex, politics, financial scandal? – lived five years off and on in Capri and was a generous benefactor to the island. Not only did he initiate the public gardens below his house, known since 1918 as the Giardini di Augusto – Krupp after the 1914–18 war being an unwelcome name in Italy – but he engaged the well-known engineer Emilio Mayer to build a path down the cliff face to the sea. A series of sharp, narrow hairpin bends, scarcely wide enough for two people to walk side by side, the turns are precipitous. Krupp, who died in 1902, had constructed out of a cave, halfway down, a two-storey building apparently for clandestine meetings, an odd idea when his own nearby villa, later used by Gorky and Lenin, must at that time have been as remote as anyone could have wished.

We could not take the road now, but had to go back up to the piazzetta, and leaving the Via Roma, which the taxis use as it is the only road for cars from Marina Grande, negotiate the steep steps of Via Mulo. On terraces planted with vines and olives shuttered villas line the steps all the way to the sea, many overhung by threatening slabs of rock. One such is the Villa Perina where Gorky is recorded to have lived in 1911. It cannot have been a bad life for a Russian writer used to a Siberian climate.

Capri is not rich in beaches, comparing poorly with Ischia, and the scatter of flat rocks, file of bathing huts and tiny curve of sand at Marina Piccola is the best on offer. But no-one in their right mind comes to Capri to lie on a beach. The coast is of a rocky, cathedral-like eminence, grotto following grotto in varying degrees of blue and green, in summer no doubt nosed by tourist-filled boats. You come eventually to Punta Carena and the lighthouse on the south-west corner. Nothing on so tiny an island takes very long to reach but since you move vertically most of the time and vistas are packed close as pages in a book you have the illusion of moving great distances.

At Marina Piccola the three Faraglioni rocks, brooding presences like a rocky animal family, the infant nursed by its parents, seemed to follow you. Scarcely anywhere in the island are you rid of them and though they are some way off by foot the closing embrace of the cliffs clicks them in like a handcuff.

Sitting in the sun on a rock watching an old fisherman pulling his boat out to sea I imagine with some difficulty Lawrence's skinny figure wanting to plunge into these foaming inlets. After a while, the day becomes wonderfully warm and we drink the silky local white wine and eat prawns outside at the Onda d'Oro. There are the shepherding Faraglioni as usual to our left, the Scoglio delle Sirene in front of us, and to the right, with tufts of pine and cactus embedded in the rockface, the cut-throat cliffs of Punta Mulo. At any moment you feel the cliffs could fall in on you, carrying with them a handful of precariously lodged villas, bits of castellated wall and the Saracenic tower. The sea, shifted now from grey-green to something near blue, swerves behind the tiny fishermen's church of St Andrew. Nature at its most picturesque and perilous all around you, it is a blessing in late January to feel the sun and sea air, soothed by wine. When we returned the next day, the weekend over, the sun had gone in and the two bar-restaurants were firmly shut. So quickly does one go from delight to gloom. On summer days, all striped umbrellas and bathers, these tiny beach-inlets must seem like Brighton.

I don't know if Lawrence ever came to the Marina Piccola but he spent some weeks in Capri in January 1920. Suddenly, in typical Lawrence fashion, tiring of the icy mountain village of Picinisco, to which he and Frieda had fled from Rome, they decided on Capri, enduring a crossing no less uncomfortable than that of the Gentleman from San Francisco: "We spent a night on board that rolling saucepan of a boat . . . the sea rose as we left the bay." The seas were running too high for boats to come out to take them off their steamer, so they had to take shelter near Sorrento. "The Italians *were* sick; oh dear; luckily we managed to keep all right."

The Lawrences rented an apartment "two beautiful rooms

Above Marina Piccola, Capri

and a kitchen we share, at the top of an old palazzo which has a staircase like a prison, not a palace. It is extremely beautiful – just on the very neck of the little town, on the very neck of the island: we can touch the queer bubbly *duomo*, almost, from our balcony."

With his customary initial enthusiasm Lawrence wrote happily to Catherine Carswell "this is the life we could enjoy together." Their friend Compton Mackenzie is living in Capri, but though they plan to stay until Easter the gossip begins to get Lawrence down. "This island," Lawrence wrote, "is covered with a small band of cosmopolitans – English, American, Russian, German – everything. The English-speaking crowd are the uttermost, uttermost limit for spiteful scandal. My dear Catherine, London is a prayer-meeting in comparison . . . The stories Mary Cannan is told are *incredible*. Suetonius would blush to his heels, and Tiberius would feel he's been a flea-bite." They should have seen the austere, deserted place, devoid of foreigners, we are experiencing.

Although Lawrence continued to make the most in letters to friends of their boat journey from Naples, "when a boat came to take us off it almost hopped on to our deck and then fell back into an abysmal gulf of darkness, amid yells unparalleled almost in Italy . . . leaving us rolling with a lot of spewing Italians," they soon settled down.

It would seem from Lawrence's descriptions that the Palazzo Ferraro in which they were camped was just off the piazzetta by the church. "Here we are, high in this old palace, with two great rooms, three balconies, and a kitchen above, and an enormous flat roof, one of the most wonderful places in the world: Ischia, Naples, Vesuvius slowly smoking to the north – the wide sea to the west, the great rock of our Monte Solaro in front – rocks and the Gulf of Salerno south. Below us, all the tiny jungle of Capri town."

They visit Compton Mackenzie in his villa. "He does the semi-romantic but I like him, he's a good sort." They meet Mary Cannan, Barrie's former wife, and Brett Young. "But I prefer the Italians."

The balmy weather leads to considerations of swimming, but appears to stop there. Lawrence writes to Lady Cynthia Asquith, "Here I sit at the top of my palace, and do nothing, sweet nothing, except go out to lunch and walk from one end of the island to the other. As for walking across it, needless: one bestrides the narrow world without being a Colossus." They are taken by the Signorina from whom they rent their rooms to look at a villa, Lo Smeraldo, to be let furnished. "It is very beautiful, and we collected wood in the grounds, and made a fire in the drawing room, and had a joyous tea, and danced on the marble floor while another Italian played the piano – altogether what one should not do – till the sun went down. It is a beautiful villa above the clear sea and the Faraglioni, all sun."

Lawrence's weeks in Capri were a brief perch in between hectic spells of travel, perhaps the most restless period of his life. Having been obliged by the war to stay in England, mainly in Cornwall, he and Frieda took off for Italy as soon as they could. *The Rainbow* had been published in 1915 and then withdrawn after the publishers were ordered to destroy their stock. *Twilight in Italy* came next and then *Women in Love*, published this time by Secker, privately at first. It was while he was in Capri that Lawrence negotiated the change from Duckworth: "I should like to be with you," he wrote Martin Secker from the Palazzo Ferraro, "because you really care about books."

In Capri Lawrence dreams up one fanciful scheme after another. "We think, of course, of South Seas or Africa. Do you know anybody in Africa, a nice climate, who'd let me live on his land and help him – no wages or anything – but I should like to help a man to make some sort of a farm in Africa, and I can always keep us two by writing."

That came to nothing, but disenchanted by what he called "the stewpot of semi-literary cats" Lawrence set off with Frieda for Sicily. They spend a year in Taormina, visiting Germany briefly before returning to Sicily. He wrote *Sea and Sardinia* after a sortie of a few days and then, in March 1922, they set off for Australia, spending a month in Ceylon on the way. The same year saw them in New York, Tahiti, San Francisco, New Mexico, and finally Mexico itself.

Lawrence soon shed his initial infatuation with Capri. Once installed in Taormina he has little good to say about Capri. "Capri was all the time like a ship which is going to arrive somewhere and doesn't." While Sicily is "beautiful, and green, green and full of flowers" Capri is "a dry rock". "Frieda loves this place." "Etna is a beautiful mountain, far lovelier than Vesuvius, which is a heap." It is not long before Taormina gets similar treatment. It is the way of Lawrence.

The Giardini di Augusto, shaped like a child's high chair, have nothing to do with the Emperor Augustus, but for diplomatic reasons were so named in 1918. They offer a green oasis among grey rock to come to in the mornings or early evening, to read or simply look. The cloisters of the Certosa, with their elegant arches and flowing lines, nest in scrub and pine below, vaguely Arab in feeling and faintly desolate in their ruin and desolation. The buildings date from the fourteenth century, but were repeatedly desecrated and plundered by pirates, and the Charterhouse itself suppressed by Giuseppe Bonaparte in the nineteenth century. From many angles the biscuit-coloured monastery and its outbuildings are almost invisible, lying in the curve of a steep slope, only its oleanders standing out in the protective green of cypress, sea-pine, agave and prickly pear. We visited the bare, single-naved church one morning, starkly beautiful, and its adjoining museum, the walls adorned by huge, utterly gloomy paintings by a resident German called Diefenbach. Capri appears not to have been lucky in its painters, surprising in an island that has been host to so many writers.

The Giardini di Augusto are equally sprinkled with seats and statues that are sensuous and invite stroking. People drop in here for a rest on their way up and down Via Krupp to refresh their eyes, and to inhale the soft balsamic air. It is like being in an aeroplane or a balloon, plunging cliffs to seaward, blue waters curdling to green, small white villas set like eyes in the island's tilted spine and flanks. The three Faraglioni from here look less threatening, their swooping, jagged surfaces given a more reduced and domestic context. The quiet, among these luxuriant ledges and terraces, flowerbeds curved under palms and cypress, is tangible, the distant sea hiss and splash of fountains only intruded on by the occasional screech of gulls. It dawns on one gradually that there is no traffic on this side of the island, only paths, not roads.

There is something suicidal about Capri, less in spirit than in geography. You have only to look over the balconies of the Giardini to feel the terrifying pull of the rocks below, a sensation repeated at scores of similar points of fall all over the island. It would be tempting to attribute this to a ghostly legacy of the time when the aged Tiberius, succeeding Augustus, was alleged to have disposed of his enemies by making them jump to their deaths off the cliff known now as Salto di Tiberio. The rumours of extreme sexual licence, cruelty and random punishments that have trickled down the centuries seem, despite the efforts of Tacitus and Suetonius, to have little basis in fact. Tiberius, arriving at Capri after a life of exemplary rectitude at the age of sixty-eight, spent the last ten years of his life in disillusioned solitude, the cares and passions of the world well behind him. During his retirement in Capri the road structure and harbours that exist today were begun and what had started out as a kind of declining emperor's playground developed into a miniature model state, the construction of new buildings and villas in places only made possible by amazing feats of engineering. When Tiberius died the impetus flagged, castles and other fortifications were left unfinished, and by the time Vandals and Saracens had their way with Capri it had returned to what it had been before, an island inhabited and cared for by a few fishermen and vine growers.

At dusk, the sky suddenly slashed pink, melancholy descends. The few people about move stealthily like conspirators.

Some years ago, when, in the incubatory period of a savage depression that was to be repeated twenty-five years later, I spent a few weeks in a seventeenth-century former monastery at Sant' Agnello. I made an effort to come to terms with the nature of my illness. The monastic quiet did not do the trick, the fabulous views across the Sorrentine peninsula made me even more nervous and edgy. I turned to Robert Burton's *Anatomy of Melancholy*, but in its baroque prose and interminable lists of symptoms and causes my attention wandered. I wanted simple answers and a simple cure. Burton was no help to me then, the situation deepening irrevocably until the tunnel had to be gone through in the hope of coming out the other side. It took many months.

I was hoping for something that Burton was not equipped to provide. He was, after all, a scholar, not a doctor. His natural home was an Oxford library, not a consulting room. But now, a further episode of affliction, when suicide was the desired solution, only a horrible memory, it seemed time to give Burton another try. Among these perfumed limestone rocks, the elusive musks of acanthus, arbutus, lentisk, pine, creating a feeling of light-headedness, there were no answers to be sought, only a strange idiosyncratic style to be engaged.

Burton occasionally refers to his own melancholy, which presumably was the starting point of his investigations, but he lived an extraordinarily limited and protected life, with few of the external pressures he discusses as being possible causes of illness. Born in 1577 in Leicestershire he went as a commoner to Brasenose College, Oxford, subsequently being elected a student of Christ Church. After serving as a Clerk of Oxford Market, he became a Bachelor of Divinity in 1614, then librarian and tutor at Christ Church. He undertook not very demanding duties as a parish priest, as a rule leaving his rooms in college only to venture as far as the Bodleian.

The first volume of *The Anatomy* appeared in 1621, when Burton was forty-four. Five further editions appeared, the last one posthumously, taking the final extent to over 1300 pages. The book is divided into three "partitions", preceded by an address to the reader in the name of Democritus Junior.

Burton is keen to present himself modestly as an all-rounder, rather than as a specialist, an attitude commended by both Plato and Montaigne. "Like a ranging spaniel that barks at every bird he sees, leaving his game, I have followed all, saving that which I should. I have read many books, but to little purpose, for want of good method, I have confusedly tumbled over divers authors in our libraries with small profit, for want of art, order, memory, judgement. I never travelled but in map or chart . . ."

Prevented from marrying, a college limitation he found abominable, Burton had no distractions of family. He was, as he put it,

not poor, not rich; "I have little. I want nothing . . ." Reduced to
the life of a monastic observer "I hear and see what is done abroad,
how others run, ride turmoil, and macerate themselves in court
and country; far from those wrangling lawsuits, I laugh at all."

What made such an apparently self-sufficient hermetic fellow
devote most of his life to what is basically a health guide, despite
all its exuberant ramifications? None of Burton's diagnoses and
remedies was particularly novel, Bright's *Treatise on Melancholy*
having appeared in 1586 and Adams's *Diseases of the Soule* in
1616. There were other health guides then available, the result
of a general feeling of unease and alienation prevalent at the
time due largely to breakdowns of confidence in traditional
views about science, religion, politics and society. "So much
science," Burton wrote, "so little conscience, so much knowledge, so many preachers, such variety of sects . . . such absurd
and ridiculous traditions and ceremonies."

The virtues of *The Anatomy* lie in the richness of its diversions.
In similar fashion to the Capri hotelier curtly dismissing the
wife of the Gentleman from San Francisco, Burton remarks,
"I resolve, if you like not my writing, go read something
else." Although *The Anatomy* is broken down into a bewildering
number of sections, members and subsections, as if adhering to
a rigid formula, it can be opened anywhere with both profit
and pleasure. Burton's basic assumption is that "the world is
mad, that it is melancholy, dotes. Examine, and you shall find
that kingdoms and provinces are melancholy, cities and families, all creatures, vegetal, sensible, and rational, that all sorts,
sects, ages, conditions, are out of tune . . . For indeed who is not
a fool, melancholy, mad? Folly, melancholy, madness are but
one disease."

Before facing the question of any remedy for this universal
madness Burton sets out plans for his ideal state: "a new Atlantis,

a poetical Commonwealth of mine own". This fetching Utopia, set forth in detail, depends upon a general acceptance that man's infirmities and imperfection are susceptible to improvement, his own task being to "anatomise this humour of melancholy, through all his parts and species, as it is an habit, or an ordinary disease, and that philosophically, medicinally, to shew the causes, symptoms, and several causes of it, that it may be the better avoided."

Moderation is the basis of all Burton's recommendations. "Nothing so good, but it may be abused." Thus, exercise but not excessively, and especially not after meat. "Opposite to exercise is idleness (the badge of gentry) or want of exercise, the bane of body and mind, the nurse of naughtiness, stepmother of discipline, the chief author of all is mischief, one of the seven deadly sins, and a sole cause of this and many other maladies, the devil's cushion, as Gualter calls it, his pillow and chief reposal."

Burton warns against too much solitariness and the dangers, so delightful at first, of lying in bed whole days. Studying and education are further causes of melancholy, as are poverty and want. "To be poor is to be a knave, a fool, a wretch, a wicked, an odious fellow, a common eye-sore; say poor and say all; they are born to labour, to misery, to carry burdens like luments, to lick salt, to empty lakes, fay channels, carry out dirt and dunghills, sweep chimneys, rub horse-heels etc."

It is one of Burton's habits that when he gets under way there is no stopping him, whole pages given up to examples and lists in support of a statement, at once erudite, fantastical, comic, poetic. The reader drowns in them, as under a great wave, willingly going under.

In general, lavishly arranged as they are, none of the symptoms and remedies remarked on by Burton come as a surprise or revelation. They are of the common sense variety, dressed up by a

rich imagination. There are wonderful perorations. I imagine
him here, in the Giardini di Augusto, enveloped by plants, shrubs,
flowers, trees, looking out at the blank, blue sea. He observes, as
at the opening of his Second Partition on the Digression of the
Air, "as a long-winged hawk, when he is first whistled off the first,
mounts aloft," that "a good prospect will ease melancholy", as
Gomesius contends. "The citizens of Barcelona, saith he, otherwise penned in, that pleasant prospect their city hath into the
sea, which, like that of old Athens, besides Aegina, Salamis, and
many pleasant islands, and inhabitants of Genoa, to see the
ships, boats and passengers go by out of their windows, their
whole cities being sited on the side of an hill, like Pera by
Constantinople, so that each house hath a free prospect to the
sea, as some part of London to the Thames; or to have a free
prospect all over the city at once, as at Granada in Spain, and
Fez in Africa . . ." So it goes on, taking in Italy, Greece, Cairo and
the Nile, Mount Sion. He concludes: "Laelius à Fonte Eugubinus,
 that great Doctor, at the latter end of many of his consultations
(as commonly he doth set down what success his physick had) in
melancholy and most especially approves of this above all other
remedies whatsoever, etc. 'Many other things helped, but change
of air was that which wrought the cure, and did most good.'"

If only it were as simple as that, a passage to Capri would
be worth all the words and potions of psychiatrists.

The *Anatomy* is a very *sensible* book; of course, if possible, one
should have a "quiet" soul, avoid fear and sorrow, remain calm
in face of provocation, "mitigate the mind with mirth, constancy,
and good hope" but these are the very things that in states of
nervous breakdown or depression one is least likely to achieve.
Burton is aware of this. "Yes, but you will here infer, that this is
excellent good indeed if it could be done; but how shall it be
effected, by whom, by what art, what means? You may advise and

give good precepts, as who cannot? But how shall they be put in practice?"

The answer is "from the patient himself the first and chiefest remedy must be had; for if he be averse, peevish, waspish, give way wholly to his passions, will not seek to be helped, how is it possible he should be cured?"

We can easily give counsel to others, Burton agrees. "Every man, as the saying is, can tame a shrew but he that hath her." Nevertheless a friend's counsel "is a charm, like mandrake wine, and as a bull that is tied to a fig-tree becomes gentle on a sudden so is a savage obdurate heart mollified by fair speeches".

A melancholy discontented person must never be left alone or idle, for in solitariness his misery "will work upon itself, melancholize". If all else fails and good advice and kind words have little effect it is permissible to divert the patient with feigned lies, strange news or artificial invention. Burton quotes Philodotus, the physician who cured a melancholy king that thought his head was off by "putting a leaden cap thereon; the weight made him perceive it, and freed him of his fond imagination."

Burton, so innocent in affairs of the heart, begins the third and final partition with a discussion of what he calls "love melancholy". He does not deny the initial pleasures of lovers who cannot contain themselves, "kissing, embracing, treading on their toes etc, diving into their bosoms, that scarce honesty sometimes," but for the most part, he concludes love is "a plague, a torture, an hell . . . like a summer fly, or a rainbow of all colours, fair, foul, and full of variation, though most part irksome and bad."

Burton lists the defects in a mistress which a man will overlook in his besottedness. They run to over thirty lines; she may have a "thin, lean chitty-face, have clouds in her face, be crooked, dry, bald, goggle-eyed, blear-eyed" look "like a squis'd cat", have "a nose like a promontory", have breath "that stinks all over the room". These are minor faults to others named as Burton's eloquence takes hold of him. She may look like "a nerd in a lanthorn", have the waist of a cow, goaty legs, breed lice, have filthy long unpared nails, but her admirer would rather have her than any woman in the world.

None of this seems to have much to do with melancholy, rather the reverse. But as a guard against the folly of passion Burton goes along with Montaigne and Chrysostom in advising the lover to look beneath the outward appearance: "Take her skin from her face and thou shalt see all loathsomeness under it, that beauty is a superficial skin and bones" and he suggests imagining the lady sick "full of filthy fleam, stinking putrid, excremental stuff; snot and snivel in her nostrels, spittle in her mouth, water in her eyes" etc.

These seem rather extreme measures, more inclined, one would have thought, to lower spirits than to raise them. But, if one is to accept that in general women have faults, just as do men, Burton adds, then it is sensible to admit them. "The worldly cares, miseries, discontents, that accompany marriage, I pray you learn of them that have experience, for I have none."

Although he strives to be even-handed Burton cannot refrain from contrasting "how free, how happy, how secure, how heavenly, in respect, a single man is" with the slavery of marriage, "what squalor attends it, what irksomeness, what charges," and worst, "all gifts and invitations cease, no friend will esteem thee, and thou shalt be compelled to lament thy misery, and make thy moan."

That is a bachelor don speaking. But there is a way of escaping from what Burton calls "the devil's paws" and "love-melancholy" whether the object of the latter is women or God.

Those of us who suffer "a most intolerable pain and grief of the heart" and who hear and see chimeras "prodigious, uncouth shapes, bears, owls, anticks, black dogs" should have comfort in knowing that Melancholy "the Devil's bath" can be routed by fresh air, exercise and faith in God's mercy. Too much fasting, meditation, questioning of God's judgements, listening to rigid preachers, should be avoided. We must take advice from physicians and divines "whose words are as flagons of wine", and above all, "be not solitary, be not idle".

Capri, despite its handful of neat white churches, does not give off much of a spiritual or religious feeling: its prevailing spirit is pagan, wild, denunciatory. What was once local here, endemic, a place for simple people living off the sea and the land, has been replaced by the fleeting, the seasonal, its inhabitants swallowed up by holiday-makers. I doubt Burton would have found it soothing or conducive to serious reflection, its changes of mood are too violent. But now in these empty, beautiful gardens it is possible to take Burton at his face value, relish the gay abundance of his imagery, the variety of his scholarship, without seeking for enlightenment or release from torment. I don't think that Burton, had I persevered with him all those years ago in my Sorrentine monastery, would have done me much good. There is sound common sense of the kind that any decent doctor could provide, but as Burton was aware, melancholy passes eventually, and by melancholy he is talking about what we now call clinical depression, not mere sadness or low spirits. There are talking illnesses and physical illnesses and most serious depression is caused by a chemical imbalance that is most effectively treated by drugs, or in extreme cases electric shock. In the almost catatonic state of deep depression words cannot reach you, or describe your feelings. William Styron in his book *Darkness Visible*, probably

The Certosa, Capri, by moonlight

came nearest to suggesting what one kind of break-down feels like, but everyone breaks down in his or her individual way, and most of us do not have words for it. At the time every moment seems endless and the situation beyond resolve. Burton displays all aspects of it with wonderful abandon, but his "anatomy" remains curiously cerebral.

Below the gardens the sea changes by the minute, peacock blue, indigo, wine-dark. The bent-double road built on the proceeds of armament manufacturing twists like a series of paperclips under us and out of sight. Walking back past the empty cloisters of the Charterhouse, its arches gleaming like ivory soon washed in sunset, we drown in the enveloping greenness, smothered in the scents of Via Tragara and our own terrace.

Capri is like a turn-table; whichever road you take the same bits of rock or promontory eventually appear but at a different angle. You lose the Faraglioni for an hour or so only to find yourself on top of them, even though you have set off in a different direction. If you follow Via Tragara indefinitely you complete a circle, exchanging a gentle passageway nursed by flowering trees and potted plants for steep, rock-edge paths, the gradients and narrowness of the paths often alarming, the waves crashing about beneath you.

A path, looked at from above resembling a leg of lamb, curves away from Punta Tragara, almost on top of the rocky sides of the Faraglioni, and winds north past the Grotta di Matermania, the steepling path never more than a yard or two from the cliff edge. This path joins on to a higher one that leads you back into Capri and closes the circle. On the level the distance covered would only be a mile or two but its switchback nature makes it exhausting.

There are various terraces at different heights from which you can take a breather and contemplate death, chunks of detached rock or savage splits in the cliff. There is a tiny beach at Porto Tragara, a mere dusting of the rocks, and some little way out to sea the sheer cliffs of Monacone, a giant stone molar with the remains of a Roman-built bath embedded in it. In this unlikely and inhospitable spot, seemingly impossible to access except by air, Augustus's celebrated architect, the Mauritanian Masgaba, has his tomb. Here too in some mysterious fashion the Charter-house monks levered themselves up for periods of retreat. Rabbits were apparently bred here during the French occupation, though beyond a few stunted tufts of scrub there is no vegetation. The rabbits must have had a good sense of balance for there is not a flat surface on the place, the wedge-shaped crown only a few yards across. There were once monk seals, a rare species of sea cow, in the transparent waters off Monacone, but though there are fragments of a Roman port below Punta Tragara itself the sea seems innocent of any such beguiling creatures.

It is impossible to imagine that anyone, unless a monk, would choose to live on this part of the coast but a few craggy bends north of Monacone you come to the equally sheer Punta Massulo. Sunk into the cliff edge is an extraordinary construction that from a distance looks like an aeroplane that has crashed into the rock and round which a circle of pines have sprouted. Closer to, the resemblance is more to a streamlined express engine, painted Pompeii red.

This bizarre edifice was dreamed up by Kurt Suckert, who under the name of Curzio Malaparte had some success with his novels *Kaputt* and *La Pelle* in the late 1940s. A punctual and enthusiastic Fascist, his quarrelsome nature and controversial writings soon got him into trouble, though not before his Fascist connections enabled him to buy and build on a hitherto strictly protected area of rare beauty.

The Villa Malaparte got underway in 1938; the architect
entrusted with the task of making a spectacular modern villa that
was to be an extension of the rock was Adalberto Libera, responsible for various Fascist buildings in Rome and a contributor
to Gruppo 7. Much favoured by Mussolini, Libera was a leader
of the school of Italian Realism. "The day I began work on a
new house," Malaparte wrote, typically envisaging himself as
its creator, "I had no idea that I would be drawing a portrait
of myself. Better than any I had drawn in my writings." While
Libera got to work, however, Malaparte departed for the Russian
front, from where his dispatches earned him Nazi disapproval
and relegation to Finland. *Kaputt* and *La Pelle*, both apocalyptic
and visionary novels about the increasing decadence of post-
war Europe, established Malaparte's fame and enabled him to
profit rather than suffer from the scandal they caused. After a
few unsuccessful plays, and an interesting film *Cristo Proibito*,
Malaparte's political and moral cynicism found expression only
in journalism of a not very popular kind.

In Capri he was able to fulfil every fantasy. There is a photo-
graph of him on the roof of his house astride his bicycle,
dressed as a racing cyclist, hands gloved and spread wide in
acclamation. Cultural critics descended on the Villa Malaparte,
after his death designated by the architectural magazine *Modo*
"the most loved and recognised work of twentieth-century
Italian architecture."

Whatever the truth of this, the villa, completed in 1949, is
certainly unlike any other house in Capri, whether a peasant's
or a film star's. Malaparte described his house as "sad, harsh,
and severe", like himself. Its futuristic lines, on two storeys leading to a roof solarium with a white sail-like curve of brick,
suggests an aircraft carrier's inclined take-off deck. There are
no extruding ledges nor balconies along the building's 177

feet length, five times its width, and the windows are inset like binoculars aimed at the sea or the Faraglioni. A long flight of gently graded, red steps leads up to the solarium roof in one direction and much more steeply and narrowly through the rocks down to sea level in the other. The interior is not for inhabiting, but for exclaiming; the exterior for wondering.

Malaparte died in 1957. His hope was that his villa, so futuristically conceived and uncluttered, would have some international cultural function. Instead, lawyers have fought over it, most of its paintings and internal features have been looted, and what was once so startling and fresh, so daring in its construction, seems destined to subside quietly like a submarine on the sea bed. Malaparte's novel *La Pelle* was filmed in 1981 round these cliffs, with Burt Lancaster and Marcello Mastroianni as the main characters. Much earlier Moravia's novel *L'Attenzione* had been filmed in Capri by Godard with Michel Piccoli and Brigitte Bardot. Moravia had a house in Capri at the time, though I doubt whether he and Malaparte were ever likely to be soulmates. The Futurists Marinetti and Prampolini, who spent time here, would have been suitable occupants of the Villa Malaparte, had it existed in their day.

The one other main phenomenon on this coast, a sight as startlingly original in its way as the Villa Malaparte, is the Arco Naturale. The path taking you back to the piazzetta winds through steep, wood-encrusted rocks, many of them hollowed out to form caves or grottoes. In the largest of these, the Grotta di Matermania, orgiastic rites were said to be practised in honour of the Mater Magna, though the bits of stucco and mosaic still remaining in the dripping darkness suggest more orderly and spiritual activities. Much research has been devoted to establishing what exactly went on in the semi-circular gloom, but the cave, thirty feet high and 6500 square feet in area, appears to have been fitted out with seats and couches for the spectators. Looking likely to collapse at any moment, the vaulted ceiling was sensibly reinforced by the Romans who levelled the floor against the natural slope. Why a place of such awkward access, requiring the agility of a goat to reach it, should have been chosen by portly emperors and their priestly attendants for their games, remains a mystery.

There is an oak wood nearby, and beyond it, arched 600 feet above the sea like a giraffe's head, the Arco Naturale is all that is left of the vault of a huge cave, collapsed over thousands of years through erosion and geological movement. What remains, rearing over water glinting like a turquoise stud through its opening, is precarious to a degree of caricature. The giraffe buries its head in thick scrub, the neck attached to the precipice as if it had been sculpted. All round it, clinging on for dear life, a rash of green scrub swarms down the cliff face.

Winter light subsides gently, the sea taking on silky cerise swathes as the last rays of reflected sun disappear behind Punta Carena. On water placid as milk a solitary tanker edges its way south towards Sicily. Two fishing boats, *lampari*, with their lamps not yet on, chug round Punta Mulo on their way to the favoured grounds off Punta Ventroso.

Dining some evenings on the wide glassed-in terrace of Virgiliano the whole gulf is spread out before you. A string of lights marks out the Neapolitan port area and its siblings, and through binoculars, on a clear night, you can pick out the great fifteenth-century gates Porta Capuana and Porta Nolana, the burly bulk of Castel dell'Ovo and Castel Sant'Elmo. The last hydrofoils slice the dark with their foaming wakes, scissoring their various ways to Pozzuoli and Castellammare, towards the smoky bruise of Vesuvius and Sorrento. A sleek white steamer moves more sedately towards the Gulf of Salerno, the pleasure look-outs of Positano and Amalfi.

Today, a Sunday, life has seemed stalled. I remember Palinurus in *The Unquiet Grave*: "The boredom of Sunday afternoon, which drove de Quincey to drink laudanum, also gave birth to surrealism: hours propitious for making bombs," perhaps Marinetti found inspiration on such a day. The original Palinurus, Aeneas's pilot who fell sleeping into the sea, and whose still living body was washed up on a beach three days later, was subsequently murdered by the inhabitants of Velia and left unburied. Connolly's attachment to sleep and its benefits made of Palinurus's exit from battle a potent symbol of disengagement still flourishing in these waters.

In the restaurant we are alone except for a young Japanese couple, the girl speaking in perfect Italian to the waiter. We order *frittura dei gamberetti* and *vino di casa*, both delectable. We watch sympathetically as the young man strives to look unconcerned at his linguistic loss of face.

There are many plaques on the walls of Capri's squares and alleyways, one of them by Pablo Neruda. He wrote:

> *Capri – Reina de Roca*
> *En tu vestido*
> *De color amaranto y azucena*
> *Viri desarrollando*
> *La Dicha y el dolor la viña Llena*
> *De Radiantes Racimos*
> *Que conquisté en la Tierra.*

Neruda, "an amateur of the sea" as he called himself, had joined the Communist Party of Chile in 1945. He was forty-one, a former member of the Consular service, a poet already famous. Two years later, as a result of recently instituted censorship of the press, Neruda was arrested and went into exile. His world travels, lecturing and reading, landed him in Italy in 1951. When the Chilean Embassy demanded his expulsion there was a demonstration in Rome – Neruda witnessed Moravia's wife hitting a policeman on the head with her silk parasol – and the order was withdrawn. The historian Edwin Cerio, whose palazzo overlooks the piazzetta, offered him a refuge in Capri and to this he went with his beloved Matilde Urrutia, though still married at the time to his wife of many years, Delia del Carril. "We came to the marvellous island on a winter night", he wrote in his *Memoirs*. "The coast loomed through the shadows, whitish and tall, unfamiliar and silent. What would happen? A little horse carriage was waiting. Up and up the deserted night time streets the carriage climbed. White, mute house, narrow vertical lanes."

Cerio, in his late eighties, tall, white-haired, white-bearded, and white-suited, greeted and then left them. Neruda describes him as "owning half Capri" and being more "genuine though not as famous as Axel Munthe".

For Neruda their stay on Capri was a romantic idyll. They went for long walks. "Among the rocks, wherever the sun beat down most, in the arid earth, diminutive plants and flowers burst out, grown in precise and exquisite patterns." They became part of "the hidden Capri of the poor", and knew where to find the best wine and olives.

In the mornings Neruda worked at his poems and in the afternoon Matilde typed them. He finished *Los Versos del Capitán*: "a book of love, passionate but also painful". Neruda records that it was the first time he and Matilde had lived together in the same house: "In that place whose beauty was intoxicating, our love grew steadily. We could never again live apart."

Los Versos del Capitán, whose poems are about both love and homesickness for Chile, was first published anonymously in an edition of only fifty copies. "We had a long celebration for this, with a table full of flowers, *frutti di mare*, wine as transparent as water, a unique offspring of the vines of Capri."

The reason for the temporary anonymity was to protect his wife, whom he acknowledges as his perfect mate for eighteen years: "sweetest of consorts, thread of steel and honey tied to me during the years when my poetry sang most".

During the twenty further years he was to live, this most travelled of poets, friend of Castro, Guevara and Allende, of Lorca and Aragon, Picasso and Rivera, wrote many more books. He was able to return to Chile, and eventually became Ambassador in Paris. In 1971 he was awarded the Nobel Prize. In 1973 his great friend, now President Allende, was assassinated. Recording this shameful occasion in his *Memoirs* only three days after the event, Neruda was not to know that within two weeks he would be dead too.

In an essay, part of a book called *Passions and Impressions*, published posthumously, this great poet, who loved dogs and collected figureheads and ships in bottles, described his Capri days as "fruitful, amorous, and perfumed by the Mediterranean onion". He went on, "One of the best times for working were those days we spent in Capri . . . Capri saves its better side for winter, the heights of Anacapri are tinged with evening purple. Bushes, weeds, and grasses spring up everywhere to greet the faithful friend who remained through winter, to live with the other island, the real island: simple stone surrounded by Tyrrhenian foam."

Presumably one of the walks Neruda and Matilde took was the one from Capri town up to the Villa Jovis, the grandest of the villas which Tiberius had built on Capri. Tiberius owed his succession as emperor to his mother Livia's marriage to Augustus. Augustus, in familiar nepotistic style, insisted on Tiberius marrying his daughter Julia. It was not a success and as soon as he decently could, Tiberius set out alone for Rhodes where he spent seven years. Eventually returning to Rome he took command of the Roman armies and on Augustus's death assumed the imperial power. He immediately had Augustus's surviving grandson murdered. Tiberius soon wearied of Rome and retired to Capri. He never returned to Rome, but he was by then sixty-eight, with many campaigns, intrigues and years of administration behind him.

Reports differ as to how he spent his time on the island, but he seems to have been solitary, bitter about the ingratitude of his friends, brooding, though this did not stop him completing numerous building projects during his ten-year stay. Augustus, more enterprising architecturally, was the first to put his imprint on Capri, visiting the island over many years, but it is curiously Tiberius's spirit, rather than Augustus's, that pervades the place.

It is a long haul from the town to the Villa Jovis but though the path is often as much a stairway as a path it takes you through real country, small peasant holdings with patches of vines alternating with elaborate villas smothered in oleander and bougainvillaea. From the Via Sopramonte, one of the wider lanes leading out of the network of arched alleys and covered ways that form the medieval centre, you take the walled Via Tiberio, rising continually through orchards and with sudden, spectacular glimpses of the sea and the mainland. The stone houses on the way are of the kind – *casetta* – that farm workers and fishermen often build themselves. Neruda, during his time on Capri when he was writing *Las Uvas y el Viento* – *The Grapes and the Wind* – relates how the country woman who used to clean for them always arrived and left very early. When Matilde asked her about this she replied, "I'm building my house, *signora. 'Una donna senza proprietà non vale niente.'*"

The house she was building with her own hands, which she invited them to inspect, was no shack but a two-storey stone building with arches and balconies. There was a tiny garden and she was making a pool. I imagine houses of this size are let for large sums during the summer. Between Capri town and the Villa Jovis near the summit of Monte Tiberio, there must be dozens of them.

During this same period on Capri Neruda was working on a long poem about China, the Revolution, and Mao, at that time one of Neruda's heroes. The cleaning woman whom they christened Olivito, because of her resemblance to a little olive tree, was meticulous in her work, including the emptying of waste-paper baskets. Unfortunately for Neruda some of the manuscript pages of this work, published eventually as *El Viento en el Asia*, had a tendency to slip unnoticed off the table and end up in the basket. In this way vital sections of the poem disappeared. Together with the Municipal Inspector, Neruda set off for the Capri rubbish dump but they were "not just hills, they were mountain ranges". The whole poem had to be reconstructed.

The houses on Via Tiberio eventually fall away, so that the last stages of the climb are left to the tramping feet of archaeologists, those lured by the extravagant anecdotes of Tacitus and Suetonius about orgies, or connoisseurs of views.

Capri is not short of the latter, and the Villa Jovis, perched close to the cliff edge of Monte Tiberio, offers some of the most spectacular. The ruins of a lighthouse tower, just to the seaward side of the entrance to the villa, are what you come upon first: built originally as a system for signalling by light or smoke, enabling Tiberius to communicate with the mainland, it collapsed during a minor earthquake while Tiberius was still alive. The imperial fleet lay at anchor in the roads off Capo Miseno and contact between it and Capri was maintained from this tower. Not much detail of its stone- and brickwork, half obliterated by scrub, still stands, but its blind-looking, decapitated bulk has a powerful brooding presence.

The lay-out and extent of the ruins – 75,000 square feet – make the term "villa" seem inadequate. Although much of the building exists only at ground level there is enough standing of the imperial quarters, staff rooms, kitchens, loggias and terraces to suggest that Palazzo di Tiberio would represent it more accurately. Water in one form or another is at its heart, a huge reservoir being central to it, with cisterns and baths leading off, symmetrically placed.

A miniature city, sliced off by time, the ground strewn with brick, stone, bits of wall. A kind of maze, leading into itself, sheer drops of hundreds of feet, meeting rooms, places of worship, an observatory. There are restored patches of brick like skin grafts, a feeling equally of fantasy and sorrow, a legacy of old games. But what games would an ancient ruler, soldier, disciplinarian, upright legislator have wanted to play here?

From the mosaic platform of Salto di Tiberio the island seems to spread itself, an attitude of surrender like a dog on its back. White houses like dice, the chill grey slab of Monte Solaro, toy harbours feathered by sails. Somewhere, bandaged by cloud, the hump of Vesuvius.

The heat begins to fade. The descent is gentle, the stone losing its glow. It is winter still, lights coming on, a man trimming his vines, another mowing, dogs barking. A fire burns somewhere, its delicious smell following us down the path, past the whitewashed tavern in which, in days gone by, a lady called La Bella Carmelina entertained visiting celebrities.

Looking back we get a last view of the church of Santa Maria del Soccorso, its white dome like a huge bald head just visible on its promontory, the cone-like structure of the lighthouse a final fling of stone in powder pink light.

So much history strewn about on the hill, so much still remaining in steps and walls and ceilings that one could believe, eyes half-closed, it was a site not in decay but in construction.

Walking slowly back in the dusk it is strange to imagine goats and cows and donkeys grazing among olive trees where there are now mostly only vines and not an animal in sight. Some, like Norman Douglas, have derided the whitewash that now covers every Capri villa, the native stone being a kind of greyish pink, but in the settling, golden light there is nothing that is not beautiful.

The piazza at night. The cane chairs of the three café-bars are pushed indoors, they are coffee and ice-cream consumers here, not heavy drinkers. This is opera, without the singers: towers and spires floodlit, the walls of the square washed in lemon light. Boats at sea are simply their lights, moving silently, waiting for the fish to rise. There seem to be pitifully few fishermen at work, not that the fish is ever worth the effort.

We are eating at Peppino's, one of the three minuscule restaurants in the honeycomb of lanes and alleyways behind the Palazzo Cerio. This whole area, designed by Picchiatti in the seventeenth century, is a mixture of the baroque and the Moorish, the cupola of St Stephen's Church offset by the arcaded front of Palazzo Cerio, with its cobalt blue balconies and rounded windows in faded pink stone. All here is curves and domes, elegant wrought iron and flights of steps, columns and pedestals, the tiny houses squashed together so that they almost meet across steep lanes. The church floor contains fragments from the Villa Jovis, but it is not the exterior that makes one linger but the perfect harmony of its setting, a tiny illuminated stage perched between mountains and sea.

The shops that form the ground floors of the covered alleys, in one of which Peppino's is housed, are mostly closed, but at every intersection there are flowers, vegetable and fruit stalls, bits of greenery, cactus or palm branches. These dark, winding alleys, conducive to a dagger in the back that never materialises, open out into terraces and courtyards, grand architecture on a minimal scale.

Peppino, a comfortable figure in striped apron, presides over four tables, the cooking area an extension of the room. Saucepans bubble on the stove, soup and pasta at the ready, bottles of wine sentinel. On a now cold night the cosiness, sturdy food and drink are welcome. We walk back to our hotel under the stars, lights doused along the Via Tragara, but trailing plants and flowering trees giving an illusion of balm. The black of the sea is sliced by a swathe of moonlight sharp as a knife.

I have Neruda's poems with me and I begin to envy him his travels, his persecution, his political exile, the experiences an English poet can only approach in times of war. As a professional diplomat his earliest working years were spent on consular duty in Burma, Siam, China, Japan, India, his poems taking on the flavour of a good cigar.

After a short spell at home Neruda was transferred to Madrid. He had not been there long when, in July 1936, Franco invaded. Neruda's support for the Republic was not appreciated by the Chilean government and he was soon on his way again, this time as consul to Mexico. He returned to Chile, was elected a senator, but fell foul of the US-supported dictator González Videla. He was accused of treason, went underground, and crossing the

Andes on horseback escaped first to Mexico, then to Paris.

During all this time Neruda never stopped writing poetry and his poems of these years, 340 of them, were put out as a single poem in fifteen sections under the title *Canto General*. Often bitter about the involvement of the United States in South American politics, and distressed by his own situation, Neruda looks back at aspects of his country's past, its natural history, its geography, its discovery, liberation, exploitation. His poem "The United Fruit Co" ends (in Robert Bly's translation):

> Among the blood-thirsty flies
> the Fruit Company lands its ships
> taking off the coffee and the fruit;
> the treasure of our submerged
> territories flow as though
> on plates into the ships.
>
> Meanwhile Indians are falling
> onto the sugared chasms
> of the harbours, wrapped
> for burial in the mist of the dawn;
> a body rolls, a thing
> that has no name, a fallen cipher,
> a cluster of dead fruit
> thrown down on the dump.

By the time he came to Capri, the surrealist influence and political preoccupation of his poems of the 1930s – *Residencia en la Tierra* – and *Canto General* had given way to a more personal, earthy, romantic style. In fact Neruda's writing was never other than romantic and down to earth whatever its subject. In Capri he was, as long as Videla remained in power, excluded but also liberated.

One would imagine that Neruda's staunch and sustained Communist views would date his poetry, but even at his most committed he writes with warmth that has a wide radius, drawing in people, places, objects, animals. His poems radiate good-will and affection, which is rarer than one might expect in poetry. In his imaginative embrace the world comes alive in its least significant details as well as in its grandest conceptions. His prolificness as a poet comes from a mind that is not compartmentalised, from a heart that bleeds easily, from eyes no strangers to tears. He is free with his emotions, with despair, loneliness, anxiety. He was fortunate to have his Capri interlude and enjoy a time of love.

Neruda's poetry, whatever the subject, has a sweep to it and through it he welcomes us into his world:

> I look at ships
> I look at trees of bone marrow
> bristling like mad cats,
> I look at blood, daggers and women's stockings
> and men's hair,
> I look at beds, I look at corridors where a virgin
>   is sobbing,
> I look at blankets and organs and hotels.

On our terrace in the early hours I picture him crouched over his desk, not far from where Lawrence thirty years earlier used to work, and writing, as in his poem "No Hay Olvido":

> There are so many people dead
> and so many sea-walls that the red sun used to split,
> and so many heads that the boats hit
> and so many hands that have closed around kisses,
> and so many things I would like to forget.

When he was on Capri Neruda cannot have been sure that he would ever see Chile again. But as a poet he made the most of wherever he was, his poetry a valise into which he stuffed everything he could. "I see a clouded rainbow hurrying, I see its water moving over my bones." In his *Odas Elementales* written on his eventual return home it was some kind of relief to be able to write poems to "simple things", long, thin poems to salt, a watermelon, a watch, a pair of socks even: "Maru Mori brought me / a pair / of socks / which she knitted herself with her sheep-herder's hands / two socks as soft / as rabbits / I slipped my feet / into them / as though into / two / cases / knitted / with threads of / twilight / and goatskin."

After Capri, as it turned out, it was never to be quite so bad again. He returned to Chile in 1953 and from his Isla Negra home, with the sea swirling at his feet, he was free to have his way with poetry.

He had many narrow squeaks in his life, as do most of us. To survive and be able to sit out on a winter night, reading Neruda in such a beautiful place with someone one loves, is more than privilege, a kind of blessing.

There are few places in Capri from which Ischia is not an invisible presence. There are as many from which it can be identified, a detached hump, more blur than anything, that has drifted out to sea. From Monte Solaro, the peak that towers over the island, you get the best view of all: all of Capri, its vines and olives, miniature white settlements and caves, its wooded slopes and brutal rocks, but also Ischia and Procida, the Sorrentine cape, the peaks of the Apennines.

Looking back, I think it was Lawrence Durrell's poetry that originally drew me to these islands. His first book, *A Private Country*, was published in 1943, but many of the poems in it I had already read. At sea in the bleakest days of the war I found these gentle, elliptical poems, scented by Egypt and Greece, magical. Durrell's syntax and pictorial inventiveness was quite unlike anything I had ever come across; Durrell himself, roly-poly, sun-loving, an Eastern Mediterranean sprite with a bouncing *joie de vivre*, a creature altogether more exotic than any of the poets I was reading. "I have no fear for the land / Of the dark heads with aimed noses," he wrote. "The hair of nights and the voices / Which mimic traditional laughter; / Nor for a new language where / A mole upon a dark throat / Of a girl is called 'an olive'; / All these things are simply Greece."

Better still were the poems in *Cities, Plains and People*, nearly all Levant-inspired, which appeared three years later, and *The Tree of Idleness*, written mostly when he was installed in Cyprus, "I shall die one day I suppose / In this old Turkish house I inhabit; / A ragged banana leaf outside and here / On the sill in a jam jar a rock rose."

In the same poem he was to remark on "the lack of someone spreading like a stain" and in the poem "On Mirrors": "You gone, the mirrors all reverted, / Lay banging in the empty house". This was a time of sadness for him, his wife having taken off, but the melancholy and beauty of poem after poem in *The Tree of Idleness* – "Style" ("The dry bony blade of the / Sword-grass might suit me / Better: an assassin of polish"); "Chanel" ("Scent like a river-pilot led me there"); "Mneiae" ("Soft as puffs of smoke combining, / Mneiae – remembrance of past lives") – I carried around in my head for years.

I did not meet Durrell then, though we later became friends and I edited his *Selected Poems*. After unproductive periods in South America and Yugoslavia, where he was attached to the Embassy, he began to write again on a visit to Ischia. While still at the British Legation in Belgrade he received a string of letters from his old friend Constant Zarian, then settled in Forio d'Ischia, praising the beauty and the cheapness of the island, and imploring Durrell to join them. This he did, in the summer of 1950, having begun to detest Belgrade.

From Ischia he addressed a long, affectionate, rather jokey letter in the form of a poem to Anne Ridler: "Dear Anne, I have been owing you a letter / From foreign parts – from Ischia where better." He describes the island as "decidedly volcanic, quite different to Greece though quite as 'punic'", they eat so much they wonder they can walk, "In octopus and scampi and red mullet / In hen and hare and cuttlefish and pullet." Of literary news, he writes, "There is a lot / Ischia it seems has fast become The Spot. / Capri is finished, everyone is here / Poets and painters too from all the nations. / And some of curious sexual persuasions."

One day on a bus ride he noticed:

> A man I'm sure you reverence as much as me
> Old Norman Douglas, worn as if by sea
> Like some old whorled and rubbed-out ocean shell
> Still holding shape and life and living well
> Eyes a Homeric blue and hands quite firm,
> An air of indefinable ancient charm . . .

Durrell, in a letter to Henry Miller, reported that he was planning to buy a house in Ischia and give up paid employment. The house he had his eye on fell through, but instead he was able, back in Belgrade in July, to offer a longish poem written in Ischia to John Gawsworth, then editing *Poetry Review*, an odd choice of recipient, one would have thought. At the same time he wrote to the Gotham Book Mart, "I wonder if you would be interested in 150 copies of a privately printed edition of *Deus*

Loci, a 100-line poem written and printed on Ischia this summer, each copy signed and numbered. The edition consists of 200 copies of which I am keeping 50. I would be glad to forward the rest of the edition to you @ $2.50 a copy." There was no reply.

Durrell wrote several beautiful poems in Ischia – "A Watercolour of Venice" and "Epitaph" – but "Deus Loci" is not, I think, despite some striking images, among them.

Capri, he wrote, is finished, and in 1950 it may possibly have seemed so. During my own several stays in Ischia during the 1950s and 1960s one had the feeling that Capri had been vulgarised beyond recall, that it was an ostentatious place for the very rich or for daytrippers. That was, of course, nonsense, though on an August weekend, the island swarming and the boats queuing up outside the Blue Grotto, it was pardonable to think so. Yet all through the next two or three decades there was no shortage of civilised and cultivated people living there.

Fashions change. Ischia had developed in much the same way as Capri did earlier, but, in truth, both have never lost their unique and different beauty. Perhaps, more than ever, they have become winter islands, recuperating and patrolled by ghosts.

Although from the Naples boat Capri looks, from halfway over, practically uninhabited, two formidable wedges of rock, one sheer, the other stretched out like a crocodile, with a low-slung hammock of green bearing a scatter of villas in between, from almost all routes out of the piazzetta you get a sense of an island with just the right amount of development. Where it is most urban, on the southerly paths to Punta del Cannone by way of Via Madre Serafina and Via Castello, you move quickly from secretive medieval to a semi-tropical luxuriance of plants, from dark damp alleys to the rioting mauves and pinks of

Above Marina Grande, Capri

bougainvillaea and oleander. Where rock takes over, the indifference of nature is chastened by the clinging shrub at its throat. The air is generally still, gulls circling; an absence of traffic, of aircraft, of ships, increases the sense of isolation.

We felt a certain reluctance to interrupt our gently meditative days round Via Tragara to climb up to Anacapri, which, although less than an hour's walk away, a quarter of an hour in a bus, seemed to belong to another time, another season. Anacapri had long been the favoured place for foreign visitors to alight, not only Axel Munthe, but many English and Italian writers, Graham Greene and Alberto Moravia among them, yet the moment did not seem propitious.

Nor was it. Years earlier I had wandered about the immaculately kept terraces and gardens of Munthe's villa with Archie Colquhoun, most dashing of wartime partisans, translator of Manzoni and Giuseppe Tomasi di Lampedusa, without ever falling prey to the place's fascination. For all the splendour of its situation, the sea and the remaining fragments of the Roman port that once held Tiberius's sea palace and bathing place a steep drop below, it has always seemed to me too meticulous, somehow clinical – a lovely sanatorium, with mosaics and statuary, bronze heads and plant-smothered galleries, for the very rich. There is nothing out of place, no dust or evidence that a man once lived and worked here. Even Munthe's motto painted on a wall, "To dare, to wish, to know and to keep silent", is faintly offputting.

Sean O'Faolain, writing in 1953, remarks on being grateful for what he calls "the happy nonsense" of Capri, recording its "musical comedy pastorale" in the season, "its golden limelight, its atmosphere of Albertines and lace, coloured umbrellas and waltz music, Blue Grottoes, donkeys, slim carriages" etc. O'Faolain preferred Ischia, as did Ibsen who spent the summer of 1867 at Casamicciola working on *Peer Gynt*, before an earth tremor drove him off to Sorrento. In 1883 Casamicciola actually did suffer an earthquake of fierce proportions.

O'Faolain, nevertheless, seems to have felt insecure in Ischia, as if at any moment the pumice and tufa of which it is composed might dissolve or be blown sky high. "We are too impressed by the primacy of the waters to be certain that land is an entirely reliable element."

O'Faolain took a fancy to what he calls "a doubtless dotty Irishman" from Waterford called Cathal. He wandered about in these parts during the sixth century and was taken up by the Italians who named him Cataldo. He became Bishop of Taranto, in due course returned to Capri and was buried near Munthe's villa, regarded as a saint.

I must have tried Munthe's book when I first came to these parts after the war, but perhaps because of its extraordinary popularity and appropriation by half the world I did not persevere and have resisted it ever since.

It was Henry James, recently naturalised, who offered to sponsor Munthe's own request for naturalisation and suggested he write the book. James had stayed with Munthe at San Michele and he was advising his old friend, afraid Sweden would be drawn into war on the side of Germany and utterly miserable, that the best remedy for chronic sleeplessness was to work.

Now in Capri I am trying again to read the writings of the much-travelled, enterprising and sophisticated Swedish doctor who wrote a legendary book as a cure for insomnia. Munthe's practising years were spent mainly in Paris and Rome but it was after his appointment to the Stockholm Court at the age of forty-six in 1903 that he came regularly to Capri and began the building of a house on the site of one of Tiberius's twelve villas.

There existed by then only a modest farmhouse, some vines, the ruins of a chapel.

Deteriorating eyesight caused Munthe to suffer in the hard white light of his own villa and it was to the Tower of Materita, one of several properties on land that he bought over the years, that he retired to work on his book.

There are two main ways up to Anacapri: the precipitous, winding traffic road or the almost vertical Phoenician steps cut into the rock wall, that lead from San Costanzo up to the villa itself. In one of the several prefaces to *The Story of San Michele*, Munthe recalls "Old Maria Porta Lettere who climbed the 777 Phoenician steps for thirty years on her naked feet carrying my letters."

From a distance the steps, apparently begun by the first Greek colonists and modified by the Romans, resemble a climbing caterpillar. At one time they were the only route to Anacapri from the Marina Grande, or indeed from anywhere else, then in 1870 the present road was built. The steps, starting just above Tiberius's seaside palace, end at a medieval arch, called Porta della Differencia, that marks the boundary between Capri and Anacapri. Halfway up, the small, simple Church of St Anthony of Padua, the local patron saint, known as the Sailors' Chapel, offers not only a refuge from traffic but a wonderful view of the gulf. Ladder-like and exhausting though the steps are – some of the local people still prefer them to the road – they have a scattering of protective greenery that makes the climb less arduous.

Lured by the tourist brochure's promise of a "panoramic" route we decided one morning to scorn buses and taxis and walk. A great mistake, because although the Phoenician steps are a challenge of one kind, to walk up the road used by traffic is sheer folly. One moment you are squeezed on to a cliff edge with a huge drop by buses and lorries hurtling round corners at a terrifying angle, the next you are squashed by climbing buses taking room to get round nutcracker bends. Sometimes the buses arrive simultaneously, barely an inch between them, forcing you to cling to the protecting wall.

The bus service between Capri and Anacapri may be the best in the world, for there appeared to be no noticeable interval between the climbing and descending vehicles, belching black smoke, forming a continuous chain. The journey takes only ten minutes, on foot a hellish hour.

Anacapri, unlike the town below, is a sorry sight in winter. Neglected paintwork, derelict hotels, a few tawdry gift shops, a couple of nondescript churches. Anacapri may once have had a lively artistic community and, away from the dim village centre, some pleasant countryside, but it lacks the style and drama so conspicuous elsewhere. We were glad to leave it.

The Story of San Michele, the discursive memoir of an overworked, wise, and good-humoured doctor who operates from a fashionable practice in Paris, goes to Lapland and choleraridden Naples, returns to Paris and ends up in Rome, is largely anecdotal, a series of short stories, some rather tall but generally entertaining. We get an occasional oblique reference to Capri, but after a frenetic few opening pages it is not until page 230 out of 350 that the villa begins to play any real part in the story.

Axel Munthe was eighteen when he first set foot on Capri. "Opposite the landing place stood half a dozen donkeys with saddles on their backs and bunches of flowers in their bridles and around them chattered and sang as many girls with the silver spadella stuck through their black tresses and a red handkerchief tied across their shoulders."

Seeing the Phoenician steps he determined to climb, against all advice that Anacapri was a dangerous place, inhabited by scoundrels and werewolves. At the top he meets an old man digging in his vineyard which encircles a small house, built by its owner Vincenzo from fragments of the Tiberius villa that once stood there. The ruins of a chapel cling to the rockface.

The vineyard was strewn with bits of columns, capitals, fragments of statues and coins. While contemplating this paradisal place Munthe is visited by a robed figure who announces himself as the immortal spirit of the place, offering him ownership of all he can see if he agrees to a bargain.

This demands that Munthe renounces all ambition as a doctor, "the sacrifice of your future". A long, tiresome dialogue ensues between Munthe and the subject of his vision and I begin to realise what put me off the book in the first place. There are numerous other bogus and fanciful intrusions and they at once lower the temperature of a memoir elsewhere fascinating in its medical detail.

One of the strangest episodes in the book concerns Guy de Maupassant, already famous as the author of *Boule de suif* and *La Maison Tellier*. The two met at the Salpêtrière, attending a lecture by Professor Charcot on hypnotism and insanity, a subject being researched by Maupassant for his book *Le Horla*.

Maupassant invited Munthe to visit him on his yacht *Bel-Ami* in Antibes, where the talk was about poisons, death, and particularly death at sea. Although Maupassant at the time was at the height of his powers, his imaginative energy sustained by champagne, ether, and a succession of very young dancers, to Munthe he was a doomed man. "The fear that haunted his restless brain day and night was already visible in his eyes." Ether appears to have been the accepted pick-me-up for the dancers in the Corps de Ballet at the Grand Opera, Maupassant's protégées providing Munthe with a steady stream of patients as their health deteriorated.

Soon after his stay on *Bel-Ami* Munthe came across Maupassant in the grounds of the asylum Maison Blanche in Passy. "He was walking about on the arm of his faithful François, throwing small pebbles on the flower beds with the gesture of Millet's Semeur. 'Look, look,' he said, 'they will all come up as little Maupassants in the spring if only it will rain.'"

There are many happy, lyrical pages describing the construction of the Villa San Michele, the digging of the foundations of the huge arches of the loggia, the columns, the cloisters. Munthe's fellow workers were illiterate and had only knowledge of peasants' houses, but they worked together from sunrise to sunset. It is curious that this fashionable doctor, who also devoted himself to the treatment of the poor, should have conceived of so ambitious and ostentatious a structure, cypress avenues and colonnades, pergolas and marble courtyards, ornate statue-studded terraces and fountains. Munthe eventually returned to Sweden and a Court practice in the Ducal Palace in 1949. During the intervening years he spent long periods in Capri improving his villa, left after his death to the Swedish state for scholarly and literary research, and writing.

The final chapters of *The Story* recount changing seasons and simple life on a small island. Munthe's own retinue appeared to include a baboon, a mongoose, an owl and various dogs, transported whenever possible from malaria-ridden Rome in Munthe's cutter that lay at anchor off Porto d'Anzio. "We rounded Monte Circeo as the sun was rising, caught the morning breeze from the Bay of Gaeta, darted at racing speed under the Castle of Ischia and dropped anchor at the Marina of Capri as the bells were ringing *mezzogiorno*. Two hours later I was at work in the garden of San Michele with hardly any clothes on."

As I read again now, of Munthe's blissful years of building and writing, his evident, infectious pleasure in the *contadini* and the land, I begin to feel more warmly about him. Half-blind at the end, he made his departure with dignity.

His final pages are the most moving, though almost wrecked by one of his imaginary dialogues, this time with St Peter and some aged Archangels. What made this rational, pragmatic man, perfectly aware of the "ill-defined borderland" between fact and fancy, go on so?

The last months of Munthe's time in Capri were not spent at San Michele but in the half-monastery, half-fortress Tower of Materita. He disputes Dante's view that there is no greater suffering than to remember our past happiness in present misery. "It is with joy and not with sorrow that my thoughts go back to San Michele, where I have lived the happiest years of my life. But it is true I do not like to go there any more – I feel as if I were intruding upon sacred ground, sacred to a past which can never return, when the world was young and the sun was my friend."

Nevertheless, "it is good to wander about in the soft light under the olives of Materita. It is good to sit and dream in the Old Tower, it is about the only thing I can do now."

His thoughts are continually about death, though he relishes the scents of spring as much as he ever did; the roses and honeysuckle climbing the stems of cypresses and the columns of the pergola, the anemones, crocuses, wild hyacinths, violets, orchids and cyclamen rising out of the sweet-scented grass. He shares the awakened pleasure in life of the lizards, tortoises, mongoose, golden oriole. But then, for this man who makes no mention on any page of a partner in his life, comes the day when he tries to tell his beloved dog that he must go away and leave him behind. "I stroked the big head, but my benumbed hands no longer felt the touch of his glossy coat. As I bent down to kiss him good-bye a sudden fear shone in his eyes, he drew back in terror and crept to his couch under the refectory table. I called him back but he did not come. I knew what it meant. I had seen it before."

In a preface to the 1936 illustrated edition Munthe remarks, "In one respect at least I can say with a clean conscience that I have not deceived my readers – in my love for animals. I have loved them far more than I have ever loved my fellow men. All that is best in me I have given to them . . ."

A decent walk from Anacapri, along a country lane cut through vineyards and olive groves, with a windmill in view – a walk Munthe must have done many times on his way to and from his tower at Materita – brings you to the remains of the imperial villa of Damecuta. Munthe, who often accompanied the British ambassador Lord Dufferin on visits to the area, wrote, "The old Emperor knew what he was doing when he built his largest villa there. Next to San Michele, Damecuta commands the most beautiful view on the island." Many fragments of the old villa were carted off by Sir William Hamilton, one-time British ambassador to Naples, whose wife was carrying on with Nelson.

This is a flatter, more wooded part of the island, much favoured by the aristocracy in Roman times for the building of villas. There is sea visible on all sides, with sheer, protective cliffs at the edges. It was from here that a beautiful, illiterate peasant girl was carried off by an English peer, a relative of the ambassador, who married her and took her to England. After his death she came back to Capri and the simple life of her childhood.

The whole plain of Damecuta is scattered with bits of masonry, the remains of farm buildings, sheds, courtyards, walls, arches. It was the imperial villa that, because of its position, was the one to suffer most from the various eruptions of Vesuvius, one of which more or less wiped it out. Below the villa area, and in better shape, the Tower of Damecuta, built much later, commands the approach from open sea. Immediately beneath the tower lies the grotto whose Sèvres-blue water has helped to make Capri's fortune.

It was not a bad place to start Roger Peyrefitte's *The Exile of Capri*, a camp, mildly entertaining novel, written in 1959, by a French Jesuit-educated former diplomat. Peyrefitte had made a name for himself with his first novel *Les Amitiés particulières*, set in a Jesuit college and describing the emotional and sexual entanglements of priests and pupils. Peyrefitte next turned his waspish talent on embassy life, not endearing himself to his former colleagues.

By now he had been nearly twenty years out of the service. His last half-dozen books alternated scathing assaults on the Catholic hierarchy with novels increasingly devoted to homosexuality and drugs. *The Exile of Capri* is one of these. At the same time, in its evocation of Capri, it is one of the most detailed.

Jean Cocteau, in a preface to the novel, writes, "To be granted dreams but not genius must be the worst of tortures. I have always liked those beings who, incapable of creating master-pieces, try to become one in their own persons."

The beautiful Jacques d'Adelsward Fersen, the real-life "exile of Capri", was such a creature. He arrives in Capri in 1897 at the age of seventeen, having encountered on Vesuvius an aristocratic thirty-year-old cavalry officer Robert de Tournel, an aspiring poet, who befriends him. Fersen is rich, a baron, a student of Rimbaud. Together they set off from Vesuvius for Capri, establishing themselves at the Quisisana. From their adjoining balconies they can see the Carthusian monastery, the Scoglio delle Sirene at Marina Piccola, the Faraglioni. The scent of tuber roses drifts up to them.

They are no sooner seated at their table in the dining room when Oscar Wilde and Lord Alfred Douglas enter, but on complaints from an English diner are refused a table. Fersen is outraged, but the older, wiser de Tournel gives him a gentle lecture on social behaviour.

The next day they make their way on foot to the Villa Jovis, standing aside for mules and sedan-chair travellers, en route discussing their respective school days, adolescent attachments. Nothing more is related of this gentle friendship except its establishing of sexual leanings.

They do not meet again for several years, for while Fersen continues his education in Paris, enjoying a dandyish social life, de Tournel is sent to India. When de Tournel reappears they go together to Venice. Soon afterwards Fersen is called up, having in the meantime managed only modest success with his attempts to break into smart literary life.

Out of the army Fersen dreams only of returning to Capri. He sets off again with Tournel, the armaments manufacturer Krupp now installed at the Quisisana, dispensing largesse, his yacht at anchor. Krupp and his friend, a German painter, share out the boys, so it is alleged. The talk at dinner is only in German, burly sailors in striped jerseys sitting amongst German dukes and princes renowned for their homosexuality.

In Germany Krupp was not so fortunate. Peyrefitte makes use of a provincial newspaper report in which Krupp is described as a "*Soldatentante*" – a queer with a taste for soldiers. A Berlin socialist broadsheet accused Krupp of being a corrupter of Capri youth, of holding orgies in grottoes, of posing naked with young fishermen. Krupp began a libel action but did not live to see it through, possibly committing suicide after his expulsion from Capri by order of the Italian authorities.

These events, and the gossip that ensued, give a documentary aspect to the novel, in which it is not wholly clear what actually happened, and what is invented. Fersen's activities in Paris involving priests, black masses, drugs and boys take him away from Capri for a time. He is arrested, mocked for dyeing his hair and wearing corsets, but in prison finds his literary reputation soaring. This was, in fact, the case.

Fersen spends six months in gaol, returning immediately to Capri, having picked up a fifteen-year-old labourer in Rome and offered him employment. In Capri he takes up residence in the Cercostella, the villa in which I am writing this now. He has brought with him the boy's brother and sister, two French manservants, a chef and a housekeeper.

The boy Nino takes lessons and goes to Mass, just as Norman Douglas's youthful servant did, so the local priest relates. Fersen and Nino do the sights, examine archaeological remains, take tea at Café Morgano or the Quisisana. At night they sit together on their terrace under the stars, Fersen smoking his opium pipes, the boy cigarettes.

All the while a new house, as grand in its way as San Michele was to be, was being built on Monte Tiberio. Krupp's disgrace and suicide was forgotten, and to the housewarming of the Villa Lysis in 1905 came the island's grandees, Norman Douglas, Cerio, Prince Giovanni Caracciolo, Marchese Adolfo Patrizi, the last two married into Capri families. Douglas soon turns the party talk to satyrs and hermaphrodites, "the ancestors of sodomy".

"For Jacques and Nino the distractions of Capri consisted of going to Desiderio the barber's for their newspapers, dropping in at the Quisisana or the Café Morgano, lunching or dining with the Lovatellis or the Wolcott-Perry sisters."

Fersen becomes devoted to his garden, its scents and sunsets and, between the pine trees, its view of Ischia. At night, lying naked beneath a silk sarong, he takes pleasure in the elegance of the opium ritual.

Gorky arrives on the island. "Jacques would have liked to mix with these real exiles. It was their mystery rather than their idealism which attracted him. But they composed a block as solid as the island's rocks and would have held his kind of exile in contempt."

Capri is at the centre of Peyrefitte's book, but he pays a diplomat's attention to events in the world outside. Sometimes their characters descend on Capri itself, Lenin, the English Queen, various statesmen. In gratitude for Capri having been protected from the homosexual scandals now raging in Germany, the vicar-archpriest of Capri's ex-cathedral organises a procession to the grotto of the Madonna of Lourdes, the local curate taking as the theme for his sermon "Our Lady and the Capriot sailor".

Meanwhile, Fersen publishes a novel about Capri, its hero a French sculptor married to an English girl who deserts him for a Russian prince. He is comforted by a disgraced young French nobleman and throws the statue of his wife into the sea, cursing the Sirens' Isle.

Although the novel has some success in Paris, it is not, to its author's dismay, well received in Capri. His friend Cerio tells him why: he has made fun of the island's priests, festivals, and officials, and presented the people as money-grabbing and ungrateful. Worst of all, the foreign visitors are described as bankrupt hawkers, corrupt lawyers, ex-croupiers, deported gentry, newly rich dishwashers, "all fraternising with old, reformed tarts, un-marriageable girls, or lesbians". Norman Douglas is no kinder, castigating him for employing staff who are not Capriots and who can expect to be left nothing when the game is over.

Nino, as he grows up, begins to flirt with girls. Fersen encounters an English girl on one of the paths outside his villa and is astonished to find himself attracted to her. She turns out to be the daughter of the Duke of Richmond's brother, who comes after Fersen with a stick. There are no further attempts at normality.

Nino's call-up papers arrive and simultaneously Fersen is requested to leave the island, a belated fit of morality having seized the Capri committee. Fersen spends the years of Nino's military service in France, only occasionally meeting him on leave from his barracks in Turin.

When Nino is released they are happily reunited, but a return to Capri has to wait until the general election of 1913. Fersen buys a new boat, a steam yacht, and they sail off towards Corfu and Greece. The outbreak of the Italian–Turkish war in the area interrupts their progress so they make for North Africa. At Biskra, Arab boys run after Fersen asking him if he knows "Papa Gide". When his period of banishment is over Fersen returns to Capri, this time on Norman Douglas's advice employing only Capriots. The Capriots, having missed Fersen's money, welcome him back with open arms.

In 1913, after a voyage to Japan, Fersen publishes a book of short stories. The same year he returns to Capri with Nino. A German, Baron Monteuffel, arrives on Capri on behalf of the Institute of Sexual Research, his object the study of penises. Following men into lavatories he often emerges with a black eye. He was not made welcome at the Villa Lysis, nor by Dr Munthe, a particular disappointment to him for he had heard of the doctor's strong, goaty smell. The baron's researches were soon sidelined by the assassination of the Archduke Franz

Ferdinand at Sarajevo and the outbreak of war. It had unexpected consequences for ex-sergeant Fersen. Obliged to report for a medical in Naples, he was rejected and ordered to enter hospital to be cured of "addiction to narcotics". Nino is called up for service in the Italian army, Robert de Tournel, long out of touch, is killed in the Artois. After years of failed disintoxication, cocaine having replaced opium, Fersen is discharged as incurable and allowed home.

Capri, with the Armistice signed, now fills up with duchesses, *principessas*, lesbians, and rich bohemians of all sexes. Douglas's *South Wind* is published, Nino is discharged from the army. Soon, too, the Marchesa Casati arrives, having bullied Munthe into letting her the Villa San Michele. In her entourage are a boa constrictor, several parrots, and an owl. Her negro lover is in charge of the leopard and two greyhounds. Baron Monteuffel, who had found his posting as a male nurse in a POW camp useful for his researches, returns to the island.

At the age of forty-three Fersen is described as having retained his youthful beauty but not his health. His eyes are sunken, the pupils dilated, his face waxen. Not content just to sniff cocaine, he now mixes it in his drinks. Aware that his time is running out Fersen decides to end it. After a final pipe with Nino and a new young friend he empties what he knows to be a fatal dose of cocaine into his wine.

Does anyone now know of the Baron Jacques d'Adelsward Fersen or of Peyrefitte's amoral novel? Yet *The Exile of Capri* evokes a period crucial to Capri's legend. Where the characters went you can go today, for their comings and goings are recorded faithfully and in detail. Half-biography, half-fiction, Peyrefitte's book is a revealing document of its time, real people, scarcely disguised, acting out fantasies in a world collapsing around them.

In his epilogue Peyrefitte claims that Fersen did for Capri what von Gloeden, the German photographer of nude males, did for Taormina, Lord Brougham for Cannes, the Empress Eugénie for Biarritz and the Empress Elizabeth for Corfu. "He is both torch and guide even to many who have never heard of him. None is more fitted to stand for Capri in its joys and sorrows, which were, and are and will be rehearsal and repetition of his own."

With Fascism came a clampdown on all those activities Peyrefitte associated with Capri and which had added notoriety to beauty. Attention, however, was focused on foreigners and Norman Douglas was one of the first to depart. Contessa Ciano, Mussolini's daughter, the Prince of Hesse, and Prince Umberto, heir to the Italian throne, were among the new intake, a rather different type of visitor.

On any excursion to Monte Tiberio you are likely to pass what is now called Villa Fersen, lying at the far end of Via Lo Capo. It was deserted for a long time, a subject of lawsuits and victim of neglect. Unlike San Michele, which does honour to the image of its animal-loving founder, Fersen's villa is a monument to nothing but corruption, self-indulgence, and vanity. Fersen lived for pleasure more obsessively and daringly than most, his moderate literary talent offset by immense wealth. His was a life lived in the Capri manner of his time, one both more corrupt and superficially glamorous than any that has succeeded it. Capri was about beauty and love and the *dérèglement des sens*. In the more staid climate of the present the beauty, on an empty, winter day, birds wheeling over the unforgiving cliffs, swooping low over vines, still exists, only it is a beauty of nature, drug free, artless. Perhaps out of step once more with its era.

A cold morning in the piazzetta, windless but sharp. A short stroll takes us past the Quisisana, cleaners visibly at work, to the great monastic complex begun by Count Giacomo Arcucci, secretary to Giovanna I, Queen of Naples, in the 1360s. Buried in a kind of bowl, pines, cypresses, prickly pears supervisory on the sides, whichever way you approach you are looking down on it. The cloisters glow in an almost subterranean light, the brick meringue-like in its cup of green. Children can be seen scurrying under the arches, trailing their satchels. After its centuries of desecration and suppression, the Charterhouse appears now an open and welcoming place, devoid of mystique. Students rather than monks occupy it, an improvement on the hotel complex envisaged until the philosopher Benedetto Croce, living in Naples, put a stop to it.

From Via Matteotti you get a good view of all the work buildings dependent on the Charterhouse – laboratories, carpenters' shops, warehouses, stables – their elephant-coloured, rounded roofs creating a sense of fluency. From here the convent of seclusion, the central part, with cells, refectory, chapterhouse and gallery area, seems solidly clamped into its rocky base, but move round a bit and you see that only a few yards separate it from the cliff edge.

It is one of the peculiarities of Capri, today happily given over to itself, that you see it nearly always as from a low-flying aeroplane. The constant switch of levels, the terracing and sudden falls, gives you simultaneously a feeling of distance and immediacy. Benches everywhere invite you simply to sit and look. Gazing at the cloisters below me I am equally aware of the Faraglioni in their blue necklace, the green scoop of the Giardini di Augusto at my back, the jagged cliffs of Punta Tragara.

It was from just above where we are sitting, late one afternoon in Café Morgana in 1924, that the Futurist Marinetti addressed a crowd. The German linguistic philosopher Walter Benjamin described coming across Marinetti in Capri and seeing him in action: "I met the framed heads of futurism. Marinetti, whom I visited for tea in very interesting company, Vasari, and the likeable painter Prampolini. Marinetti is certainly quite a lad. He performed a 'noise poem' to great effect: neighing, boomer guns, rattling carts, machine gun fire, etc. In addition he told stories of his stay in Fiume during the decisive days of the campaign by D'Annunzio, with whom he fell out on account of the latter's Caesarism."

George Steiner has spoken of Benjamin as one of the "spell-binding literary philosophic presences of this century". References to him pop up everywhere nowadays and writings about him far outnumber his own few collections of aphorisms and essays. Born in Berlin in 1892, for most of his life he struggled to make a living, translating, doing odd teaching jobs, reviewing and broadcasting. He failed to get a permanent post at the University of Frankfurt-am-Main. But, despite his hand-to-mouth existence, he managed to keep constantly on the move, spending several months in Moscow, Ibiza and Capri, before going into exile in Paris in 1933. He published his reflections on contemporary Germany under the title *One-Way Street*, a pretty despairing look at German life during the Weimar Republic.

It was as a means of escape from the ominous events of 1923 in Germany – the French occupation of the Ruhr, Hitler's failed coup in Bavaria, communist uprisings in Saxony, serious inflation – that Benjamin decided on his journey to Capri. The Brechts were in southern Italy and a number of other German intellectuals in the area. Ernest Bloch he already knew and in Capri they spent many evenings at a beach bar discussing books and philosophy.

Benjamin seems to have taken his Capri adventure seriously. "To get back to my trip," he wrote, "people in Berlin are agreed there is a conspicuous change in me. The exaltation with which

I prepared for it in the spring by fasting and similar excesses and with which, not without Dora's intensive support, I struggled to achieve this change both externally and internally, was not in vain."

Benjamin's stay in Capri, which he used for daily letter writing and reading, as well as explorations of the island, resulted in his "Capri Chronicle" in which he remarks on everything from local housing and living conditions to conversations with friends and reflections on political philosophers. Benjamin, with his steel-rimmed glasses, heavy moustache and shock of dark hair, must have seemed, as he sat with his books and papers in one of the piazzetta cafés, the very embodiment of a German intellectual. But he was an intellectual, despite his gifts and intelligence, without any secure base, politically or in the terms and conditions of his subsequent life. With the coming of the Nazis, Germany became lost to him, both as a home and as a recipient of his writings.

Those who write about Benjamin agree that his months in Capri not only acted as a refuge but effected a change in his thinking. He came to realise that in the altered circumstances of Germany, philosophy had a need to be practical.

After leaving Capri, Benjamin travelled in the next year to Spain and Lithuania. He published his *The Origin of German Tragic Drama* and wrote extensively on Proust, Kafka and Baudelaire. His essay on Goethe's *Elective Affinities* was the most striking and typical of all his critical pieces, the similarity between the situation in the novel and his own personal predicament making for a passionately-felt involvement.

Benjamin's last few months, after a brief internment on the outbreak of war, were spent mainly on the run. He was in Paris, attached to the Sorbonne, when the German army reached the city, leaving it at the last moment with thousands of others making their way south. Benjamin made for Lourdes, then Marseilles, where he hoped to collect papers enabling him to get to America. These did not materialise.

The French were by now handing over all emigrants to the Germans, in whatever parts of France they were living. Benjamin, with a few friends, decided to cross into Spain over the mountains. They managed to reach Port-Bou, a small port badly damaged in the Civil War. The plan was to make for Lisbon by train and there to seek visas for the United States. At Port-Bou they reported to the police only to find that their transit visa had been cancelled and that all refugees were to be sent back. For Benjamin this would mean return to French internment followed almost certainly by a German concentration camp.

The Spanish police allowed the party one night in Port-Bou, after which they would be escorted back across the frontier. Benjamin took the opportunity to take a fatal dose of the morphine that he always carried with him. Had he hung on a little longer he might have survived, for almost immediately the Spanish authorities eased their restrictions and allowed the rest of the party to continue on their way.

In 1979 a small plaque was erected in the terraced, seaside cemetery at Port-Bou. Then, in 1994, the Israeli sculptor Dani Karavan used a passage from Benjamin's "On the Concept of History" as a text for his extraordinary monument, *Passages*: "It is more arduous to honour the memory of the nameless than that of the renowned. Historical construction is devoted to the memory of the nameless."

I am reminded of my friend and neighbour R. B. Kitaj's long obsession with Benjamin. In a note to his 1972–3 painting *The Autumn of Central Paris (After Walter Benjamin)*, Kitaj wrote, "Dear Benjamin is now a truly chewed over cultural spectre . . . his wonderful and difficult montage, pressing together quickening tableaux from texts and from a disjunct world . . . his personality began to speak to the painter in me – the adventure of his addiction to fragment-life, the allusive and incomplete nature of his work (Gestapo at his heels) . . . Benjamin thrills me in no small measure because he does not cohere, and beautifully."

That seems fair. In Kitaj's painting, set in the autumn of 1940, Benjamin, cigarette in hand, is at the centre of a café, apparently talking, only his head and spectacles visible. He is hemmed in by groups of people and by an assortment of red tables. It is not plain what the painting means in anything like literal terms, but it is dominated by the black cliff of Benjamin's hair and the swarming red of the tables and chairs.

That a writer with no completed, let alone major, work, who to the very end was never quite sure what he represented or really thought, should have such influence, in all countries, on all generations, is a kind of triumph. Uncertainty, it would seem, is more seductive than conviction.

The piazzetta begins to fill up, dogs making rendezvous. Soon the Sorrentine and Neapolitan necklace lights up. It is cold enough for topcoats and scarves. For so many refugees and exiles Capri was a temporary haven, a time out of time. A far cry from the orgiastic version handed down by unreliable Roman storytellers.

I never discovered where the Villa Discopoli was, even if it had retained its name since Rainer Maria Rilke stayed there in the autumn of 1906 as the guest of Frau Fähndrich, the sister of the Rilkes' friend the Countess Schwerin. I thought it might be one of the villas lurking behind a walled garden and guarded by palm trees in Via Tragara, just below the balcony where I am writing, or on the way to Villa Jovis where Peyrefitte's sad, beautiful "Exile of Capri" held court. Alternatively, it could have been a neighbour of Gorky's establishment on the steep path to the Marina Piccola, or somewhere on the slopes of Anacapri.

Rilke was thirty-one, exhausted in his usual fashion, hard up, longing for solitude. He had a wife, the sculptress Clara Westhoff, and a small child, but was happier apart from them, fond though he was. His own needs always came first. Although his great works, the *Duino Elegies* and the *Sonnets to Orpheus* were some way off, he had a reputation. He had been to Russia, travelling with the Russian-born, intellectually ambitious philosophy student Lou Salomé, published a book of poems, failed to become an officer in the family tradition, and most recently put in a stint as secretary to Rodin in Paris, about which he wrote a memoir.

Dependent as he frequently was on the hospitality of well-born women, Rilke usually managed to keep a part of himself separate. When he arrived in Capri he was so determined to get down to work that he barely noticed where he was. Frau Fähndrich gave him a cottage to himself and the inhabitants of the villa, two old ladies and the young Countess Solms-Laubach, never imposed themselves on him. When he did emerge to look about him he found "the indisputable beauty" of the island a challenge and rather depressing.

Much of Rilke's time in Capri was spent in working on his prose book *The Notebook of Malte Laurids Brigge*, writing poems, and firing off letters to family and friends. His wife Clara called in for a day on her way to Egypt.

Despite the attention shown to his needs and the comparative peace of his surroundings Rilke began to long for Paris, where of all places he seemed to work best. However, his restlessness was cured by his sudden discovery of the country round Anacapri into which he began to make daily climbs. He felt, somewhat surprisingly, that it was like being in Greece. "For no landscape", he wrote to Clara, "could be more Greek than this, no sea more filled with the distances of antiquity than the land and sea that I see and experience on my walks to Anacapri. That is Greece, without the works of art of the Greek world, but almost as though they had not yet come into being."

He came upon the disused Church of Santa Maria a Cetrella on the cliffs behind the village. "I have begun to write some verses for the poor forgotten Madonna up there. The little church is shut, so I say all sorts of nice things to her through the door."

A visitor to the Villa Discopoli, of some value as it turned out to Rilke, was the fairly elderly, stout and red-faced Swedish evolutionist Ellen Key, with whom Rilke had been corresponding. Her startling views and appearance caused some upset to the German inhabitants of the villa, but it was at her suggestion that Rilke began his translation of Elizabeth Barrett Browning's *Sonnets from the Portuguese*. Ellen Key did not stay long enough to disrupt the quiet rituals of the household too damagingly, but she interrupted Rilke's regular explorations.

He did, however, spend an evening with the newly arrived Gorky, reporting by letter to the departed Ellen Key: "Gorky spoke well and simply about Verhaeren and Hofmannsthal. But the 'democrat' he is at such pains to exhibit stands between us. The obstacle is all the greater in this case, because I feel that the revolutionary is a contradiction both of the poet and the Russian."

It had begun to warm up by the beginning of May by which time Rilke had spent six months in a kind of hibernation, one not without results. But he was ready now to return to his spiritual home of Paris. Later he was to remark that he could not have undertaken the labour of writing *Malte* without those quiet evenings at the Villa Discopoli where "nothing happened except that I sat with two old ladies and a young girl and watched them doing needlework, and in the end one of them would peel an apple for me."

In the daytime the only sounds on Via Mulo are your own footsteps on the descent to the sea. At night, with the various villas nesting on either side in green caves, there is no sound at all. Darkness has withdrawn all noise, were there criminals about they could operate in icy secrecy.

It was, however, down here that Rilke came to visit Gorky. In 1905 Gorky had been locked up in Peter and Paul Fortress in St Petersburg for protesting against the Bloody Sunday massacre of 9 January. Involved on his release in the armed rising in Moscow he fled Russia to evade arrest, eventually settling in Capri. Recently separated from his wife, he had taken up with Maria Andreeva, with whom he arrived by boat from New York, where he had gone on a fundraising trip on behalf of the Bolsheviks.

Although Gorky was aware that a return to Russia in the near future was out of the question he was not isolated in Capri, which was turning into a home from home for exiled Russian writers. Soon after his arrival he wrote to the publisher Ladyzhnikov: "Many Russian writers are here at present . . . and gloomy people they are. They sit with knitted brows as they silently contemplate the vanity of all earthly things and the insignificance of man. And they talk of corpses, graveyards, toothache, and headaches, of the tactlessness of the socialists and other such things . . . Flowers wither, flies expire, fish die, stones pull faces, as if they are about to be sick."

Gorky's colleagues from the Znanie publishing collective did not all approve of his revolutionary involvements at the expense of his literary activities. Leonid Andreev wrote to a friend from

Capri, "Life here is not good. The only real person is Gorky and even he is not right somehow. He has become extremely narrow, and his brains are well and truly scrambled."

Gorky had formed a group in Capri known as "the God builders", whose view was that Marxist ideas would benefit from a healthy infusion of religious spirit. Gorky had been on good terms with Lenin. This new religious zeal was not to the taste of the firmly atheist Lenin, who took it upon himself to call on Gorky in Capri. Gorky's fame internationally was comparable to Lenin's own, but although their cooperation was important to the Bolshevik cause Lenin left Capri for Switzerland with no narrowing of the gap between them.

The next months saw them moving still further apart. Gorky and his "God-building" friends decided to set up a political school for Russian workers on the island and though it prospered for a while it was finally undermined by Lenin who set up a rival establishment in Paris.

This failure, of both friendship and philosophy, cast a shadow on Gorky's time in Capri. Lenin came again to Capri a year later but they could not agree, either about religion or political strategy.

Gorky by now had serious financial problems, though he managed to finish his novel *Confession,* into which he put all his new ideas. His relationship with Andreeva had become less exciting than it had promised to be and it prevented him from seeing his twelve-year-old son. By 1913, his health was deteriorating and he was ready to leave.

During his time in Capri Gorky, as well as work on novels and many literary and political articles, wrote hundreds of letters, many of them to his wife. He constantly invited her to Capri, well aware of the awkward situation that would result with Andreeva living in his villa. In his letters to her he makes plain how much he suffers from their separation, how much he misses his son, how devastated he is at the death of their five-year-old daughter.

In one of his letters to his wife Gorky gives some idea of the kind of life led by the Russian exiles. "Andreev left after creating a fine scandal on the island. He got dead drunk, wanted to shoot himself as usual, fell down, smashed his forehead, pushed somebody into the water etc. I have a hard time with him . . . All these writer fellows of today are mentally ill, pathetic and perverted; to hell with them."

Gorky is not kind in his letters about many of his fellow writers. "Blok is simply remaking the bad half of Paul Verlaine in a Russian manner . . . his petty talent is drying up completely, a conceited boy who is too greedy for fame and whose soul is without trousers and heart." Sologub "is an old coquette who is in love with death, always flirting with it in the fearful expectation that it will give him a crack on the skull". Tolstoy "is an artist of genius, beyond comparison, but I don't like him. He is an insincere man who is excessively in love with himself. His humility is hypocritical and his desire to suffer is offensive."

Gorky seems surprised that his wife is unhappy. "You shouldn't be sad. Look at what wonderfully interesting times we are living in." He tells his wife that he is studying mathematics and Italian, soon starting on English. Gorky gives little sense that he ever goes out of doors or is in the island at all. His thoughts are only about Russia, its politics and literature, so he might just as well be writing from St Petersburg.

A savage earthquake on the mainland, which caused 100,000 deaths on 28 December 1908, breaks up the obsession with Russia briefly and in a long letter to Bunin praising the latter's novel *The Village* he begs Bunin to visit him in Capri. "What magnificent quarters we will find for you, oh my! Facing south, sun all day, a covered balcony." Capri, he remarks, is a "lovely stone set amid the sea".

It was just this time of year, mid-winter. Gorky writes in another letter that the Russian visitors "behave like pigs, and rabid ones to boot". He reports to his wife that his personal life is "abominable".

Although Capri was Gorky's base for seven years he made occasional sorties out, to London for a conference, to Paris to see his wife, to Alassio and other places on the Italian mainland. In November 1912 he informs his wife that Andreeva has taken all her things and won't be returning. "I have a bad cold," he writes. "I'm coughing like an old dog, my head aches. I don't go out of doors, of course, anyway the weather is rotten – it's windy and rainy." He confirms that he is living alone, so could be visited, or his son sent on his own.

In fact, none of this came to pass. After the isolation of the Capri years he was only too glad to be back in the thick of Russian publishing and politics. On 31 December, having been granted some kind of amnesty despite being a political "undesirable", he arrived at St Petersburg's Warsaw station.

At moments it is still winter and we huddle in overcoats. Hours later the sun beats down and we sweat. On benches along Via Tragara the old women sit knitting, there are long days to get through before scarves and gloves can be discarded. In the Giardini di Augusto dogs chase each other watched over by old men with rheumy eyes. Smoke from bonfires curls up into the thin, colourless air. A solitary freighter pushes almost imperceptibly north. It takes time for the spring, and for the day to get going.

I have begun a life of E. F. Benson by Brian Masters, largely because of Benson's association with Capri, where he spent an increasing amount of time in the summer pre-1914. For me, he had always been one of those writers known largely by family association – with Rye, where he became Mayor, with his brother A. C., who wrote a life of E. F. ("Fred") with his father E. W., who became Headmaster of Wellington and Archbishop of Canterbury. He was friendly with Lord Alfred Douglas and Wilde, with the Somersets, one of whom had been forced into exile because of an infatuation with a seventeen-year-old boy, and another involved in the Cleveland Street scandal relating to a male brothel in London. Fred had a taste for booze, not a matter for approval by the Archbishop. But he was on good terms with Henry James, who had a sentimental attachment to his brother, A. C., who became Master of Magdalene College, Cambridge.

E. F. wrote a great many novels, stylish, good-humoured, rich in diverse characters, among which the Lucia series brought him fame and fortune. They are not, however, revealing about his own life and feelings. Unlike some of his contemporaries he was secretive about his homosexuality, though made no bones about his pleasure at being in the company of homosexuals like Somerset Maugham.

In fact, when Benson chose to have a home in Capri, he shared it with Maugham, usually absent, and the homosexual John Brooks, failed writer and husband of the renowned lesbian artist Romaine Goddard. Brooks, a permanent resident of Capri, arrived in 1895 and died there in 1929. He liked the best of everything but had to rely on others to pay for it. He occupied himself with some unpublished translations from the French and was not slow to denounce Benson's novels. "Fond as I am of him I *cannot* read his stuff. It seems to me deplorable trash."

Benson was in Capri, at his Villa Cercola, with Brooks when

the 1914–18 war broke out. He was too old, at forty-seven, to have to join up, he was more or less indifferent to world affairs, and if ever there was a place remote from politics and war, that was Capri. But he returned home eventually and was put to work at the Ministry of Information, one of his tasks being to report on Italy and the Pope's probable allegiance. He was free to visit Capri.

Sadly for Benson, the owner of Villa Cercola decided no longer to rent. He offered it to Benson and Brooks, but Brooks had no money and Benson had just taken on Lamb House in Rye. He remained at Rye until his death from cancer of the throat – he had smoked heavily all his life – in 1940. Capri had, in the end, proved only the sweetest of interludes.

As it had proved for us. A month out of winter, hot one minute, frozen the next. Our only conversation was with each other. Left to our own devices, there were no distractions to disturb the jostling voices of the past. We languished in memories of other people – of Bunin, Benjamin, Benson, Neruda, Gorky, Rilke – lulled by seductive scents, by the siren songs of a compulsive sea.

Aeolian Islands: *Late Spring 1998*

FROM CATANIA, IN the dark, past the lemon groves and shorelights of Acireale, perched, like Taormina to its north, high above looping rocky bays and sprints of sand. This is puppet-theatre country, one of the few surviving areas of it in Italy, where also the handsome Piazza del Duomo, in an otherwise uninteresting urban sprawl, hauls in students of Sicilian baroque. Acireale has three times gone under to lava streams, the last time in 1693. There are sulphur baths still, their rancid, cloying smell drifting over the railway station. Behind us, offshore, lie the rocks of the Scogli dei Ciclopi.

But now we are driving under the stars inland, Taormina glittering on its slopes on our seaward side. We pass through endless tunnels, the road cut into the foothills of Etna, its peak glowing at intervals like a cigar gently drawn on. Just beyond one of these motorway tunnels, in a villa on what was then a bare hillside behind the spectacular Greek theatre, later reconstructed in the gladiatorial Roman manner, D. H. Lawrence spent three exhausted years trying to recover from his indignities in the 1914–18 war.

Lawrence, at some stage, tried his hand at translating the novels of the great Catania-born novelist Giovanni Verga, *I Malavoglia* and *Maestro Don Gesualdo* among them. Verga was much travelled and sophisticated but returned home to write earthy, passionate novels, set in the mountainous country we were travelling through, of a kind calculated to excite Lawrence.

It was late when we reached Milazzo, too late for a boat

anyway. It being Sunday night the *passeggiata* was in full swing under the stout palms that line the *lungomare*, the girls in fire-fly dresses boldly flaunting their immunity, the young men in groups eyeing them tentatively and smoking. Occasionally a motorbike would roar past.

What we could see of the port looked handsome gone to seed, a semi-circle of plain, nineteenth-century buildings with ornate balconies, and next to them similar buildings either boarded up or decrepit. Boats were drawn up on the shore and the moon on the water contrived a semblance of magic.

The end of the line in more ways than one, Milazzo must once have been dignified. Garibaldi won his great victory here and before that Milazzo's strategic importance caused it to be repeatedly squabbled over, from the Greeks in the eighth century BC to the British during the Napoleonic wars.

The town is dominated by a citadel, its magnificent forti-fications the equal of any in Italy. The Inquisition flourished here and it feels like it. Built on the site of the Greek acropolis, itself Arab in foundation, it reached its present incarnation under the Spaniards in the seventeenth century. It would have been a brave prisoner whose heart did not quake at the sight of this grim fortress, with its cells, tunnels, and remedial keeps.

Unfortunately for Milazzo, the romantic if alarming associa-tions of this part of the town are offset by the oil refinery in the docks at the eastern end. From its chimneys belch yellow, curdling fumes that lie like a duvet from under which the ferry and hydrofoil docks barely extricate themselves.

We sleep in a hotel that has the size and contours of a barracks. Opposite, apparently closed, the Dominican Chiesa del Rosario, whose convent was the scene of some of the worst Inquisitorial excesses, presents a bland face to the world.

*

Next morning the quays, newly washed, glisten, and between the palms fishermen lay out their silvery catch. Remove the oil refinery and Milazzo would be a resort to be reckoned with.

More imposing still does it seem, when we look back from the stern of the sparkling white ferry, the *Piero della Francesca*, as we steam out past the long thin claw of the Capo Milazzo headland – sandy half-moons enclosed by low, salmon-pink cliffs. The mildewed stone of the fearful citadel buildings with their rusty gates on its hill top, the snow summit of Etna behind, the languorous beauty and repose of the old city, the fishing boats beached under stolid palms – if you saw only this you would be surprised Milazzo was not more of a place in itself instead of simply a port of embarkation.

Shut off by a beak-shaped promontory from the narrow straits of Messina and easy access to the coast of Italy at Reggio di Calabria and Villa San Giovanni, Milazzo has only the Aeolian islands to serve. Cefalu and Palermo to the west are better reached by road and train, and it is from Palermo that regular ferries run to Naples, Cagliari and Genoa.

The nearest of its starfish archipelago, Vulcano, a mere ninety minutes' sailing from Milazzo, was soon visible, one of several mauve smudges on the horizon. Although seas here are often rough, islands being cut off from each other for days at a time, the regular criss-crossing of steamers and hydrofoils creates fellow-feeling.

The sea today is calm, to the point of being almost gelatinous. On the chart the seven islands seem like rocks carelessly dropped from an aeroplane. All, in varying degrees, are tent-shaped, the villages sliding off the sides of a central crater. As we came to know them better their differences of style and feature became more apparent and almost always wisps of smoke were visible from below the crater's rim. There was a Magritte-like element to it, a surrealist giant in a bowler hat puffing on a cigarette.

There are only a handful of passengers, the Milazzo football team on their way to a match on Lipari being the largest component. Most of the players have collar-length hair in the lush Ginola style and their coach harangues them in extravagant fashion from the moment of departure. They pay not the slightest attention, lolling unconcernedly or gazing out to sea.

From a distance Vulcano, where we are basing ourselves, appears to be joined to Lipari, though there is a narrow half-mile channel between the two. To the east the smaller shapes of Panarea and Stromboli, in line ahead formation, can be discerned.

As we tie up the first whiff of sulphur hits us. The small harbour of Porto di Levante, host to a single waterfront hotel, the Faraglione, contains a fishing boat or two, some port buildings. Dominating it is a forbidding wall of rock, steep and fissured, that is the opposite of welcoming. At different times of day, in various lights, it changes colour, dove grey, to lilac, to deep purple. Most of the time it wears a thin spurt of steam.

From port level this cliff is inaccessible. Separated from it by a road, to which most of the village clings, is a dislodged out-crop of volcanic rock, mustard-coloured and porous. The volcano's rejects lie about like abandoned toys.

The Gran Cratere, from which the island descends, looms ominously over the harbour, a huge, lanced boil whose discharges solidify to form rivulets of lava. Later we saw a more gentle side to it, layers of dune-like, black sand dotted with gorse. A path winds above a flat plain to the crust.

The volcano's aspect from the sea – apparently it is one of the oldest, on its last legs – would deter most sailors from landing, especially if they came upon it from the east, where cliffs like

the legs of giant elephants, creased and scaly, run almost vertically into water.

In the circumstances it is astonishing that anyone ever
ventured here, especially since it was only in the eighteenth
century that the island was settled. The frequency of eruptions,
the sulphuric smells, the general feeling of inhospitality and
danger, encouraged sailors to give Vulcano a wide berth long
after the other islands were in play.

In a bizarre gamble a reckless Scotsman called Stevenson
bought the island in the hope of exploiting the sulphur and
alum. He hadn't got far in his ambitious project when a further
series of eruptions – the last of which rolled on from 1886 to
1890 – sent him and everyone else scuttling off to Sicily.

On the way to our hotel – set like Malaparte's villa in Capri
on the edge of a cliff – we pass for the first of many times the
fanghi, the foul-smelling mud pool in which there are always a
handful of stout customers of both sexes wallowing. Sometimes
they lie motionless, only heads exposed, like hippopotamuses.
The more fervent and arthritic cake themselves in mud, face
included, or rub one another, a more sensual than therapeutic
activity. Emerging, they look like warriors in war paint, though
their figures often belie it.

A sulphurous beach adjoins the pool, the sea peacock-blue
in patches; then the road winds into Vulcanello, a tiny after-
thought of an eruption, whose birth in 183 BC was excitedly
recorded by Pliny and Livy. Vulcanello is joined to Vulcano by a
narrow isthmus, a black sand bay on one side, scrub on the
other. A lane rises and twists through gardens and flowering
trees to a slight mound, the whole like a kind of half-risen
pastry, with a skirting of green. Once installed, we look over
more or less empty water to the west, on the far horizon
the hazy shapes of Alicudi and Filicudi, furthest points of the

starfish. To the north we face across a few hundred yards the southern heights of Lipari, vertical splinters of rock, miniature versions of Capri's Faraglioni, not quite attached to it. Beyond, Salina seems to rest on Lipari's shoulder, with Panarea and Stromboli just visible to the north-east. Sometimes all seven islands of the archipelago are in sight.

These are art-less islands, unpainted, unwritten about. The Fascists despatched their political prisoners here, mainly to Lipari. The system of *domicilio coatto*, by which supposedly non-violent criminals were merely exported to remote islands, without obligation to work, caused Norman Douglas in *Old Calabria* to comment scornfully, "It is a school, a State-fostered school, for the promotion of criminality."

These prisoners received free lodging, a daily allowance, and two suits of clothes a year. Far from wishing to escape from their state-supported indolence many prisoners re-offended at the end of their sentence in order to return. The wine was cheap, the climate good. Douglas, who had stern, if inconsistent views about crime and punishment, was incensed at this abuse of privilege carried on at local tax-payers' expense. On one of his leaves from his posting to the embassy in St Petersburg, Douglas worked on a report on the pumice industry in Lipari. The publication of this in 1895 led to the abolition of local child labour. "One of the meritorious acts of my life," he later wrote.

In Capri I had discovered an antipathy to re-reading Douglas. At one time or another I must in my youth have read most of his books, but over the years his corrupting habits and obsession with boys, which made him *persona non grata* in one country after another, and his digressive pedantry, began to bore me. Michael Sheldon, in his biography of Graham Greene, suggests that in the years after the war Douglas and Greene hired boys together in Anacapri, but though Greene was up to most things there is no evidence for this. Some aspects of Douglas's life are distasteful, his views often silly – John Davenport called it "a sort of pink Nietzscheanism" – but I would try and come to terms with him again here, in waters that he loved.

To get the most out of Stromboli, and the nightly erupting firework display – not guaranteed – you need calm weather and clear skies. One such day came up immediately.

We left Vulcano in a gentle haze, our small boat making about twenty knots. Within minutes we had rounded the southern hump of Lipari and were abreast of the town proper, a fastidious arrangement of castle, cathedral, quays and port buildings secreted behind a headland. Gradually, like an envelope being opened, the whole bay under its volcanic pyramid reveals itself.

We soon leave it behind, the water a transparent green-blue. You expect to see dolphins and flying fish, but today only an occasional fishing boat and a scudding hydrofoil are on view.

Panarea announces itself with a scatter of islets, the largest, Basiluzzo, once inhabited but now used only for the growing of capers. Some of the islets, like Dattilo, are finger-shaped and aggressive, guarded by screaming gulls, in others, like Lisca Bianca and Bottaro, tiny rinds of white sand soften their ferocious profiles. We nose in amongst them, close enough to be glad we are not without lights on a rough night, then skim away leaving Panarea like a recumbent monk to port.

Stromboli now lies directly ahead, appearing to be volcano and nothing else. It produced, at some stage, a tiny appendage half a mile off, now a lighthouse, whose keeper manages to haul himself up a sheer cliff on steps cut into the rock like a rope ladder.

We inspect this weird multicoloured basaltic lump, which

has its own name, Strombolicchio, and which possesses from certain angles the outline of a Romanesque cathedral. There is no indication from sea level that it consists of anything but inhospitable rock, though on closer inspection a kind of platform at the top of its fifty-yard circumference reveals a green smearing of prickly pear and caper.

Stromboli has no harbour as such, but eventually we glide alongside its solitary jetty, surprised slightly to find round the skirts of the volcano, gently puffing like the funnel of a steamer, a green swathe embedded with white villas.

We have a number of hours to fill before dark, when we shall return to the boat and work our way round to the best vantage point for the fireworks.

Stromboli, away from the solidified lava streams, the *sciara del fuoco*, which give a terrifying aspect to a slab of the west coast, has a rural look to it. Not much of the island is built on, but a shoe-shaped wedge to the east of the jetty, contained within two leafy lanes parallel to the sea, has the feel of a small village. The two lanes eventually form a circle, within which the Church of San Vincenzo dominates a square with a couple of cafés, a bar, a chemist. From the square the steep, narrow Via Roma leads one way to the quay and the other, turning into the Via Vittorio Emanuele III, loops its way through villas, smallholdings, handkerchief-sized vineyards, and lemon-filled gardens, to the black sand beach of Piscità and the dock.

We dawdle the afternoon away, pausing at the modest pink villa where Ingrid Bergman and Roberto Rossellini lived in 1949 during the making of their film *Stromboli*.

It is strange to think of the emotional dramas taking place here nearly fifty years ago. The idea for the film came to Rossellini early in 1949 when he stopped at a refugee camp for Eastern European women outside Rome. He had spoken to a sad and depressed Latvian whose lonely situation haunted him. The film would be about her meeting a fisherman from the Aeolian islands with whom she has nothing in common but who might offer the chance of a new life. She accompanies the Italian to Stromboli where, though the fisherman in his simple way loves her, she pines for the country and friends of her youth. Though soon pregnant she decides to kill herself in the volcano's crater. On the last few yards she collapses, crying out to God to save her. Salvation comes in sudden acceptance of her situation and the realisation that there is comfort and peace to be had on the island after all. The film was to be called *Terra di Dio* – God's Land.

Rossellini, the distinguished director of *Roma, Città Aperta* and *Paisà*, was at the height of his powers, with a wife and a string of women, including the actress Anna Magnani. The Swedish Ingrid Bergman, recently made famous by *Casablanca*, was beginning to weary of Hollywood and the kind of films expected of her. She was bowled over by Rossellini's work and wrote to him with the approval of her manager husband – the rather unappreciative dental surgeon Petter Lindstrom – saying she would always be available if he could use her. To Rossellini her letter out of the blue was an unbelievable stroke of luck. He was finding it difficult to get American backing for his various projects and the possibility of one of the most famous actresses in the world working for him was likely to be crucial.

Neither speaking each other's language, they eventually met in Paris, with Bergman's husband present. Bergman was thirty-four, Rossellini forty-three. Despite endless difficulties connected with work and their respective obligations they were able to meet again in Hollywood, where Rossellini outlined his vague plans – he never worked from a script. After being turned down by Goldwyn, he managed, with Bergman's help, to get Howard

Hughes, owner of RKO, to put up the money for *Terra di Dio*.

With the deal completed, Rossellini set off for Rome, Bergman following a month later. Perhaps because of their undisguised attraction for each other, their involvement began to be publicised as something other than a professional arrangement. It was put about that Bergman had decided to leave her husband and daughter without any intention of returning. What at that stage was little more than a flirtation was turned into a scandal, Bergman, in the eyes of the Hollywood studios and the American press, a depraved whore whose films should be banned.

From Rome Rossellini, a collector of fast cars, and Bergman set off for Amalfi, staying at one of Rossellini's old haunts, the romantic monastery-hotel Albergo Luna Convento, with cloisters, a medieval tower, and gardens overlooking the sea. After a few days here Bergman wrote to her husband, telling of her love for Rossellini and her wish to remain with him.

In April the director, the star, and the camera crew of *Terra di Dio* set sail for Stromboli. The fisherman was to be played by a real-life fisherman Rossellini had come across in Salerno. Their quarters, rented from the local teacher, were without water and all food – mostly tinned – had to be imported.

Bergman's own situation soon came to resemble that of the character she was playing, for amongst a crowd of amateur actors, their actions improvised, the dialogue made up and changed on the spot, she felt completely at sea. Exasperated, she turned on Rossellini, threatening to leave. "He doesn't need actors," she remarked later, "he just makes pictures naturally – with people." Rossellini forbade her "to act".

In a letter to a friend she wrote, after a few days of this, "This way of making a realistic picture leaves you dead . . . And to have only amateurs to play with when you have as little patience as I have. But all the bad weather and hardships I take gladly when I work with somebody that is really remarkable . . . He writes the dialogue just before the scene. He chooses the people a couple of hours before the work . . . His violence, if something goes wrong, can only be compared to the volcano in the background. His tenderness and humour come like a surprise immediately after. I understand well that people call him crazy, but those are the people I always loved, isn't that so?"

Rossellini certainly put Bergman through it during the making of the film, asking her to climb the volcano in bare feet, though the fumes burned her throat and eyes, and made her sick. It was not quite what she imagined but she stuck it out.

In the midst of filming, Bergman's husband arrived and the two met in Messina to discuss their future. Rossellini threatened to kill himself if Ingrid returned to her old life. Any possibility of that was ended by Bergman becoming pregnant. Stromboli, as the film was being finished, had one of its more violent eruptions, inundating half the island, but on the side away from where they were working. It seemed an omen.

There followed months of acrimonious divorce proceedings between Bergman and Lindstrom, Rossellini seeming to get off more or less scot-free from his various entanglements, his wife even agreeing to an annulment. It was, nevertheless, some time before there was any hope of a marriage, their child being born illegitimate, the cause of a great deal of Hollywood fuss and hatred.

After filming, the couple moved to Rome, where the child was born and final touches put to *Stromboli*. When the film was released it was panned, not on moral grounds but for its tediousness. The scenery couldn't save it nor Bergman's acting, though her performance was described by Donald Spoto, author of an excellent biography of the actress, as one of "controlled panic . . . a textbook on how to convey implications of longing and imprecations against an inhospitable society".

The marriage took place by proxy in Juarez, Mexico, and for some years all went comparatively well at the seaside villa Rossellini had bought at Santa Marinella, north of Rome. Two more children were born, Ingrid's career flourished, despite Rossellini's reluctance to let her work for other directors. The films they did do together, *Europa '51* and *Viaggio in Italia*, again made without scripts and with little outline, were no more successful than *Stromboli*; the films she later made with others, for they needed the money, were well received and financially rewarding. Rossellini resented Ingrid's revived fame, even more so when he was sacked from a film he was directing that starred Richard Burton and Joan Collins.

The marriage was stranded, both emotionally and geographically. Rossellini went to film in India and took up with an Indian actress by whom he had a child. Bergman was being courted by the Swedish producer Lars Schmidt, whom she later married. After many happy years together, he left her for a younger woman. She returned to the stage in Paris and London, becoming an even greater star. Her relationship with Rossellini turned into friendship, lasting until his sudden death at the age of seventy-one. With Schmidt too, she remained close friends. Only Lindstrom, growing increasingly bitter, continued to revile her.

Whether the film or the volcano means more to people nowadays is not clear. Even if the film is slow and lacking in incident there is always Ingrid Bergman's beautiful face to look at, less moving than in *Casablanca*, more life-scarred and tough, as she was meant to be. Rossellini's way of directing may have made her feel awkward amongst the local cast but she never looks other than a real person, with her cut legs and her choking fits.

*

The sulphur smell here, though maybe not at the crater up to which we watched a band of Germans struggling, is less noticeable than in Vulcano. We spent the day walking among vineyards and along the black beach, and after drinks at the Bar Ingrid and marvelling at the sunset we boarded the *Cala Junco*.

It was quickly dark and as we sailed slowly between Strombolicchio and Punta Frontone the last layers of pistachio, cobalt and yellow faded from the sky. Soon there was only the obscured core of the volcano.

We anchored and waited. There was no sound except the peaceful lapping of water against the sides of the boat. At intervals the peak acquired a pink veil, then lost it. There were suggestions of increased light as if a fire was being worked up by a pair of bellows, then these too subsided.

Perhaps the volcano was not going to perform tonight. Half an hour or more went by and then, just as we had begun to look away, a great jet of fire shot out of the crater and in a kind of parachute of flames, scattering stones in its wake, slowly descended.

Within seconds it was over. We hung on for another hour, there was a second, smaller gust of flame, and then nothing. The volcano had done enough for the evening. It was time to go home.

It had been worth it, for although the action was only momentary the visual impact was lasting. It is one thing to see fireworks, however spectacular, knowing them to be man-made, but here the earth was giving a great heave of its guts, an exhalation of the entrails, that in times past had decimated whole areas, demolished many lives.

On the north-west of the island the tiny village of Ginostra – a harbour, a few houses, some donkeys – lies on the very edge of the lava stream. A strip of green like marzipan holds olives and prickly pears, but why and how this minute settlement should have broken away from the rest is a mystery. A coating of black dust covers plants and houses, and towering over everything the volcano and its ancient, bleak rockscape stands as a permanent reminder of disaster.

Stromboli has erupted ten times this century, four times in the 1950s, the last time in 1966. The worst was in 1930, but because the lava flows always in the same direction, within defined limits, the islanders don't suffer too much.

Sometimes people hoping to see the dragon spit out its fire have to wait days, other times it indulges at regular intervals through the night. In daylight there is nothing to be seen, except from the sea a plume of smoke. Photographs show, at its most spectacular, cockades of fire alternating with spreads like a peacock's tail; less dramatically, but even more beautifully, scarves of smoke, a faint orange-cerise, swathe the island.

Sailing back to Vulcano we watched Stromboli's lights diminishing, the stars coming out in a haze over Lipari and Panarea. In the swish of the boat's wake Ingrid Bergman's face wavered like a watermark.

Overnight the weather changed beyond recognition. Filicudi and Alicudi, earlier solid smudges to the north-west, had disintegrated and the steep cliffs of Lipari became black and forbidding. The boat had been ordered to take us to Panarea so there was nothing for it but to go, in spite of the scudding cloud and squalls of rain.

There are three kinds of boats that ply between the islands: the ferry steamers such as the *Piero della Francesca* on which we had sailed from Milazzo, the *aliscafi* or hydrofoils, enclosed, small, and very fast, but dependent on conditions, and motor yachts, the kind of boats we were using, slightly longer than the

Eruption at Stromboli

hydrofoils, not much slower, but with some deck room as well as a cabin.

It was not a comfortable journey, the boat yawing and rolling, but making good headway through the spray. Panarea, the smallest of the inhabited islands, nineteen miles to the southwest of Stromboli, was described to us as the nearest to Capri in sophistication, but in this weather, as we approached, was more like the Orkneys.

Landing, and restored by several *caffè corretto*, coffee with dollops of cognac, we set off in the rain up the narrow lane that carries, on either side, villas in lush gardens. There was an orderliness of design quite foreign to the other islands, whose buildings straggle arbitrarily across bays and up hillsides, and then for no obvious reason peter out.

Here, every inch of available land – not much of it, in fact, for the cone is steep and the cliffs savage – has been precisely calculated. The villas, white, flat-roofed, each with shady palm and trailing bougainvillaea, give off an air of prosperity, though, used as holiday homes by rich Italians from the north, were shuttered. You could be in Greece, though Panarea is rockier and greener.

Lower in profile than Stromboli, smoking away in the distance, Panarea's solitary lane takes you past a series of scooped out, sandless bays, that lead in due course to the headland of Punta Milazzese. The hills hereabout are a tweedy, green-brown, swift grassy slopes cut short by contorted rock. Punta Milazzese, mustard-coloured and like an antler in shape, divides two beautiful inlets, each with a resident white yacht but as yet no buildings. In 1948 a number of shelters dating from the fifteenth century BC were discovered, a rocky and precarious site for any settlement, its whole extent being no more than a hundred yards, the sea crashing about beneath.

The museum in Lipari houses various pieces of Minoan-style pottery taken from here.

From Punta Milazzese back to the port is a mere twenty minutes' walk. There is no more to Panarea than that. Islets coming in and out of the rain are visible from every turn in the path and in good weather Panarea's bijou housing and secluded rocky coves must seem relaxing to a Milanese or Naples businessman. There are no cars on the island.

Had one an inclination to stay on – and were they open – there are a couple of nicely situated hotels, a few *pensioni*, a bank, some modest restaurants set in gardens or by the harbour. It is a very private-feeling place, where connoisseurs of sunsets could spend a week or two indulging themselves. Islands without incident or diversion have their place but the restrictions of Panarea, its lack of people and space, might, despite its evident prettiness, soon begin to pall.

The sun emerged in the early evening and we returned to Vulcano on a sea like a millpond, the milky water the dustiest of pinks. Already our near neighbours, Salina and Lipari, seem like old friends, the offshore and hazardous chippings of rock that make sailors keep their wits about them apparently no more harmful now than a shoal of seals.

Do the year-round inhabitants of these small islands feel content with their lot, never hankering for new experiences, new sights? If you asked them it's unlikely they would know the answer.

Vulcano. A few days off the sea and a chance to read and explore the island, which turns out to be larger and more leisurely than at first sight. In Porto di Levante there is no indication of anything other than the volcano, but once on the road that skirts the mauve rust of the crater itself you come across a series of tiny plains and valleys with grazing sheep, goats and donkeys, and an occasional small farm. The acid yellow gives way to soothing green, the road twisting and turning between Monte Saraceno and Monte Rossa. Except for the fissured crater of the volcano area and the pumice cave on its western flank, this switchback of wood and copse, of vine and olive, could be anywhere. Vulcanopiano, the only plain of any significance in any of the Aeolian islands, stands like a kind of billiard table balanced on the steep legs of the surrounding cliffs.

There are no internal villages, but at the southern-most point of the island a rough track leads through fields of mulberry and caper to the lighthouse settlement of Gebo.

From the higher ground, looking back, the island appears oval, with the tongue of Vulcanello added. A collar of black sand softens the spiralling crater rim and beyond the lacy cliffs, which seem to hold the island together, Lipari, Salina and Panarea ride like battleships. Photographs of the crater taken from the air show a mushroomy bowl of colour, in certain lights, often used by Ben Nicholson in his reliefs. Looking north from Monte Saraceno the island stretches out like some squashed animal, paws flattened and coat moulting.

A freighter catches the dipping sun as we look, seeming on fire at one moment. The sea floods with light, the outlines of the other islands hardening. The freighter's wake draws a white line, gradually blurring, over indigo becoming violet. The experience of these places is to do with light, an almanac of it, whose every line, every page, yields something different. In the end, books come to seem irrelevant.

All the same, there is a limit to what you can make out of landscape. Huge lemons, hibiscus, jacaranda, jasmine, flop over every wall, rock plants of every shade – yellow, red, white, cornflower blue – sprawl over the cliff edge, even a snake slithers into the gorse that is the most vivid of all the colours, but in the end they cannot compete with the lavishness of the lava and the monstrous rock shapes that rear out of the soil. Not far from the hotel, in the Valle dei Mostri, a whole menagerie of creatures – dancing bears, elephants, giraffes – gesticulate and prance, grimace and sneer. The lava, however rigid, is never idle.

There is no island in these parts on which Norman Douglas did not leave an imprint. He used to go gecko hunting on the islets off Panarea and Stromboli, he tells us in *Looking Back*, and on Panarea, where the Bishop of Lipari, Giuseppe Cipolla, planted 3000 olives, he was mistaken for a doctor, his interest in geckos assumed to be medicinal. Summoned to the bedside of a dying girl, he quickly jumped into his boat and cleared out.

I had no knowledge of any works on the Lipari islands but on a 1908 visit Douglas came upon several handsomely illustrated books by geologists and engineers. One of these, by the Archduke Ludwig Salvator, published in Prague in 1893, runs to eight volumes.

Remembering his time here a quarter of a century later Douglas is brought to one of his more eloquent passages. "Savagery and opulence touch hands on these waterless islands; I liked the quality of the landscape. I liked the harsh colours, the violent perfumes of earth, the monstrous cactus hedges, and all those scattered rocks that rise out of an incredibly blue sea and shift their profiles with every step you take . . . A panoramic region; it fills you with a sense of Homeric limpidity. It takes you back."

A doctor by the name of Johnston-Lavis, based in Naples, cruised these islands looking for minerals. Through his findings of obsidian on Lisca Bianca and Bottaro, he evolved a theory that these half-submerged rock islets were all part of a larger island, and if the sea bottom was raised a few fathoms their combined identity would form something the size of Lipari. The realm of Aeolus? Douglas asks, though it was thought to be on Stromboli, Homer's "floating island; and around it all a wall of bronze unbroken, and smooth ran up the rock".

Johnston-Lavis as a young man was part of an 1889 expedition made under the auspices of the Geological Association of London to study south Italian volcanoes. The volume they published ran to 342 pages and contained sixteen photographic plates.

The guide they used on Lipari, one Bartolo, produced a notebook and asked the members of the group to add their comments.One of the names was Guy de Maupassant.

In his book *La Vie Errante* Maupassant describes his first view of Vulcano: "*fantastique fleur de soufre, éclose en plein mer*" and his ascent of the crater. He went on to Salina and reported on malvasia, the wine of the island, "*on dirait du sirop de soufre, c'est bien le vin des volcans, épais, sucré, doré et tellement soufré, que le goût vous en reste au palais jusqu'au soir: le vin du diable.*"

Douglas observes scathingly that there is not an ounce of sulphur on Salina and there is no sulphurous taste to malvasia. Douglas puts Maupassant's error down to the first signs of the venereal illness that killed him. However, in reputable wine lists, malvasia is today usually described as having a sulphurous as well as sweet taste and honey colour. Maupassant certainly had a thing about sulphur; he later wrote, perhaps with more justification, advising Jules Clarétie never to eat French grapes, "all French grapes are poisoned by sulphur".

The weather seems to have relented. Having sailed past by Lipari numerous times I am looking forward to going in. It is the shortest of journeys across the straits from Vulcano, the

Lipari

clouds high and fleecy, the sea the deepest of blues. Rounding
Punta della Crapazza, the cape that blocks off the rest of Lipari
from Vulcano, there are at first few signs of life: steep, grey
cliffs carpeted with low scrub, gorse, small untenanted bays,
humps of terraced hill dipping and rising precipitously as they
approach Monte Guardia.

Lipari, superficially secretive, hides its best places behind
headlands. Yet once the folds have opened out, the boat nosed
in, you are presented with a view of dazzling promise; a rich
green backcloth sloping up gradually to the curled, lava-stained
greenery of the volcano. But the volcano here is a docile, unthreat-
ening creature, a matter of suave curves and amiable grassy
outcrops with none of the tension and contortion common to
the other islands. Two wide, generous bays, separated by a chunk
of fierce rock that stands out like a guard-dog, hold an assembly
of freighters, steamers, hydrofoils, yachts, small craft and fishing
boats. On the dividing rock a cluster of fine buildings, including
a handsome castle and adjoining cathedral, both sixteenth-
century Spanish with later adjustments, a number of baroque
churches in various states of dilapidation and a convent, are
reined in from the sea by thick walls apparently impacted on
the rocks beneath them.

This is a view to be reckoned with, on a par with the harbour
of Porto d'Ischia.

The hottest day so far, though still only April. Once ashore
we make, through narrow shady streets and the gardens of
Piazza Mazzini, for the upper town, the citadel, that houses
the Bishop's Palace and a group of museums. From the Via
Garibaldi that runs up from the port and curves down to the
smaller port, Marina Corta, a long flight of wide, steep steps
leads you to fortress level.

The Museo Eoliano, its rooms dispersed around the cathedral, is famous for its collection of Greek theatrical masks, allegedly the most complete anywhere. Not all are genuine but there are realistic models of actors doing their stuff in the plays of Sophocles and Euripides. Herakles and Hades, and the three-headed Cerberus, entwined by snakes, whom Herakles dragged to the upper world, scowl convincingly. There is an engaging, stagey feel to the terracotta group of dancers and actors, many found in graves in the Diana area behind the port. These places often have a dusty, deserted air but this citadel of Lipari, the sea all dazzle and shimmer beneath its walls, glows with activity.

The Museo's archaeological section, next to the Bishop's Palace, has enough stone weaponry, blades made of obsidian, flints and knives, removed from burial sites, to satisfy the demands of the most bloodthirsty of the children tumbling about and draping themselves on the half-excavated tombs, of which there are several. Death has been around here, and confinement too, but they have left no evident deposits. The decorated vases on the classical wing, ranging from the ninth century BC to the works of the man known as "the Lipari painter" a century later, depict every kind of jolly recreation – bathing, making love, sacrificing, doing acrobatics, playing the fool and the flute – acted out by clowns, courtiers, gods and satyrs. There is a pretty garden outside, with engraved stones and tombs, under palms and cypresses, and a small Greek-style theatre, from the upper rows of which you can watch the ferries gliding in from Milazzo.

This is an enchanted area, half-cloister, half-playground, the houses of the old town climbing up past the Diana necropolis to the peaks at your back and little avenues and alleyways twisting among ecclesiastical buildings, stopped short every so often by wedges of sea and sky. From the balustrade on the south side of the theatre you can look down at the tiny port of Marina Corta, its triangular waters crammed with many-coloured dinghies. On the further quay the grey-white fishermen's chapel, the Chiesetta del Purgatorio, rounds off an elegant exercise in the picturesque.

The Piazza Sant'Onofrio, which lies just off the port, has no equivalent in the other islands: a line of open-air cafés, bars and restaurants under striped awnings, a bold actorish statue to San Bartolo, jostling fishing boats, careering dogs, music, and a general sense of energy and bustle. The main street leading to Marina Corta, the Corso Vittorio Emanuele, is closed to traffic after six in the evening, so the *passeggiata* spills out until dark without fear of interruption. The other islands haven't a hope of competing: space too cramped, too few people.

Lipari can hold its own with any of the smaller Greek, Yugoslav or Italian islands and it is more than just a capital. The road that runs in a kind of skeleton shape round the central bony ridge is a scenic ride that can be travelled by bus in either direction, a journey of less than an hour, none of it flat. Once past the long pebble beach of Canneto and the tunnel that cuts through the Monte Rosa headland you come to the pumice quarries of Campo Blanco. It was here that Norman Douglas performed his "meritorious" act, writing his report and getting children out of labouring in the caves.

For a mile or two, up to Porticello at the north-eastern tip, the coastal hills look as if under a dusty sheet. Workings on the pumice have produced smooth chutes that slide into the sea, turning the water the pale blue-green of pastis. A coating of pumice dust lies like Johnson's baby powder on the roofs of the little village, which in winter must seem like snow.

The pumice industry appears to be flourishing, small coastal ships being loaded off rickety-looking piers as we passed. The pumice is nowadays exported to be used in anything from toothpaste to bleach, from light bulbs to fertiliser. Above these white flanks the crater of Monte Pilato, site of the last eruption in the year 700, bears a green covering like a tonsure. The men going to and fro from cave to boat look to be wearing make-up or extravagant sunblock, and they appear as remote from their fellow workers in Lipari as if they were on another continent rather than a few miles away.

By the time you reach Porticello the white has begun to run out, there are no more cranking machines lifting and loading, and the sea off the pebbly beach has resumed its normal colour. There are other small, equally tree-less villages in the north, like Acquacalda, with their own quarries, equipment and piers, but once past the curiously-named Puddino valley with its two isolated churches, "*chiesa vecchia*" and "*chiesa nuova*", there are varieties of plain separating the mountains from the sea. The coast bends and falls and at one point, on the edge of a lush, poppy-spotted valley, you can look back at the *faraglioni* between Lipari and Vulcano, dramatically reduced in size by the towering cliffs of the Costa di Ponente. From Quattrocchi, "four eyes", so-called because engaged couples come here to be photographed, Vulcano looks bald and shabby.

But we are back there before nightfall, seeing, from another angle, a peachy sunset framed by the *faraglioni*, eloquent last blessing of the sun on a softly melting horizon. A solitary fishing boat makes its way into the shelter of the cliffs, sails folded back like a crow at rest.

Vulcano. We shall go next to Salina, whose double dromedary humps we can just discern beyond Lipari. Meantime it is salutary to read Compton Mackenzie's remarks in his *My Life and*

Times on the reception of his Capri novel *Vestal Fire*, described as a sequel to Douglas's *South Wind* (still unre-read by me), by a very young Cyril Connolly, "as feeble as sequels are". "To enter into such vain and obvious competition with a masterpiece like *South Wind*", Connolly wrote in the *New Statesman*, "is to merit deserved and speedy misfortune." Mackenzie seems not to have been ruffled by this and his novel, with similar background and characters as in Peyrefitte's *The Exile of Capri*, acquired many admirers. "The theme of the book", Connolly wrote, "is the infinite time it takes an American colony to discover that a man, if he is a French Count, young and rich, artistic, handsome, and polite, can still be an intolerable bore." The book is 400 pages long and Connolly's verdict was that Mackenzie had been on Capri too long and accumulated too many scores to settle. In due course *Vestal Fire* was banned in Italy on the orders of Mussolini on five grounds: for making fun of the *carabinieri*, for making remarks derogatory to the State; for mentioning the unmentionable; for injuring the *réclame* of Capri; for being *contra bonos mores*. I read *Vestal Fires* so long ago that I can no longer remember whether any of this is valid. Most likely, as an undergraduate, I was impressed by its worldliness, sophistication and mild malice.

There is an agreeable restaurant by the port in Vulcano, Maurizio, where you can eat in a garden and be served by theatrical waiters. The wines are light and delicious, the honey-coloured malvasia slightly cloying, but not a whiff of sulphur in the air or in the wine. We could now, after numerous excursions, walk the mile or so from Vulcanello to the port blindfold, guided entirely by the smell, first of flowers, next of the salty lagoon, finally of the sulphur baths. The port itself, as far as I can detect, has no smell at all, except for a faint odour of diesel.

*

Salina. Sky clear and rinsed of cloud. We take the west coast of Lipari this time, Vulcano always in sight behind us, Salina obscured at first. It is a gentle journey under ferocious cliffs and among pointed islets occupied by terns. Gulls make sorties over our boat. An hour out and Salina's craters are ahead, one much larger than the other.

The port of Santa Marina Salina is unusual among these islands in having a fine, tree-shaded promenade running parallel to the beach. Dominating the village, behind which the main volcano rises very steeply, is the khaki Chiesa Madre, a domed church rather out of proportion to the rest, which seems to double as a lighthouse. A wedding was taking place as we arrived.

The volcano is tightly covered here with myrtle and broom, the effect as close-curled as a negro's scalp. Narrow streets, with tiny alleyways crossing them, are reached from the harbour by stairways, the village being on several levels. Tiny though it is, boutiques of one sort or another are interspersed with fruit and vegetable shops, and the place has a convivial air.

Salina's ancient name was Didime, meaning twin, the modern term for which is *gemella*. But though the name derived from its twin craters, at sea level there is little sign of the smaller. A bus route leads in a northerly direction to Malfa, the island's other main town, from where a road sneaks across the island between the two craters. Approaching the coast a series of hairpin bends drop you to Rinella, the possessor of a strip of black sand, a church, a score of houses, an array of fishing boats attached to a jetty.

The land here is terraced, the rocks saffron-pink. In some old photographs waves give the coast a ruff of spray, covering the houses. Another equally modest settlement, Leni, sits like an eyebrow halfway up Monte dei Porri. Ferries and hydrofoils rather surprisingly find it worth their while to call at Rinella, though quite what for is not clear. The landscape, in its savagery of cliff and tortuousness of approach, is one calculated to deter strangers. The soil, curiously brown on the slopes, turns to a kind of marzipan green higher up.

These small ports of Salina are attractive each in a different way. To the north-west Rinella Pollara, straddling a flat cliff-top, has no boat access to the sea, raised as it is over sheer rock far above water. There is a half-moon crater of a sort, the site of Salina's last eruption, leaving a dark crust bisecting the sky to the north of the village. A tiny split in the rockface leaves just enough room for determined swimmers to reach some black sand.

The way back to Santa Marina involves an almost vertical climb to the Val di Chiesa, the twin peaks of Salina on either side, the more southerly one, Monte Fosse delle Felci, being the highest in the archipelago at 3000 feet. The seventeenth-century Santuario della Madonna del Terzito nests in thick woods, from where you can, in late afternoon, look through the feathery splay of palm trees at the sun sinking over rocky islets, the horizon turning from mauve to coral pink.

Lingua. A few hours in hand before the evening boat so we decide to walk the coast road from Santa Marina due south to Lingua. Most of the way you are on top of the sea, the road climbing and swivelling at intervals, with either inlets or small vineyards struggling to get a hold in the rocky lava.

You see the village, far below, from a long way off, a mirage at first in sun hotter than bargained for. The road dips down then flattens out to run through orchards and gardens until blocked off, at sea level, by a white church with tiled roof. A few boats are drawn up on black sand and at the end of a brief promenade a small square, with palm trees planted in paving stone, contains a bar and a restaurant with red chairs outside. The three houses, each with balconies overlooking the square, are white, their windows and doors outlined in peach or aquamarine.

Nearby are salt lagoons and a bog separated from the sea by the spit of land that gives the village its name. This is malvasia country, as well as salt, and there are worse ways of spending an afternoon than sitting in the pretty piazzetta after lunch and feeling the cool, honey-gold liquid run down your throat.

Houses are few and far between, pink or white rectangles set in green scrub. There is always the volcano at your back but it has long been tamed here, the land innocently lolling in the spring sun. The island has a soothing and serene presence, its dramas of contour muted.

Back in Vulcano we gaze every evening across at Filicudi and Alicudi on the western horizon, the sun slipping out of sight behind them. These, the most westerly of the islands, are the largely undeveloped, poor relations of the archipelago, remote from Milazzo. Each island has a small hotel and Filicudi a church in the last stages of collapse. As you approach Filicudi you are confronted by a 250-foot rocky obelisk rising sheer out of the sea, with a small duck-shaped fragment accompanying it. Filicudi, too, boasts a grotto, the "Bue Marino", or sea cow, whose startling blue compares well with Capri's own Blue Grotto. Among the ferns of Capo Graziano, there are remains of a Bronze Age village, compared to which the other few settlements are scarcely livelier.

These are dreamy, dozy places, Alicudi, shaped like a perfect breast, with a faint scatter of hollow-eyed houses, even more so. They made the beautiful film *Il Postino*, about the exiled Pablo Neruda and his touching relationship with a postman, here. The actor who played the postman, desperately ill throughout, died after the last day of shooting, giving the film an added poignancy. Neruda would have been moved. Alicudi has no cinema, though there is no shortage of TVs for the inhabitants to enjoy their moments of recognition.

Ericusa, from *erica*, Latin for heather, was the island's ancient name and the steep slopes still have a purplish tinge. Alicudi Porto, a few dinghies drawn upon its shingle rind, consists of several layers of houses, white two-storeyed blocks like pieces of Lego. The coast is punctured all along its circumference by caves. There are no flat surfaces on the island, the central peak Filo dell'Arpa, 2000 feet, reachable only by a stony track, which climbs past the ruins of a castle. Who could have thought it worth fortifying such an insignificant place? Presumably this decrepit building was felt good enough to house the *mafiosi* who ran riot here until fairly recently.

In the last few years electricity has been installed. The Hotel Ericusa, open for only four months in the summer, has twelve rooms, a restaurant and a terrace overlooking the sea. Food and fruit has to come in by boat. An ideal place for those of an unsociable disposition.

The simple life carried to extremes. Flowers grow well among the heather, houses are draped in bougainvillaea; silence is broken only by the braying of donkeys. There is a tiny church, the Chiesa di San Bartolomeo, though hardly enough people to warm it unless they all arrive together.

Boats for the 150 inhabitants are their livelihood and their lifeline. Distances, even to the mainland, are not great but there is little curiosity, nor enough money, to set forth more than once. Mostly, families stay put, generation to generation.

The seven islands of the archipelago, rarely out of sight of each other, are not much in touch either, Alicudi least of all. Naples to the north-east, Palermo to the south-west, define their worlds, cities on the edge of the imagination.

At last, when we have no plans, *South Wind* beckons. Why has it become so difficult to face it? I'm not naturally much of a re-reader and its comparative bulk, 422 pages, is offputting. Yet its opening sentence, "The bishop was feeling rather sea-sick. Confoundedly sea-sick, in fact", and its last, "For it was obvious to the meanest intelligence that Mr Keith was considerably drunk", have remained with me for years. Not much of the rest, unfortunately.

By the time Douglas came to write *South Wind* in 1916 he was forty-eight. He had published three travel books, *Siren Land, Fountains in the Sand* and *Old Calabria*, all of which have honourably survived the passing of the years but which made little impact at the time. He had been married to a cousin and divorced, the five years of his marriage having produced two sons. He became a pederast, though until he was fifty he had the occasional heterosexual affair. It was only after his move to Capri that he seems to have given women up. Douglas's exile, if one can call it that, was hastened along by the first of many criminal charges laid against him, initially in London, but repeated in various countries elsewhere.

In Capri he finished *South Wind*, but though the island remained his spiritual home it was only for the last five years of his life that he returned there. He lived mainly in Florence – until asked to leave – the South of France and Lisbon, but was constantly on the move. In 1942 he was allowed to return to London, not the best of moments for a natural pagan to settle in after twenty-five years' absence. He died in Capri in 1952 and is buried in the cemetery.

In *South Wind* Douglas gives the island the name Nepenthe. "The social atmosphere of Nepenthe", he wrote, "is distilled out of Capri – out of the Capri as it always should have been and as it never, alas! yet was or will be. I have taken what liberties I please with the place. For example, I have located it nearer Africa and made the soil volcanic, whereas it is limestone." About the notion that it is a *roman à clef* he wrote, "I have never tried to draw a figure from life, as they say . . . a human character, however convincing and true to itself must be licked into shape, otherwise its reactions, in a world of fictitious characters, would be out of focus."

Nevertheless, to old Capri hands, several of the characters seemed to bear an undeniably close resemblance to real people. How much is fact, how much fiction, is neither here nor there, for Douglas's novel is essentially about talk. It is generally complained that *South Wind* lacks plot, but if that is so, there is no shortage of incident: blackmail, fraud, murder, death by mosquito bite, a volcanic eruption, a riot, a festival, an earthquake, a forgery.

The novel's events take place during the fortnight which the Bishop of Bampopo "in the Equatorial Regions", on a visit to his cousin, Mrs Meadows, spends on the island. The Bishop, "resembling a broken-down matrimonial agent", according to the indolent and worldly local priest Don Francesco, soon finds himself at the centre of what passes for expatriate society, its members meeting every forenoon in the piazzetta to gossip and inspect new arrivals. The leading players are the Duchess of San Martino, an elderly, high-church American, Don Francesco, "too fat to run about – he could only talk" but "a fisher of men and of women"; Madame Steynlin, a Dutch lady whose hats were proverbial but who was uncompromisingly Lutheran; Miss Wilberforce, seventy-five years old, still mourning her lost sailor lover and frequently drunk and disorderly; the scholarly Mr Ernest Eames, obsessed with Latin; the rich, owlish, hedonistic and longwinded Mr Keith; the American millionaire Van Koppen. Also resident on the island is a Russian sect, who call themselves "Little White Cows", their leader a Rasputin-like figure; an absurdly handsome youth called Denis who attends on the Duchess; and a distinguished-looking Italian, Count Caloveglia, a sculptor, who lives a hermetic life. There is a club of sorts, the Alpha and Omega, its President the dictatorial Mr Parker, an English remittance man whose boisterous good humour masks "a remarkable combination of malevolence and imbecility". His shady existence is protected by his unpaid post as Nicaraguan Financial Commissioner for South-Eastern Europe, an appointment made solely to get rid of him from that country. There are few Italians on show, the chief of them the wily magistrate Malipizzo who has to concern himself with the disappearance of one of the new arrivals, the smarmy and vulgar Mr Muhlen, whose presence on the island no-one can quite account for.

Vulcano is not Nepenthe and the characters of *South Wind* in comparison with the simple inhabitants of the Aeolian islands belong both to another age and another society. *South Wind* takes place during a sirocco, everyone slightly unbalanced by the heat. Here, looking across at the carbon shapes of Lipari and Salina, the weather moving from winter to spring and back again in the course of a day, it is difficult to imagine heat. The characters in *South Wind*, however, suffer from the weather rather than enjoying it. They pre-date beach culture, their pursuits largely verbal and sedentary. Douglas knew these islands well, his knowledge of their history, antiquities, flora and fauna, conveyed always in a relaxed, conversational fashion. However his eagerness to inform, whether about the life and martyrdom of Saint Dodekanus, patron of Nepenthe, or about the Crotalophoboi, cannibals and necromancers whose eyes grew on the soles of their feet – both encountered in an early chapter – results in a narrative that often grinds to a halt.

Parts of *South Wind* could, it seems to me, have been written by Wodehouse. However erudite the disquisitions and speculation – about oriental art or viniculture, chastity or diet, education or puritanism, glucose or apples, the way to eat red mullet – farce is never far away. The Bishop and Mr Keith, the Bishop and Mr Eames and Count Caloveglia, engage in talk of a kind seldom heard these days except possibly at High Table, scholarship and inquiry and the digestive process happily entwined. There is, despite their advanced years, something schoolboyishly innocent about the old buffers.

The Bishop witnesses a murder, his cousin Mrs Meadows disposing of the blackmailing Mr Muhlen, who turns out to have once been her husband, off a cliff to preserve her present, possibly bigamous, marriage and the happiness of her children. The Bishop makes no moral judgement in the circumstances. "He approved. Mrs Meadows had saved her family. She was perfect of her kind."

This is morality above the niceties of the law, and in *South Wind* people behaving for the greater good but committing actions not strictly legal always earn the Bishop's approval.

In Douglas country, I am enjoying his novel more than I expected. You can doze off with impunity, despite evocative and seductive passages about Capri's operatic scenery which has no equivalent in these islands. He describes the slender palms, a gleaming precipice, the distant sea. "Gardens appeared to be toppling over the houses; green vines festooned the doorways and gaily-coloured porches; streets climbed up and down . . . windows were aflame with cacti and carnations, slumberous oranges glowed in courtyards." "There are no half-tones in this landscape," the Bishop remarked to Mr Keith, "No compromise." "And yet perfect harmony," Mr Keith replies. "They are all true colours. I hate compromise . . . that is why I cannot endure England for long. The country is full of half-tones, not only in nature."

Douglas's scientific, botanic training leads to accurate, specific descriptions. Although *South Wind* is part poem, part philosophic treatise, there is nothing of the romantic in Douglas. In contrast, a character like Ernest Eames, with his frozen classical mind, blossoms under the stimulus of Perrelli's *Antiquities*, studied in this sunny climate, and the annotation of which becomes his life's work. "He entered upon a second boyhood – a real boyhood, this time, full of enthusiasm and adventures into the flowery by-paths of learning." That is Douglas's own poetry, too. It is an austere one.

Writing about *South Wind* years later, as an introduction to one of several editions published in the late 1940s, Douglas remarked, "*South Wind* was the result of my craving to escape from the wearisome actualities of life. To picture yourself living in a society of such instability, of such 'jovial immoderation' and 'frolicsome perversity' that even a respectable bishop can be persuaded to approve of a murder – this was my aim."

After thirty years he found little to change in the text although, he reflected, in more sober moments, "Certain passages strike me as being ornate to the point of flabbiness. Let them stand. The most original chapter is the twenty-fourth, a study of the progressive stages of alcoholic exhilaration. I would not alter that chapter."

South Wind, in one of its aspects, is about people discovering themselves, yielding to the humanising effects of the landscape. "There is something in the brightness of this spot which decomposes their old particles and arranges them into fresh and unexpected patterns." Mr Keith remarks to the Bishop during a short boat trip, "That is what people mean when they say that they 'discover' themselves. You discover a mechanism, you know, when you take it to pieces."

They are off the cliff precipice known as Suicides' Rock. The old boatman produces a blood-curdling account of the victims whose deaths he has witnessed. "Many is the poor Christian I have pick up here. He throw down himself. Him dead. Often in small pieces. Here blood. Here brain. Here leg and boot. Here finger."

The Bishop is troubled by the frequency of suicides. "It is the scenery," Mr Keith explains, it unnerves people. "Don't you feel its effect upon yourself? The bland winds, the sea shining in velvety depths as though filled with some electric fluid, the riot of vegetation, these extravagant cliffs that change colour with every hour of the day? Look at that peak yonder – is it not almost transparent, like some crystal or amethyst? This coastline alone – the sheer effrontery of its mineral charm – might affect some natures to such an extent as to dislocate their stability."

There is nothing unnerving of this kind in the scenery of the Aeolian islands. Nerves are not strung up here, you are not constantly presented with precipices of seductive vertiginousness. The islands bask rather, seal-like shapes with their sparse villas and tiny ports in the skirts of more or less extinct volcanoes. Clouds drift across the sky, changing the colour of slopes and cliffs, mauve to silver to heather to black. The islands are without bustle, their dramas belong to long ago. A little fishing, a few vines, the odd cow, it's enough. From almost any point on each island you can watch the ferries from Sicily, see through the smoke of Milazzo the snowy, ashen cone of Etna, smell the sweet scent of broom flowering in tufts through cracks in the lava. A culture of boats, on their many small journeys.

"We discourse like sages and drink like swine," says the excellent Mr Richards, Vice-President of the club, in *South Wind*. "It is a good island." Indeed, these are good islands, out of season, left to themselves and free of marauding visitors, which they are for nine months of the year.

We sail into a westering sun, incise fine lines into indigo sheet metal. To circle Lipari you steer north in the lee of gull-flapped cliffs, turn east in the passage before Salina, and then it's a straight sail south of Vulcano. You move from the bare and bleak west to the softly commercial east, the high fortified walls and domes of Lipari town a reminder of invasion and squabble, of the piratical assaults of Barbarossa.

It is a bit of a let-down to return to Compton Mackenzie's *Vestal Fire* and *Extraordinary Women*, his two Capri novels published in 1927 and 1928, a decade after *South Wind*. Mackenzie, who wrote too much and too fast, and never put enough store by his own (or anyone else's) writing, has lasted less well than Douglas. There are no mysteries in his life, as his biographer ruefully remarked, for he published ten volumes of autobiography, four war memoirs, seven volumes of various kinds of reminiscence.

In addition, he plundered his own experiences in whole series of novels such as *The Four Winds of Love*, *Carnival*, *Sinister Street* and others. He was less a creator of character and plot than an imaginative recorder and adaptor.

Mackenzie differed from a more fastidious artist like Douglas in that he was happy to turn his hand to anything. He wrote on the Duke of Windsor and tobacco, on whisky and gramophones. Altogether, as well as becoming a radio and TV personality, he published more than a hundred books. He realised eventually, as he remarked in Octave 6 of *My Life and Times*, that "versatility would be counted a vice until I became old enough for it to become a virtue", but his optimism proved a delusion.

He accepted that his telling of the Count Fersen story, later dramatised in Peyrefitte's *The Exile of Capri*, and for which he had already chosen the title *Vestal Fire*, would have to wait until more of the main characters had died or departed. Douglas's *South Wind*, moreover, "had made a novel set on a Mediterranean island out of the question for some time to come".

When he did get started he took more care than usual. "I did what I had never done before and have never done since; I made a false start with forty pages which had to be torn up." He was worried about making his old American ladies too convincing, and he was frightened about shocking his large middle-brow public. He decided to treat the homosexual aspects of Capri life as comic, not erotic. Mackenzie was not a writer to take risks against manners or taste.

The main other technical problem, which Douglas did not solve, was how to introduce a large cast without confusing the reader. *South Wind*, it occurs to me, would read much more easily if there was a descriptive list of characters as in a play. But while *South Wind* covers only two weeks in the lives of its characters, *Vestal Fire* is spread over fifteen years, 1905 to 1920, and divided into three books. The main characters, Anglo-Americans, enjoy vendettas and petty rivalries in an atmosphere of drugs and decadence, and as in *South Wind*, congregate in the piazzetta café to gossip and to observe. There are the usual rich old ladies, aspiring and unpublishable writers, effeminate young men, a replica Count Fersen and a Norman Douglas sibling.

Life revolves round parties and most specifically round the failure of the Count to join up. "Why do perfectly good parties come to an end? Why can't we go on enjoying ourselves forever?" Even less happens than in *South Wind*, the talk is less stylish. But time, though slowly, does pass, the villas empty, the chatter dies away.

Gerald Gould, a habitually generous reviewer, wrote that

though the "whole story of decay and drugs" is treated as comedy "there is no cynicism and little satire". On the contrary, "there is an extraordinary tenderness, the characterisations merciful".

Vestal Fire, in fact, slips down as easily as a cold Campari. *Extraordinary Women*, based on one of Capri's more notorious lesbian relationships, had a more difficult passage, Mackenzie's original publisher Cassell refusing to publish it. *The Well of Loneliness*, Radclyffe Hall's lesbian novel, had just been withdrawn by Cape, so it was something of a gamble for Secker to take on *Extraordinary Women*. *The Well of Loneliness* is earnest about its subject, Mackenzie is frivolous. Sex, of all kinds, is treated as fairly ridiculous, an aberration that can usually be indulged without harm.

Mackenzie always took trouble to relate his fictitious characters accurately to real places and events. Three of the four women in *Extraordinary Women* were based on friends of Mackenzie's wife; the fourth, a caricature of a practising lesbian, is described as having been a trainer of women boxers before coming to Capri and equipping herself with a monocle and bowler hat.

Mackenzie's novel is light-hearted entertainment, no more, no less, but Raymond Mortimer, for one, took Mackenzie to task for his levity, curiously calling the book "an expression of male pique and wounded vanity". Did he imagine Mackenzie wanted these intriguing and sexually amoral women for himself?

The Mackenzies, in the immediate post-war period when Capri seemed to revert to its former pleasure-loving self, appeared to enjoy an open marriage. Mackenzie often played chess with his wife's Russian lover, one of several, and in his sociable and non-committed way had affairs of his own. For much of the time they were apart, not usually from choice. Capri, with the arrival of Romaine Goddard, rich, talented, striking-looking, became increasingly a haven for lesbians and Mackenzie became fed up with their machinations and with the influx of writers. "I object to living on Capri because every quill driver in England apparently thinks that is the key to success . . . I dislike the literary world, and if I want to talk about civilisation, I prefer to talk to a doctor."

Nevertheless, he remained, a flamboyant figure in his silk shirts, bow-ties, cloak and black velour sombrero. He was kind and generous to new arrivals, finding villas for Lawrence and Brett Young. "He does the semi-romantic," Lawrence wrote to Catherine Carswell. "He is nice. But one feels the generations of actors behind him and can't be quite serious."

In these islands you have to bring your own ghosts with you.

Alicudi Porto

Ischia: *Autumn 1948*

BY SIX, WITH a grey-blue light moving off the deserted quay, Naples still hung under a thick haze. As night receded, the pall of smoke from the waterfront was already taking its place. Out at sea a mauve bandage of mist blindfolded the islands.

A few ships were tied up at the jetties, small, white-painted steamers of varying sizes that made daily trips to the islands – some to Capri, some to Procida and Ischia, and some south to Sorrento. At the moment they lay motionless on the green, oily water, silent under their awnings as occasional birds flew heavily on to the rainbow patches of oil that surrounded them. Above the cobbled quay the yellow- and pink-washed houses stretched up the hillside behind, the morning light breaking into the privacy of their sleep, probing the black holes of windows. Inside them the gradual comprehension of another day sifted thousands of minds, turned over thousands of bodies that resisted it and faced away to the walls. The familiar strings of drudgery tugged at them with a nostalgia for what was not there; in stained tenements where grime was closer than a friend; in one-night rooms where the wallpaper was less strange than the adjacent body; in flats where men and women opened reluctant eyes to an allegiance no longer desired, yet who could never break away.

Along the Via Marina, up the Via Duomo and along the Corso Umberto, discarded fruit and rubbish festered with flies as the sweepers moved along brushing up the dirt. Along the quay, sailors and dock-workers stopped at the Bar Rosa for coffee before going back to their ships. Girls with brown, dusty legs hung about with their dresses half-unbuttoned and shifted chewing-gum from their gold-filled teeth. From the tenement balconies women padded about in nightdresses or shook brooms over the decaying square. The crumbling stone of the Castel Nuovo seemed to close up on itself.

On the cobbled stones of the quay a solitary policeman exercised his dog.

We left in the smallest of boats at a quarter-past eight. Like a Thames riverboat, it had one funnel and awnings along its whole length. By the time we sailed, about thirty or forty passengers had come on board, mostly middle-aged peasant couples with children; a cargo of ice had already been piled in the hold.

The journey to Ischia is about eighteen miles and takes exactly two hours. We came slowly out into the bay, past British submarines and an enormous American aircraft-carrier, its decks black with aircraft; sailing boats and launches came past us all the time and Naples grew clearer and cleaner as we got further away. Ports should be preserved on the mind's periphery as they are on the sea's, beautiful and chaste, full of promise and illusion. Every moment, as the boat turned, Naples, like a restless creature in the morning heat, stretched out some new promontory, flexing and unflexing lines of dazzling white houses and sand, like muscles.

The water became Pernod-green, gradually changing from electric to ink blue, emerald to turquoise. Ischia and Capri lie at opposite ends of the arms that form the Bay of Naples, and going north-west to Ischia, the mainland drags beaches dotted with villas. To port the sea stretches out to a horizon that tilts then recovers. Fishing boats drift with their oars folded, like wings of birds, asleep on the satisfied water.

The boat altered course westward, following the northern arm of the bay, and leaving it for the open sea. A thick, smoky-purple haze still blotted out visibility beyond five miles and extended over Naples, so after a while, behind us, only the upper contours of the mountains could be seen, like suspended effigies, high over the hidden town. Somewhere Pompeii, Amalfi, Sorrento, refracted sun off their bony white stone. The world of ordinary people had been rubbed out in between.

We gradually pushed the haze away in front of us. The sun began to slant hotly under the awnings, mixing with the heat of the engines. Men began to lie out on the benches asleep.

At about a quarter to ten, the islands came into view. There was now nothing of the mainland to be seen; all one's ties had been cut. A tiny break had been made in continuous time, like forcing open a circle of wire that would gradually close again. In that space, life, a past and future, could be re-assessed. The untidy ends, the stray garments of involved relationships might sort themselves out. For one's isolated, exaggerated problems, the sea would be an unction; the island noise of cicadas the noise of personal history. Or so one hoped.

The boat sounded its siren. The sleepers got up and stretched. The green, pock-marked hills rose up out of the water in front of us, deeply indented; first Procida like a small prehistoric animal, in its belly a fabulous, glittering port, a cluster of soft, pastel-coloured houses curling away from a beach where waves broke lazily in powdered edges and scanty olive trees emerged above terraced vines – then Vivara, a hump of scraped, green rock, ringed with trees, a house perched near its summit and, beyond, much larger, Ischia, where a skeleton castle stood out from the island at the end of a narrow causeway.

We sailed past a beach with parasols dotted over burning sand, behind it white, flat-roofed villas half-hidden in pine trees. We turned sharply round a lighthouse into the port itself.

The sun was almost overhead. We nosed through the narrow entrance of the bottle-shaped harbour, pink and blue houses encircling it. The opening just allowed a steamer to squeeze through. Nets covered most of the quays, off which dozens of small fishing boats, a dredger and the smart launches of port authorities were tied up. A group of brightly dressed people waited at the barrier. Layers of different green – lemon, olive, vine – stretched in tight, pubic curls up the mountain that rose immediately behind the port. A road bordered with pink and white oleander wound up over the hill to the right.

Porto d'Ischia

THE TOWN IS fairly recent, a gradual development sliding downhill from the original site on the rock where the derelict castle now stands. Two decisive events have shaped Ischia's growth – a volcanic eruption in the fourteenth century and an earthquake in the early nineteenth. The latter destroyed a large part of the north of the island. The new town has a lively, holiday air, something coquettish about it. The mile of road joining it to the old port at the foot of the castle is flanked by seaside shops and hotels; in side streets off it neon-lit bars and cafés under faded awnings reach to the beach. At night, coloured lamps, green and pink, give a dance-hall look to streets endlessly paraded, the whole area on the move, families, lovers, children, dogs.

A porter carried our cases to the Regina Hotel, set back from the beach in a pinewood. The noise of the cicadas was deafening. Then, suddenly, it would stop, as if a switch had been

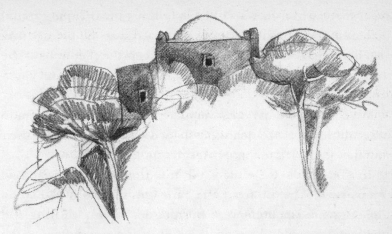

Promontory at the entrance to the harbour at Ischia

turned, the silence almost as palpable. Now, as we walked through freshly washed streets, past up-turned café tables and piazzas being cleared of the night's refuse, the cicadas were a shrill acclamation of arrival. The pinewoods surrounded the hotel like a cordon; inside, it was hospital-clean, the white-coated waiters, like medical students, pushing trolleys over rubber-lined floors. The island had already taken on a therapeutic air.

The sea was just visible from the verandah that joined all the rooms, a thin strip like blue velvet. After three days' travelling it seemed at first one more fatal mirage. The war was still close enough, it left too many half-heard voices. It was time now to be set free.

A few fishing boats were drawn up on the beach. The sea was cool salt, a lotion to plunge one's body in endlessly. The sea bed glittered like green marble and under the surface the sun made golden squares on the watered-silk weeds.

Afterwards, on burning sand imprinted with footsteps, we lay watching the water ripple like flints in the heat and the haze turn the horizon into soft blue wool. A gramophone ground out nostalgic Neapolitan tunes from a bar at the pines' edge. We drank iced Cinzano and tried to keep the flies at bay. The beach now looked chic and slightly overbearing; the sand wafer-coloured.

We lunched out of doors, very late, in the shadow of a lemon tree whose fruit, like delicately-shaped breasts, imprinted their outline on the leaves that protect them.

In the shade we waited till the worst of the heat had spent itself. The air from the pinewoods came over like an opiate; some labourers were burning leaves in a clearing and the wood seemed like a church full of incense. Below us the beach had completely emptied; the whole of the sand was now covered with fishermen's nets. Along them, at intervals of a few yards, fishermen squatted, cross-legged, in blue dungarees, striped jerseys and small, flat straw hats. They sewed, with scrupulous care, the fine nylon squares, drawing the mesh like silk stockings over the lumps of their knuckles. There was something erotic in watching it. Rolling up the netting in strips, they carry it draped over their shoulders, walking, five or six of them in single file, across the sand.

Fishing boats go out across the green skin that settles, like skim on milk, over the sea at dusk. The mauve blindfold lifts slightly off the horizon and Vivara and Procida grow nearer, as if through telescopic lenses.

The sun sinks, orange and cerise, below Epomeo, the extinguished volcano. The light changes from golden to peach, from blue-grey to green and purple, then in darkness the islands, so present earlier, are rubbed out. The cicadas, silent in the afternoon, begin clamouring again as cocktail-shakers are brandished for a clientele fresh from siesta.

At about seven, streets begin to fill. Waiters move expertly among the tables with *gelati*, coffee and vermouths; *carrozza*-drivers crack their whips over their mules, and the soundtrack from the open-air Giardino cinema is a crackling montage to conversation.

The line of light behind Procida flickers down the coastline from Pozzuoli to Sorrento. During the day one can feel cut off, but at night the links with the mainland are re-established; and incessantly, until morning, the lights of the islands and Baia throb amongst the lighthouses and beacons that mark the extremities of the bay. Within them, in a ring of their own, the brighter, smaller lights of the fishing boats – the *lampari* – float their hypnotic patches on to the water.

The fish round the islands are disappointingly poor; nearly all small, *sardinelle* or *alici*, mostly head and tail, *lacerte* or *seruzze*, without any recognisable flavour. Because of this the Ischians, except for the poorest, have almost abandoned the *zuppa di pesce* about whose ingredients Norman Douglas wrote in *Siren Land*: "They have colour and shape, these fish of the inland sea, but not taste; their flesh is either flabby and slimy and full of bones in unauthorised places, or else they have no flesh at all – heads like Burmese dragons but no bodies attached to them; or bodies of flattened construction on the *Magnum in parvo* principle, allowing of barely room for a sheet of paper between their skin and ribs; or a finless serpentine framework, with long-slit eyes that leer at you while you endeavour to scratch a morsel off the reptilian anatomy."

From sunset till midnight the aperitif drinkers, the *gelati*-sellers, the *carrozza*-drivers, compete against the hoarse dialogue of ancient American films. Then, for what seems hours, the noise from the Monkey Bar, Ischia's one *boîte*, spills out into the resinous dark, slowly turning into pinewoods. Tonight when sleep came, it brought a train of unambiguous associations; generously breasted women conversing on the decks of blue-sailed barques, dwindling into playing-cards above an olive sea.

Ischia is shaped like a tent, with Monte Epomeo in the middle and vine-terraced hills like canvas reaching down to the sea on all sides. The six towns, amongst which the 40,000 inhabitants are distributed, are fairly balanced, with Forio, the largest, near the middle of the west coast and Porto d'Ischia in a corresponding position on the east. To the north Lacco Ameno and Casamicciola nearly meet, and in similar positions, a mile or so inland to the south, lie Serrara Fontana and Barano. A good, asphalt road, running in a sort of inner circle round the whole island, connects them. Communications in general are good, with regular ferries and buses leaving Porto for a complete circuit. Or you can hire your own boat, to sail or with an engine. There are few points on the island which can't be reached on foot within three or four hours. In the winter it gets very wet, but now in summer we travel everywhere by boat or walk when we go inland.

On most days early cotton-wool clouds lie over the hills but by midday these have disappeared and a hard blue stare lasts until sunset. The sun dazzles off flat, white roofs or is absorbed in vine-scrubbed hills. The sea scalds, a grey-blue that smokes itself out on the coast.

This morning we walked to Fiaiano, a small village a third of the way across the island from Porto d'Ischia, right up in the hills. The narrow path cuts through the pinewoods of La Mandra that cover the whole of the Lava Dell'Arso, the great wedge-shaped area, arid till quite recently, which was destroyed by the eruption of 1301. Now it is all planted with trees. A small mule-track runs up at right angles from the main, circular road, a track like a dandruffed parting walled with jagged stones. Lizards detach their surreptitious lengths from lichened crevices and butterflies – white admirals, fritillaries, clouded yellows – fly languidly from the dust-coated vines. The vine terraces reach from shore to skyline; the grapes very small and sour, unsightly in comparison to the olive trees that originally covered all these hillsides. A poor investment today, there is only a fragile olive industry left. A few scattered villas, stone eyes in shabby green lashes, break the monotony of vine and scrub. Most of them are Roman, with wide porticoes and pillared balconies, set well into the rock; the vines reach right up to the verandahs, the only approach to them through specially hollowed tunnels.

During the day the sun sucks up vitality from the hills, but at sunset everything is given back. The sea, changing from blue to chromium, is the only constant, an ignored but glittering margin to the rock-centred life of Fiaiano.

Looking down from the village, the island falls like a cloak, its hem trailing into blue crêpe sea. Fiaiano itself, rarely visited despite its beauty, is quite different from the coastal villages. A narrow, cobbled street separates two lines of houses, each house freshly whitewashed and hooded with clematis or trellised vines. In each is exhibited, in miniature, a cross-section of the island's export life. The doors all open on the street and small, grey-eyed children with grave, lovely faces sit on the steps of rooms where bent old women in shapeless black weave baskets or turn flax. Their men sit in dark, cool caves, working on leather, the raw smell of wine from barrels stored in rock-vaults drenching the air.

The men of Fiaiano are taller and better-looking than the fishermen, Greek in appearance, with a solidity and strength the others appear to lack. The women sail past in biblical majesty with their water-jugs, their brown legs fastidiously certain on the cobbles and their breasts pressing upwards against the thin material of their dresses. Their carriage has a functional grace.

On the roofs of the houses tomatoes, cut in half and laid out in rows or put on a stick and hung up outside doorways, dry in the sun. Two of the larger caves, pasted with pin-up girls and cigarette-cards, act as grocery shops and wonderful fresh lemons lie ready to squeeze into glasses of crushed ice and sugar. The stalls are packed with boxes of aubergines, figs, peaches. Best of all, the small, beautifully flavoured pears refresh us after our long hot climb.

We leave Fiaiano in time to bathe before lunch. Halfway down the hill, black-eyed boys come running after us with their hands full of blackberries, which gravely they proffered and gravely we accepted.

Porto d'Ischia is in reality two separate places, Ponte being its other half, different in function, in architecture and in date. The circular harbour, originally enclosed by rocks and part of a lake, was opened in 1853. The modern town dates from this period. Port buildings and cafés reach most of the way up the hill to the pinewoods. The harbour is a bowl, with steep sides, the lights of villas in the evening and the lighthouse on Punta San Pietro joining over the water.

The original, old town, Ponte, early sixteenth century, with narrow, honeycomb streets in the Genoese fashion, has developed between the narrow spit leading to the castle and the Spiaggia dei Pescatori, an area today more functional than recreational. The pink, blue, yellow houses have a decrepit elegance, the main street, with its palm-shaded restaurants, church and workshops, always in sight of the castle. During the day, their refuse crawling with flies, the narrow, congested alleys

fester, but at night the houses glow, the beach beneath them
reduced to a meringue-coloured, foamy strip. The whole population, the buildings themselves, seem released. Lights come
out singly in windows doubled on water; small bulbs burn
over complacent religious effigies inset into leaking walls. Old
women, barely visible in the darkness, crouch over their door-
steps, children asleep like weights beside them. The causeway
to the castle is lined with old fishermen, silently sitting and
smoking clay pipes. They look as if they have been there for
ever, meditative, self-absorbed, wary.

At the seaward end of the bridge the Aragonese castle straggles down from the top of an enormous rock, the decaying
buildings a shove away from sheer drops. The castle, even the
shell that remains, is both dramatic and sinister, the scene of
terrible events that have left brooding presences. Approaching
by boat there are rocks everywhere, the water startlingly
transparent and peppermint-green. Out of the sun, the castle's
forbidding contours about you, it is not hard to imagine the
despair of its former inmates, mostly prisoners there for life.
Landing, you enter from a small bridge tacked on the end of
the causeway. The road up is steep, winding through tunnels
lit with electric candles burning over images of saints. Off
the tunnels small rooms, strewn with rusted tins and straw,
are gouged out of low walls. A smell of donkey droppings, and
either as tantalisation or comfort, a glimpse of sea and islands
through slits in the walls.

Little of the original castle, built by Alfonso I of Aragon,
remains. The walls have crumbled away and the church, with its
painted crypt and decorated chapels, is derelict. Early crude
murals are still visible under networks of cracking plaster, somewhat extravagantly claimed by the Ischians as Michelangelo's,
because of his friendship with the poet Vittoria Colonna

who lived in the castle. Some of these faint illustrations, in powdery blue and gold, of religious themes, are beautiful. More to the taste of the caramel-headed boys who show us round, are the rooms where aged nuns of a resident order came down to die. There are two adjoining stone crypts, in the walls of which are seats cut into the rock. On these the nuns who thought their hour had come sat and waited for death. When it arrived they were moved into an adjoining vault, in view of the others, where the bodies of their predecessors lay. Our small guides thought this good theatre. In the semi-darkness, small piles of bones lay carefully arranged round the walls, occasionally disturbed where mongrel-dogs had dragged a crunched femur into the light of day.

The nuns of the Castello, Ponte d'Ischia

The castle, a microcosm of the history of Ischia, was built in the middle of the fifteenth century, 150 years after the final unifi-cation of Ischia with Naples. Before this, the island underwent a series of occupations: the Saracens and Pisans in the ninth and twelfth centuries, later the Emperors Henry VI and Frederick II. The castle's appeal is romantic as well as historic, being the birthplace of Ferdinando Francesco d'Avalos, Marchese di Pescara, the Italian general, hero of Ravenna and Pavia. Pescara died of wounds in Milan in 1525 and his wife, the beautiful and talented Vittoria Colonna, spent the rest of her life in the castle where her husband had been born. Their relationship forms one of the great love stories in Italian history and the Castello d'Ischia is a setting that does justice to it.

Vittoria Colonna's years of mourning here came to symbolise for future generations *l'amor divino* – the spiritualisation of love as a counterpart to the cynical marital infidelity of Renaissance Italy. Vittoria herself, not only in her relationships with Castiglione and Michelangelo, but in her general enslavement of what Burckhardt calls "the most famous men in Italy", created and projected a myth by her unattainability, inspiring a respect and adoration almost unknown outside literature.

Emerging from the damp vaults of the castle, where one is lucky to survive the sudden flaws and holes, the unexpected wells, it is a relief to encounter bright sunlight. Romantic legends are all very well, but the sense of doom in these sunless rooms outweighs everything. The castle is something to be looked at, a magnificent enterprise in its own right, but I doubt many visitors return there.

San Montano, the prettiest beach on the island, is on the extreme north-west, two hours' walk by the coast, which is what we did today, though usually we go by boat to Lacco Ameno. The road climbs and falls, a switchback between oleanders and vines, small bays crinkling between headlands. The hills rise sheer on your left, Epomeo dominating the other peaks which from different turns in the road look nearly as high. Villas in the wooded hillsides command spectacular views, like boxes in a theatre.

After an hour's walk Casamicciola stretches out on the left of the coast road, a quarter of a mile of houses heaving themselves gradually from level to level. You pass a line of shops selling fish, mussels, baskets and postcards, which comes to an end in an L-shaped piazza where two or three bars with outside tables are set amongst flowers. On one side a few carriages blister under palm trees, behind them the beach; on the other a road rises sharply up to hill-villages, and to various, strategically placed, hotels. Somewhere up there Ibsen's old villa lurks. A lighthouse like a pepper-pot marks the end of the stone jetty to which boats come in every day from the other islands or from the mainland on their way out to Ventotene and San Stefano, the prison islands halfway to the Ponziane islands. Suitably black-painted steamers with yellow funnels carry away a flutter of white roofs in a green bay as their last look at normal life.

Striped beach umbrellas lay in rows; beach boys and their cronies guarded different areas or idly watched children diving off the pier, coming up like wet dogs. We continued past them under cliffs with caves stacked with wine barrels reaching far into the rock, their entrances barred by huge, bolted grilles. Further along, the beach became a dump for old oil-drums, the picture postcard effect suddenly ruined. Half a mile on and round one more headland the buildings of Lacco Ameno, a fishing village about half the size of Casamicciola, spread out at the foot of Monte Vico, the old Greek capital. We stopped and bought melon and peaches, had a drink in a wine shop. A hundred yards out to sea a large rock, mushroom-shaped, sticks out of the water and acts as a raft for swimmers; the rowing boats going out to meet the mail steamer rest there. There is a myth about an underwater house attached to it, the result, it is said, of a building falling into the sea during one of the many coastal landslides.

Just beyond this we arrived at the square of Santa Restituta – the patron saint of Ischia – with its pink buildings, its third-century church with Byzantine decorations and murals, and thermal baths to which people still come, hobbling in off the boats from Naples.

San Montano, on the other side of Monte Vico, lies in a kind of gulch, ending in a small half-moon of sand. On either side scrubby headlands, separated by a narrow strip of sea, enhance its privacy. Cactus grow here in great abandon, along with olives. A few thatched huts, a couple of boats attended by a man with stocky legs and a straw hat, are the only signs of life. We could have been in Africa, so deserted was it, so off the beaten track. The green, milky sea barely bothered to break. Out of the sand, hot springs bubbled. The water was a blessing, and we spent all afternoon in and out of it.

We left when the sun had gone behind Epomeo, stopping only to drink glasses of iced wine on the way back. By the time we reached the hill above the harbour of Porto d'Ischia the water in the port was the colour of wine, streaks of sunset running through it.

I read in the mornings on a terrace facing the pines. Away from the beach, the only noise is of the cicadas. At intervals girls go by carrying jugs or baskets on their heads. I follow their vase-like figures as they swing through dappled paths in the woods. A blue chink of sea is just visible over the fringe of trees and occasionally, when I look up, white sails curl like irises over the water.

A carriage clatters by, the driver flicking his whip over the mule; now a tiny donkey, the size of a dog, draws an enormous

load into town. From my book I am learning something or
other, though not as much as from just looking. Towards
noon we go for a bathe, dry out in the sun, drink a Cinzano,
lunch about two. Life reduced to the minimum. I used, in the
Arctic, to dream of such indolence.

The streets empty, though sometimes a priest can be heard
toiling up to the school where they teach. Shopkeepers fan
themselves on chairs outside their shops, humped like dolls
with the sawdust running out of them.

At night, the waterfront crushes out the day's heat on its stone
transfer. The sea changes colour as you look at it; houses, losing
their daytime stains, acquire a mellow bloom. Girls in the semi-
dark become romantic, elusive creatures, turning from peasants
into icons. Old age is becoming to the matriarchs on their door-
steps. Every so often a boat slips out, its powerful lamp probing
the sea. Lighted windows outline the silhouettes of men playing
scopa, the card game that is a day-long ritual of fierce intensity,
no laughing matter. Women cool off on steps, worn beauties
replete in their seasons.

Classical form in modern dress is evident everywhere, especially
lower down the social scale. Peasants especially seem perpetua-
tions of paintings, embodiments of the varieties of female
beauty that Firenzuola catechised so precisely in the sixteenth
century. Yet today the illusion of purity, coupled so often in
practice with extreme sensuality, has vanished with the cult of
the contemporary woman, whose freedom of movement has
taken beauty out of the *salon*, an art of pastiche, into the fresh
air. The practice of oiled sun-tanned skin has brought with it an
unaffected elegance and healthiness, a physical assertiveness that
at the same time reduces the excitement of concealment and

unavailability. These half-naked women have lost m
sexiness. Sailors at sea might find this hard at first to

Afternoon. Two girls play with a huge, striped ball on the beach,
stumbling and falling over the uneven sand like colts. Hair
corn-coloured, wind-tossed; legs whose muscles are still insecure,
a prey to the sinews' impulse. A yacht keels over like a dancer
on skates; the sea arches its back as waves break like tissue. The
island seems to wheel in a light wind.

Above us the slopes of Epomeo have folds of vine, the foliage
dense save for a jagged scar. Along the skyline a frieze of palm
trees gestures resignedly, skimpy and lost in undergrowth. At
sea level the glare shimmers, almost hallucinatory. The resinous
scent of pine drugs us as we let sounds drift over us, the sirens
of liners in the gulf, the stamping of horses, clink of *carrozzas*,
fidget of cicadas, throatiness of frogs. We are insulated from
ourselves by the glass wall of heat, impervious to the silver eyelid of an aeroplane, the whine of mosquitoes, the dipping of
honey-coloured oars.

We sail this evening to the Grotta del Mago. The heat is already
slackening and there are two clear hours of activity before dark.
We turn out past the pinewoods, the Spiaggia dei Pescatori and
the old town, rinsed and serene now at sunset, then through
the small gap between the causeway and the *castello*. The water,
like cut-glass, is quartered like a chart on the sea bed. We edge
through rocks, past fishing boats and beyond the pier under the
crumbling cliffs of Sant'Anna. The original tower, like so many
Ischian buildings, has crumbled into the sea, leaving a slither
of grey rock. There is barely an islander who has not lost, at some
time or another, one of his relatives in a landslide or cliff accident.
The isolated beach at Sant'Anna is only reachable by boat, for

the rocks come sheer down to the shingle, cultivated to the very edge with vines. The whole way along the coast, on straggling, awkward pieces of cliff and jutting headlands, there are olive trees and precarious, but neatly terraced, vines so not a foot of land is wasted.

An hour's sailing and the rocks become increasingly indented – great fissures cut some of the cliffs in half, so they protrude at alarming angles. Everywhere the rough volcanic surface looks as though some huge hand had grasped the lava while it was still warm and clenched it up like plasticine.

The Grotta del Mago is the largest of the coastal caves – we can stand up in the boat as we go through. Inside it widens out, stalactites like dentists' equipment suspended from rock. The water has turned into shades of blue ink, an illusion of concealed lighting. Twenty yards in, a tiny channel leads into the middle of the cliff where the rocks reach down to two feet above the water. In the sticky darkness nothing is visible except the O, like the opening of a pencil-sharpener, of the entrance.

Inside, a silence of magnified echoes. Our boatman seems to be in a state of prayer or else he's fallen asleep. Perhaps he was out fishing all night, or more probably playing cards. He's old, and the passing days may have little to distinguish them. Water, rock, cave, scarcely perceptible changes in weather or temperature: a simple life, though who knows what he may have gone through during the Fascist period or the war. He was unlikely ever to have been an enemy of the state, these islands being mainly unaffected by mainland politics. Except for those who voiced anti-Fascist opinions, in which case the *castello* would have become their home. Only when the war was ending did Allied troops occupy Ischia, and then only for recreation.

We come out into the sunset. The dazzle has gone from the sea, and the sky is smoked over. Through blue-grey mists the uneven humps of Capri tilt like a foundering ship.

The stars harden into bits of cut-out tinfoil as we return under a following breeze. By the time we reach the old waterfront, moonlight is splashed across our bows, a chromium sash behind the pinewoods as we round the cape and tie up at the jetty. The gramophone is playing in the small bar at the edge of the pine and we drink two Negronis before going back to change.

Soon after midnight I awake, naked and restless under the open window. The heat is unrelenting. The cicadas have grown quiet; only the occasional whine of a mosquito penetrates the breathless darkness. The moonlight catches the end of the wall near the balcony and sitting up in bed I can see the sea-glitter thrown backwards and forwards as if in a chain net. I have become senselessly anxious, a prey to bad memories. The Arctic still seems to retain its images, the clank of steel doors and the crackle of flame, a ship half-capsized. Does it never quite let go?

I watch the night tick its way into dawn. Under a wafer-thin layer of sleep, a factory of ideas grinds itself out.

Then suddenly, through the half-open shutters, my eyes open to the ruled blue of the bay.

Another afternoon, reading Byron's letters. Autumn seems to have insinuated itself into the landscape. Or is it only imagination, an uncertainty about the future that comes from watching fishermen wind up sunset in their nets? The beach is still like a picture-postcard. But there is a premonition of something ending, a hint of rust in the wooded hills.

Is life preferable with or without security? Surviving was for so long the best one could hope for, but now at twenty-five, I want plurality, other kinds of experience. Would one like to be able to look even five years into the future? I wonder.

Casamicciola

BASED HERE NOW we have the gulf on a new bearing. Procida and Vivara are hidden behind the Punta della Scrofa and, opposite us, the Bay of Gaeta, with Capo Miseno to our right, makes the distance from the mainland seem much further. The bay dazzles and glitters, a sieve of blue splinters, beyond which a thin froth of sand and surf off Gaeta squeezes itself out like ectoplasm at sea level. Only up here, on the scrubbed hillside, can one see where the mauve coast actually reaches the water. Named, according to Virgil, after Aeneas's nurse, Caieta, Gaeta is a compact secreted town of alleyways and cobbled streets on the far headland from Naples. Across five miles of sea it remains only a blur, which comes into focus through binoculars.

Casamicciola's main street, bordered with oleander and palms, runs in a straight line along the sea's edge. The piazza contains rows of cafés that face each other uneasily through trees. Horse-drawn carriages outnumber taxis, giving the town an agreeably old-fashioned and leisurely appearance. From the piazza cafés everything and everybody can be, and is, observed; the input and output of local buses, the arrival of the Naples steamer, the doings of fishing vessels and motorboats. The scruffy beach makes few concessions to fashion, swimming here being a family affair arranged round vast picnics – ham, bread, grapes, wine. The men wear braces and striped fishermen's jerseys, as if they were sitting for Seurat or Cartier-Bresson. Lacco Ameno is just round a corner, but it is a world away, minding its own business. Political slogans and manifestos scrawled or pasted up on walls

round the piazza seem more like decoration than calls to action.
One could live here, just as some people can live in Hastings
or Bexhill.

Each Ischian town has its own bay, backdrop of mountain
and a pair of headlands marking out its territory. The distance
between them is negligible, yet each has its own distinct, unmis-
takable character.

Casamicciola has a rather engaging, off-season quiet, villas
and hotels each muffled in their own gardens and vineyards. As
a resort, it's pleasantly informal. The three hotels, the Bellavista,
the Suisse and the Pithecusa, all overlook the harbour, perched
on different slopes of Epomeo. The Villa Ibsen (where Ibsen
wrote *Peer Gynt* at the same time as Boecklin was living in
Casamicciola) has the best view of all – a rambling white building with flowers growing up all over it, a rose garden and
trellised terrace, under which the whole bay – sea, quayside,
town – drifts in a heat haze.

Waking is effortless, a surfacing to light. Through the shuttered
window a surprisingly hot sun turns the room into an aquarium –
rippling patches of aqueous, honey light. We breakfast on the
terrace; coffee, brown bread, boiled eggs and figs. By eight o'clock
the sun has begun to glint, the sea, despite the lateness of the
season, already feverish and throbbing. In the bay, sailing boats
have settled like butterflies, hardly moving. The fishing boats
have been in for hours, and now the first mail steamer is off Baia
on its way to Porto d'Ischia. Below, in the town, fruit stalls are
being set up along the main street; waiters wash down the exact
areas – no more – of pavement outside their cafés, chairs are being
put out in the Giardino restaurant. Off the promenade, under the
oleanders, pomegranates, mussels, watermelon are on offer. Up
here, we sense, rather than hear, the bustle of people on the quay

and the sellers by their stalls. Occasionally, as if a door in between were being opened and shut, a gust of noise comes up with the heat from below. Or else voices ring clear and sharp like gun-fire across the flat water. Life at sea level seems fore-shortened, stereoscopic. Each new day promises nothing more than itself.

Trying to educate myself I read Burckhardt under a lemon tree. It's hard to take anything in. Rows of grapes are staked out for fifty yards all round. The hotel wine is made on the premises, though it is still early for picking and pressing. In another three weeks the whole island will seem to be on the move, the pickers working their way up the hillsides, starting from the coast. The air will feel as if it has been drenched with a wine-spray and the island itself seem to be bubbling, unable to contain itself any longer.

At midday we walk over to San Montano to bathe. Going through Lacco we meet Raffael, the local postman, one of the few obvious eccentrics on the island – habitually drunk, always meticulously polite, very cultured in appearance. A straw hat is squashed over battered, soggy features which still preserve, like the half-erased head on a coin, outlines of nobility – a Wodehouse character somehow turned renegade, a gentleman's gentleman broken loose. By late afternoon, when the main post of the day comes in, he is usually beyond carrying out his duties and goes, or is carried, home singing and blowing his whistle, a satchel of undelivered mail on his shoulder. He wakes very early and begins his delivery-round before dawn. By then his head has cleared, and, filled with the elixir of a new day's drinking ahead of him, he stops at every house, whether they have mail or not, to blow his whistle as a reconciliatory, social gesture. Calise is, as usual, in his shop – an effusive, good-natured caricature Italian who has done his time on the New York sidewalks, and now, retired to his native village, talks nostalgically and repetitively about Manhattan. We sit with him and his wife sometimes in the evening, enjoying the sunset and watching the white lights come out on the hillside, the only sounds the gentle swish of surf. Raffael is teased by Calise, who eggs him on to drink more and more, until he can only giggle and blow out his cheeks like a whale. Calise outlines his plans for a salted-herring industry to make his own and everybody else's fortune. Only native apathy, the reluctance of provincial people to take a risk, he says, is holding it up.

We buy our lunch at Lacco – ham, brown bread, white wine, grapes – then lie on the nearly empty Montano beach till dusk. The sea is viscous, olive-green. The waves have hardly the energy to break. Although autumn is upon us the heat has not declined. We had storms a few weeks ago but the tail-end of summer has taken on a new lease. The valley behind us is rich in reeds, ferns, bamboo. We float, rather than swim, meditative, inactive. It is hard to recall another life.

At sunset, under an oyster sky, we return along the sea road. The dust has settled, the air pure, noiseless. The sun has an effect of noise: as it sinks, a persuasive silence spreads over the landscape. Outside the church of Santa Restituta two nuns flutter through the piazza, their starched cuffs a reproach against the sensual indulgence of local life. Not everyone comes here for pleasure. Old leathery peasants, doubled like hairpins and noses to the ground, men as notched as the sticks they lean on, take cures in waters that in Casamicciola are supposed to be the best in the island. In the evening the clients parade in striped cotton pyjamas, grisly reminder of other sorts of victims in recent photographs. Three main baths are supplied from the *gurgitello*, a thermal spring of 135 degrees Fahrenheit – the Manzi, the Belliazzi, and then, at the far end of the town, the Monte della Misericordia for the very poor.

Traces of the earthquake of 1883 are still visible. Three thousand people died, nearly as many injured, in a few seconds. Running up from the coast road a kind of crushed stone walk stretches, through bare patches of hill, to the centre of the island. In winter, when the trees are leafless, the vines have the look of skeletons.

Every evening at sunset between Lacco and Casamicciola, a pair of cows are led down to the beach. At intervals, villagers arrive with jugs, holding out different-sized containers, and wait patiently while the cows are milked. The sky changes colour behind them, going through its usual antics. The milk hisses from rich udders, singing against the tin jugs. By the time the cows are led away, broodingly indifferent, up the hill, night has fallen.

The piazza smells of incense, of dry leaves. Young girls, in pairs or more, parade, handkerchiefs fluttering from their wrists, their scent mixing with the sour sweat of old fellows stapled to their benches. A time of reading the *Corriere della Sera*, of gossiping. Steamers are arriving and leaving. There is an undercurrent of desire, a covert, oblique establishing of relationships as young men, giving nothing away, smoke, observe. Nothing escapes them. All is serene, untroubled, on the surface. So it must have been before an earthquake or the outbreak of war. Here the Fascists are only smeared graffiti, daubed slogans fading fast.

Festa della Santa Maria Maddalena. Clouds have appeared from nowhere. A southerly wind has whipped the bay into a spumy, olive-coloured mass, changing the whole aspect of the island. Occasionally, the now autumnal sun throws splinters of light through the sky's masonry. Without heat, the landscape's human qualities, indolence, self-sufficiency, the feeling of leisure, collapse; it is as though some faculty, necessary for the rituals of living, is missing. The island seems suddenly bleak, a northern outpost of variegated greens and stiff foliage.

The beaches are empty, only a few boats bobbing indeterminately off the Punta della Scrofa. The routine mail-boat, normally met by small dinghies and swimmers, arrives alone and unmolested. No other boats come in all day. A large, black-sailed fishing smack dwarfs the silent and sallow quay. The noise of sunlight, the scissoring of cicadas, the simmer of sea and rock, are absent, as if short-circuited. The island's whole life and landscape are animated by sun – without it the land is lifeless. The empty hours are like dead skin that people absentmindedly scrape off in an enforced idleness.

During the day there are various explosions in different parts of the island and in Procida. The amount of noise made during a *festa* indicates the degree of pleasure the people wish to give to their saint. The structure of Ischia, its rocky crags and hollows, makes the slightest sound, the most anaemic firework, echo like a thunder clap. It would not, one imagines, be difficult amongst these reverberating valleys to propitiate the most implacable of deities.

At six in the evening a band begins to play in the piazza. The wind, still strong, catches the music in gusts, so it comes up to us as through swing doors. In the dull light a crowd begins to form in procession behind a priest, who emerges from the church at the head of a small choir. The priest and choir carry torches and at various places down the main street light flares which flicker and belly like sails in the wind's eddies. They circle the piazza several times, chanting as they light huge oil-stoups spaced out on the sea-front. Then, retracing their steps along the line of raffia shops, fishmongers, fruiterers and bars, they regroup under Boecklin's statue in the square, the whole town

aflame around them. Why Boecklin, who died in 1901, is celebrated here is something of a mystery, since he was the most
casual of visitors, painting his mythological scenes either in
Florence or his native Switzerland.

At moments the air burns and bellows with music and flames;
at others the wind engulfs the whole piazza in its embrace,
putting out brass band, choir and procession like a hose. As
it grows darker the flames are extinguished and the waterfront floodlit; boats are lit all over, their profiles glittering.
The procession begins to wind back to the church, returning
by small streets behind the town. Muffled singing floats disem-
bodiedly behind them, losing itself like smoke on the hillside.

The wind drops during dinner, leaving the air sultry and
sluggish. The *festa* was being held in a village near the top of the
hill and by half-past nine groups of people wander up the
narrow lane towards the music. At the entrance to the village
a great tiara of light hangs over the road. On either side
neon lights are strung along telegraph wires. Wax images of
Christ, hung with flowers, smile beatifically from small alcoves.
Reproductions of Santa Maria Maddalena, pieces of melon,
rattles and fireworks, chromium cribs and model mangers,
bars of thick, gluey *torrone*, figs, balloons, rosettes, neckties, are,
in the name of the Virgin, hawked noisily at the village gates.
Above, on a flat piece of wasteground, a band plays on a
decorated dais, its lights flickering and dying. Sometimes the
musicians are plunged into total darkness, the majority aban-
doning their music; a few lonely trumpets struggle on like
drowning swimmers. Every so often lights revive, leaving the
bandmaster, like a harassed referee, to fix an arbitrary place in
the score and rally his orchestra into some semblance of unity.

We buy *torrone* and melon, sitting down to eat them on the
low walls of a lane, which rises vertically out of a dried-up

ravine. Every few minutes fireworks unfold in umbrellas of pink, green and violet, suddenly fading to leave the sky black and empty. More people arrive, from below and from above, walking abreast across the road, then coming to rest near us on the walls. Rockets and Catherine wheels spin colours across their faces. Arches of neon glitter in haloes over the hill, the church, its doors wide open, illuminated like a ship. Children and black-shawled women shuffle into clouds of incense; inside, the muffle of intoning voices testifies to habit and duty.

Tonight there are no boats out; the fishermen, uncomfortable in formal clothes, stroll past stalls of devils and crucifixes, religious postcards and silk underwear. In their oasis of light the dark-suited band plays operatic arias with touching gravity. There is no dancing or drinking. The spectacle itself is enough – gunpowder and gaiety, incense and Madonnas, paper flags and rockets. It is the homage that is important, the proprietary manner of the celebration. For it is not just anybody's festival, but the personal thanksgiving of one particular community. The rest of the island sleeps unconcernedly out of earshot. It is not their affair.

At midnight the crowd starts to disperse. Children lie bundled on the laps of women or stagger with rubbed eyes round gaudy stalls. The fireworks begin to run out. Only the church, all its lights burning, sails like a galleon into the dawn.

The cloud and wind last for three days; according to local wisdom their normal duration. Then, in a cleansed blue sky, the sun gradually reasserts itself. Sea, hills and trees grow into sharper outline, as if some tonic was at work. The paintwork on fishing boats takes on new life, the beaches look cleaner. Where vines and olives looked dusty, their leaves glow with inner health.

We row one morning across the bay to Lacco Ameno, tying up below the church of Santa Restituta. From the sea the island seems wonderfully free of diesel and dirt. On the climb to Monte Vico, threading our way through vines, cactuses and sweetcorn, we come across a derelict chapel encircled by trees. On the edge of a rocky spur a neglected war cemetery is just visible through the undergrowth. Narrow inlets, a brilliant turquoise, afford shelter to fishing boats which are stationary below us, a few red floats marking the netted areas. Nothing is on the move.

Little remains of the old capital and Greek settlement. Recent excavations, mostly by Germans, have produced some relics, scattered fragments of stone now in the museum at Porto d'Ischia; lack of proper funds has made any serious archaeological survey so far impossible. The information and relics in existence are due almost entirely to German settlers, like the Buchners, who run the museum and whose enthusiasm, despite lack of local interest, has created a basis for future work.

High on the hill, above the beach of San Montano, a naval signal-training station now stands, surrounded by barbed wire and flanked by two crumbling buildings. The larger of these is occupied by the family which owns the surrounding vines and from their outhouses, hidden in the undergrowth, chickens scamper anxiously across the narrow paths. Although none of the ports are far off as the crow flies, these rocky slopes, heavily wooded, have a sinister indifference to them. They do not belong to the coastal life and the few settlements that there are have a hermetic quality. On the horizon, dimly discernible, is the prison island of Ventotene and beyond it Ponza, and the atmosphere of imprisonment and exile – the Princesses Julia and Octavia finished up here – seems to have drifted across the intervening water.

We could look down on the green, transparent slit of San

Montano, the sea listless. A troupe of fat women waddle off
the beach, venturing up to their knees. They lie out later,
good-natured, gossipy, maternal. They age quickly here, their
adolescent desirability a matter of memory.

We row back from Lacco Ameno over crinkly water, the sun
still overhead. The pink, confectionery columns of the thermal
baths promise pleasures that have to be postponed. A hot bath
is some hours ahead.

There is no bank in Casamicciola. Planning to move on today
by the first steamer to Forio, I get up early and walk the coastal
road into Porto d'Ischia. A few lizards slither into and out
of crevices in walls, like vagrant hotel guests returning in the
morning to their own rooms. The air is heady with scent. As
I round the bend the scale and shape of Porto seems to me
perfect, an ideal sea-settlement come to life. Fishing boats,
coalers and launches lie like poor relations beside opulent
yachts on the curved waterfront. The quays are scrubbed, shining. I change some money, have a black coffee at one of
the cafés, buy an illustrated magazine with cavorting models,
politicians and film stars and catch the newly washed bus back
to Casamicciola. The day's first boat from Naples comes nosing
into the harbour just as I arrive. At eleven, the *Pythecusa*, a small,
sleek-white liner, sidles over a long swell, the gale's residue, and
backs up to Casamicciola quay.

By the time we sail the boat is nearly empty, the weather –
there was still a breeze – persuading most of the passengers to
continue their journey by road. A few peasants clasp unhappy
hands to ample stomachs, clutching at baskets of rolling vegetables as the boat lurches and swings, propellers revving in space.
A priest, his triple, pale jowls like ruffs, leans over the side, his
breviary held away like a cup of tea, the sea's spume dripping

like shaving soap from his apprehensive features.

Sailing round the north-east corner, the coast becomes wilder, more romantic, old, disused buildings, abandoned look-outs, scattered on the edge of promontories. A few terns and puffins waddle over stray patches of grass on cliff-tops.

The Punta di Caruso terminates abruptly, giving way to slivers of sand. The beach of San Francesco, sheltered by its headland, stretches for a mile or more to the harbour of Forio, its domes and turrets visible over a clutch of masts. On the near slopes, stretching back from the beach, the villas of Montevergine lie among bamboo and vine. The hills are gentle behind the coast road, then, shedding their burdens of brick and scrub, rise to stony peaks.

Forio

FORIO, THE SECOND town of Ischia, is the industrial capital, an old Saracenic outpost put to commercial purposes. It has little in the way of accommodation, no hotels worth speaking of. But people are beginning to come here, renting rooms or villas for next to nothing. The streets have a homely, non-touristy feel, more workshops than boutiques, a wonderful sailors' church, Chiesa del Soccorso, high on a cliff. It is on Maria's café, one of two among trees off the main square, that social life centres.

Architecturally, Forio is Spanish-Arab. Twice in its history the town has been occupied, once each by Spaniards and Moors. Forian girls were obliged to marry the invaders, all the local men having been expelled. Arab features are evident and there

Chiesa del Soccorso, Forio

was a time when Forio had its own native quarter. It's not hard to imagine the steep alleyways winding out of the harbour as a casbah, the lanes part of a souk. Houses, behind huge wooden doors, open into courtyards, sometimes with a palm tree in the middle.

Our *pensione* overhangs the beach. The mornings are sultry, though gusts of wind soon tear the clouds apart. The town, walled in like an old garrison, seems to be falling apart, its secret enclaves crumbling to expose rough plots, given over to goats and dogs. There are more boats below us than people. In the sea walls, under ancient watchtowers, wine barrels are shifted about in cellars, their sour smell drifting up to us. We are the only people in the building, the owners sleeping elsewhere and returning early in the morning. I am reading James Hanley and Henry Green, recent friends, and despite their different backgrounds, friends of each other. Green's dialogue, whether spoken by factory workers, firemen or the upper classes, makes out of idiosyncrasies of speech something both sad and comical. Hanley shares some of Green's mannerisms and can often be funny but it is essentially a bitter humour. As a sailor he knew a different kind of life and the experience never really left him.

From our bedroom a cool, stone-floored room with mosaics and Moroccan paintings on stuccoed walls, we look across the bay to Montevergine. Below us, in the morning, the noise from the beach sounds like an orchestra starting up, the sky an egg-shell slowly cracked by the sounds of day. At this moment of our lives a tin jug and basin, a gilt dressing table smeared with lipstick, framed reproductions of religious scenes, a scarf draped over a bedpost, sandals and suntan oil are all we possess. There are other bits and pieces of clothing, mostly in suitcases, a few books. It is enough. Everything else we can buy as we want it. Being here is more like living than visiting. It is a quite different feeling, as far as I'm concerned, from anywhere else on the island, and from anything I've ever known.

A yacht like an inflated petal curls into the bay. At noon the mail boat slides over the silken water to drop anchor. A queue of boatmen jostle off her gangway for mail and for passengers. From our balcony we watch the ships' officers, brilliantly white against the decks, supervise the unloading; "Santa Lucia" drifts lazily into the heat through the ship's loudspeakers. I was never happier, I realise, than when coming into port after a successful patrol: leaning over the bridge of a destroyer, observing Wrens swishing alongside in their launches bringing the mail, watching all the small processes of tying up. The sound of sirens – it never fails to move, even when one is no longer part of it, as here.

The curved jetty bisecting the bay cannot take steamers, so they have to lie some way off. Porto d'Ischia has the only harbour in the island where boats can come alongside comfortably. Every day at Forio the mail boat lies off shore until four o'clock, then begins the return journey to Naples via Casamicciola, Porto d'Ischia and Procida. Not a bad life for the crew, if rather a tame one.

At a restaurant last night we made friends with Baron and Baroness A. from Florence. The food was unpunctual but plentiful, the same as usual. There was a small band. F., an Italian ex-army officer, whom we have met before, sits opposite. Always in uniform, he struts in to meals, his fair, wiry body as if on a clothes-hanger. He must have some kind of official status, though he can hardly still be a soldier. His stiff, toothbrush moustache twitches impatiently as he waits to be served, irritated by flies and delay. He smiles, then switches off his smile like an electric light. Openly Fascist, he calls himself a "positivist" in our periodic talks. Man, he says, must be master of his own fate. From this, it follows that the social system must allow him infinite expansion, both for good or evil. The development of the individual and democracy are incompatible.

"I would kill myself," he repeats, banging the table, "rather than live in a Communist Italy." I believe him. The vision of Mussolini and Clara Pettacci's corpses strung up by their compatriots, their near-naked bodies swollen, does not mean to him the end of an idea. Pale blue eyes stare inhumanly above his niggling lips, his frustration only too evident. But F. is not an isolated phenomenon, only one of many, in whom a delight in uniforms and all that goes with them has been unkindly thwarted. A porter and a stationmaster, a bus conductor and a ship's steward, now look as swanky as officers once did. Uniforms are not only seductive for Italians however. I, too, sometimes hanker for the old days, the feeling of being a swell. "Soldiers half a crown, Sailors if they're willing / Big fat men, two pounds ten / Little boys a shilling." So the song went when I was in bell-bottoms. I think, though, on the whole I preferred a naval officer's uniform, the more so since, once an ordinary seaman, I never expected to wear one. With what childish excitement I went up to London on my first leave as an officer, only, after exchanging my new uniform to go out on the town in battle dress, to find on my return in the early hours my hotel room non-existent through a bomb, my uniform unwearable.

Last night there was a dance to celebrate the opening of a new café. We went to dinner with Eduardo Bargheer, a refugee from Nazi Germany, now an Italian citizen. Bargheer, who lives in Forio, is a painter, primarily a watercolourist, whose romantically felt scenes of Ischian life have many admirers. Fishermen mending their nets, women bearing pots on their heads, boatmen rowing, his is an ancient, yet also a contemporary world. At one with nature, his figures endure the same seasonal crises and pleasures, the same simple activities as occupy Matisse and Bonnard, though the light is Italian.

We reach the café at ten o'clock, when it is already crowded. Beyond the rocks the chromium sea glitters, the sky hazy with stars. Two naked bulbs, fixed into vine pergolas, light up a square of cement across which a number of couples are tangoing. In a ring outside the dancers, like spectators at a boxing match, a thick cordon of shirt-sleeved men, brown faces shining, blue-black hair glistening, sit at trestle tables in semi-darkness. Beyond this dance floor *pizze* are being served in an alcove. The noise is appalling, the music hoarsely relayed on gramophone records through a huge horn loudspeaker. Speech is scarcely possible. We buy bottles of white wine, uncomfortably settling at a wobbly table. The dancing is taken seriously, total concentration on the dancers' faces. No smiles or jokes. There are a few Valentino types, with oily hair and sideburns, but they come in all shapes and sizes, fishermen, farmers, shop girls, the last fingering their crucifixes nervously and sweating. The owner of the wine shop and his wife sit side by side, as if on an inflated cushion, somehow adrift from the proceedings. They look straight ahead, expressionless.

Every so often a tipsy figure pushes his way through the remorselessly jigging dancers. A few politically abusive epithets are hurled and then he disappears. The sea is awash with moonlight. The café seems like a brilliantly illumined raft cut off from its moorings. There are daubs of light on the mountain, its peaks jagged above us. The women's scent and the musk of the flowers mingle. The dome of the church and the battlements of the old castle are outlined on the harbour like transfers that will be gone by morning. On such a night in 1931, the Italian poet Laura de Bosis flew his plane low over the streets of Rome delivering anti-Fascist leaflets. As he flew out to sea Italian air-force planes followed and killed him.

At midnight we return through moonlit squares, shadows knife-edged on walls. Out of earshot of the café, silence hangs like a conspiracy. In the empty streets, our footsteps echo over cobbles. We might be under siege in some Arab oasis. Later, through the open window the sound of the sea, feathering over the beach, seems like a rehearsal of release.

The main roads out of Forio, the ones that circle the island, discourage pedestrians. Apart from the perilous shore road to Montevergine, the only way we can walk is along the rough track through the vines leading to Epomeo. In the heat of the day the closely cultivated slopes sag in the sun, bunches of grapes hanging down like udders. As you climb, you are aware only of blue sky above the sweep of vines tenaciously struggling into ripeness. Stones glint like quartz where the sun catches them; lizards spin out of the undergrowth. Nearer the summit we look down at the layers of vegetation, the scatter of houses, streets that are sugary lines of cinnamon, cobalt, yellow, the soda-white walls, on which the waves break up after their long journey.

We have missed by a few days the triumphal return of a Forian cardinal. The cardinal, owner of a private palace outside the town, arrived in a cloud of pageantry, accompanied by Vatican escorts, for his summer recess. Now inferior only to the Pope, he was of humble birth. When it seemed likely at one time that he might even become Pope, consternation prevailed in the town. "Fancy! A Pope from Forio!" The people hold up their hands in horror, "How could we have lived it down?"

*

Tonight, under a clear moon, the town looks like a box of white bricks. The hills behind are dark smudges, mere intensification of darkness. We look out from Nettuno's flat roof, sea syncopated behind us, at small Arab-like streets of mud huts. In the bar rows of bottles, like medicines in an old-fashioned pharmacy, suggest hygiene as much as intoxication. This is the poorest section of the town, families sitting out in front of their houses, a man clapping his hands, another one chanting. I watch the smoke from their cigarettes curl up, the glow as they inhale, and am struck by a feeling that this is the real, real world. I am conscious of experiences greater than my own, though I know equally this is not so. In harsh conditions we memorise pleasure, only later like Rimbaud see it as death.

Another exchange of cattle and wine took place today. A freighter came in during the afternoon and rowing boats went out to meet it, towing barrels through the sea behind them. The boat's hatches were lowered and teams of cattle, like parachutists, were pushed out into the water. There were about twenty cows and oxen, pulled in on ropes, only their heads like mounted antlers visible above the sea.

Every evening, under green palms, the sky curdling above them, men sit playing *scopa*. Dark-throated, they wear short-sleeved white vests and faded blue linen trousers. Fishermen, café proprietors, labourers, clerks. An atmosphere of coarse tobacco, of stale sweat and pomade. Flies settle on white enamel lampshades, on bottles behind the bar. Cicadas strive for attention. None of the men ever drink.

The bay unusually full of boats, the sea at its flattest. *August for the people and their favourite islands*. Table-tennis and girls, their breasts whiter where their *maillots* have clung, crucifixes swaying; old men in straw hats asleep in the shadow of boats. Fresh and pungent, paint dazzles where always someone is repairing his boat, someone with rolled trousers leading a donkey, his cart full of rubbish. *Limonata* and Nazionale cigarettes, newspapers uncurling in flurries of sand, remote headlines trampled under classical feet. A boat rounds the headland, sails breasting the air for a moment, then slowly subsiding; it circles gently some distance off, then, like a dog coming to heel, runs in, shaking itself. Over-ripe bits of fruit, cigar-ends, a litter of seaweed, *frutti di mare*; the beach smothers and drains us, while blue, patronising skies, days without difference, burn incontinently ahead. *Passo quel tempo, Enea / Che Dido a te penso ...*

Sant'Angelo

THE MOST SOUTHERLY point of the island. We came yesterday by dinghy from Forio, a two-hour journey in boiling sun. The sea was molten lava, a grey-blue treacle that seemed at any moment about to congeal. The coastline, extremely bare, is streaked with pink, yellow and grey strata of rock. Isolated green tufts stick up round the cliff edges like hair *en brosse*. Above the strip of coast road the peaks of Epomeo and Monte del Monte stretch like velvet muzzles above the original crater.

We left Forio soon after midday, the only time we could get a boat. We hired one of the owner's friends – a sailor on leave from a luxury Italian liner – to sail the boat back before sunset, so it could go out again for the night's fishing. We took lunch with us – hard-boiled eggs, salami, bread, tomatoes, a bottle of Chianti and some peaches.

The south-west corner of Ischia is deeply indented, scattered rocks lying in shoals off the cliffs. Navigation near this brusque coast for any but the smallest boats is hazardous. No sandy bays break the severity of rock. The cliffs jut out threateningly, only scrub above them, the topsoil arid and without cultivation or buildings. There is evidence everywhere of landslides, of erosion. The island suddenly seems harsh, unwelcoming.

The sea this afternoon, in a westering sun, is like old gold. We pass isolated rocks, miniature offshore islands – Pietra del Cavallone, Pietra Bianca, Pietra Nera – steering round the Punta Imperatore, the most westerly point. Across the bay behind us the sweep of Spiaggia Citara, with its thermal gardens half-hidden from sight, balances the beach of San Francesco, twin watery wings on the village of Forio. The Chiesa del Soccorso, virginal white on its promontory, is a calming presence for us as we skirt La Nave, a barque-shaped rock which seems like a solidified wreck, its crew frozen in terror. It is as though the rocks and the sea have taken control here, humans allowed only fleeting passage.

Soon, a breeze lifting us past the steep cliffs of Punta della Cima, we get our first glimpse of Sant'Angelo – a honeycomb of white settled on a sandy isthmus, the long beach of Maronti beyond and a great hump of headland at the seaward end of the port. The ruins of a castle decorated this mound, not the most elegant of shapes. There are fishing boats everywhere, and terraced slopes reach up more gently than elsewhere to Epomeo. There was scarcely anyone about and the little speech we heard was in German.

Sant'Angelo, a fishing village at the foot of steep cliffs, is unreachable by bus or *carrozza* and in winter almost isolated. Compact to the point of seeming self-sufficient, a community whose families are so integrated into a local pattern that it is impossible for outsiders ever to break in. Their world of a few square miles suffices for the kind of life they lead. The sea takes up their nights, the wine caves where they play cards, their days. There is no cinema, two bars, two cafés. If you wanted to escape prying eyes this would be the place, and a small group of Germans have made their way here. I try to work out which species of refugee they are.

The mountains protect and at the same time add to the feeling of claustrophobia. We row over every morning to Maronti where above the beach the hot springs of *fumarole* smoke like run-aground steamers. The vines covered in dust look like powdered perruques on their sticks. Stranded in time we discard dreams like skins. To want something here is to have it and be rid of it for ever.

The sky feathers over at sunset, clouds collecting round the peak. All day fishermen have played *scopa* in cool wine-shops; boys have mended nets or painted boats in the blistering heat. On washing lines women's underwear anticipates the comfortable folds of flesh.

Usually we consume our *zuppa di pesce* and pasta alone, but now at the weekend there is an influx of visitors to our table. An Italian lawyer, an enthusiastic amateur artist who dines in a white cap, sits on our right with his wife, a meringue-like blonde, and their ailing pre-Raphaelite daughter. He bubbles like a cauldron over her, shouting out jokes to other tables, growing swarthy with wine. On our left an elderly, timid Swiss couple descend for meals as though fresh from meditating or income-tax study. The wife is reading Karl Jaspers, his works like a bible by her place; her husband discourses to all and sundry on music and mountaineering, unlikely subjects in this context. A retired Italian naval officer, so Roman in appearance he is a caricature, sits with his wife, a generous but outsize Isolde, on the verandah. He gives the impression of still being at sea, which in a kind of way he is, for the waves break only a few yards below. When the meal ends the chatter subsides, cigars are lit, grappa produced. We watch the boats with their riding lights lift and fall in the harbour. The hills are like the heavy, ribbed wings of bats. A day ending like many another, sun-burned, salt-encrusted.

This morning we have lain in the rock-pools at the bottom of *fumarole* so hot they have to be cooled with fresh sea. Above them, through a cleft in the rocks, a ravine winds into hills pitted with caves. Most of the caves are inhabited. At sunset the inhabitants troop down in families like one has seen monkeys do in India; they bathe and wash clothes on the beach. Some caves have small terraces, flattened out of the rock and over-looking the dried-up gorge. Mats, hammocks, sometimes chairs are set out. At sunrise whole families venture out of the black cavity, rubbing their eyes at the light.

Further up the ravine, whose rocks on either side, with stray cacti, make it seem like a Mexican canyon, special thermal baths have been sculpted from the cliff. Each bath is a hollow dug out of rock and irrigated by boiling spring water. The rock is divided into compartments, each with its sunken bath fed by a narrow runnel, and each flanked by a flat, six foot slab on which the bather rests in towels for an hour or two after bathing. Each time we went up, some child or woman would be lying motionless in a steaming colander.

At five in the evening, the inhabitants of Testaccio, a small rock-village, dawdle to the beach and join the troglodytes in long lines across the sand. Only the boys actually seem to bathe, the women paddling in black dresses, occasionally squeezing out clothes in the surf. Though living so near the sea, they fear it, just as they fear the sun on their bodies. They are vigilant against exposure. On the rare occasions when they venture beyond waist-level, a whole second set of garments, fixed by a network of lacings, becomes visible under their black, shapeless costumes. In dress and social development there is a time-lag of nearly half a century between the people inland and those on the coast. On the coast every gesture reveals a relaxed attitude to life. Inland, the villagers move in period costume, like faded, yellowing pictures from family albums.

Reading Browne's *Religio Medici*, the sun hot, the sky an aching blue, one is persuaded to accept his definitions of happiness. We are rarely *consciously* happy because consciousness makes us continually aware of a thousand miseries and cruelties. But we can, largely by sensuous means, be induced into a traumatic condition in which the only reality is the immediate present. Browne writes:

> There is surely a nearer apprehension, of any thing that delights us in our dreams, than in our waked senses. Without this I were unhappy; for my awaked judgement discontents me, ever whispering unto me that I am from my friend, but my friendly dreams in the night requite me, and make me think I am within his arms . . . And surely it is not a melancholy conceit to think we are all asleep in this world, and that the conceits of this life are as mere dreams to those of the next, as the phantasms of the night to the conceit of the day. There is an equal delusion in both; and the one doth but seem to be the emblem or picture of the other. We are somewhat more than ourselves in our sleeps; and the slumber of the body seems to be but the waking of the soul. It is the litigation

of sense, but the liberty of reason; and our waking conceptions do not match the fancies of our sleeps. At my nativity, my ascendant was the watery sign of Scorpio. I was born in the planetary hour of Saturn, and I think I have a piece of that leaden planet in me. I am no way facetious, nor disposed for the mirth and galliardise of company; yet in one dream I can compose a whole comedy, behold the action, apprehend the jests, and laugh myself awake at the conceits thereof. Were my memory as faithful as my reason is then fruitful, I would never study but in my dreams, and this time also would I choose for my devotions; but our grosser memories have then so little hold of our abstracted understandings, that they forget the story, and can only relate to our awaked souls a confused and broken tale of that which hath passed. Aristotle, who hath written a singular tract of sleep, hath not, methinks, thoroughly defined it; nor yet Galen, though he seem to have corrected it; for those *noctambulos* and night-walkers, though in their sleep, do yet enjoy the action of their sense. We must therefore say that there is something in us that is not in the jurisdiction of Morpheus; and that those abstracted and ecstatick souls do walk about in their own corpses, as spirits with the bodies they assume, wherein they seem to hear, see and feel, though indeed the organs are destitute of sense, and their natures of those faculties that should inform them. Thus it is observed, that men sometimes, upon the hour of their departure, do speak and reason above themselves. For them the soul begins to be freed from the ligament of the body, begins to reason like herself, and to discourse in a strain above mortality . . . we term sleep death; and yet it is waking that kills us . . .

*

The beach a gleaming copper, the sea turquoise. A motorboat
came over from Capri today, unloading two middle-aged couples,
white-fleshed and plump, in time to launch them for short
spells in the sea before lunch. Boatmen, unnaturally obsequious,
set up umbrellas, unpacked hampers of ham, pie, fruit, olives and
wine, and spread out garish towels on the sand. The two women,
one blonde, with pink, peeling skin, the other dark-haired and
hirsute, squelched up the beach, breasts and thighs shaking.
Behind them two bald, pigeon-legged, tight-faced men followed
with mincing steps on the scalding sand. They ate while we
swam and when two hours later we returned from lunch, were
all four laid out like bottles in a row. In unison the four bodies
rose and fell, rose and fell . . .

Our room is over a wine-cellar. All day, but especially after sunset, the sharp, raw tang of wine comes up in great draughts
outside the window. The bedroom has only a black, gold-knobbed
bedstead, a china bowl and jug on a wooden stand, a small rug on
a stone floor, but from our bed I can see the bay through the
shutters. The few villas on the opposite hill dazzle like salt, their
whiteness too brilliant to look at. Their owners have departed.
We wake with the sound of barrels being moved below us.

After a twenty-four-hour gale, the good weather is back, the
sea like a green slide, transparent over a seaweed kingdom.
Growing restless, we sail the dinghy miles out, at last bored with
sunbathing. To have reached such a state is an accomplishment.
This initially exquisite Mediterranean inertia, an enervation
we accept so readily, daily begins to lose its hold. A crisis devel-
ops between submission and escape. The Ischians themselves
emigrate in great numbers. They return, but in the meantime

live the middle part of their lives away. To them Ischia is a place to return to, to retire in when the real business of living is over. In our small boat anywhere is possible, nowhere out of reach. Ponza, Pontellaria, Panarea, Egadi . . . A delicious reverie interrupted by a speedboat cutting across our bows nearly overturning us.

Yesterday, after many postponements, we climbed Epomeo, a steep, three-hour journey either by mule or on foot. After some hesitation, principally because it is very easy to lose the way, we decided to take mules and guides, letting them descend the same night while we returned ourselves at dawn. There was, we knew, a small hermitage, inhabited by a peasant-monk who, for a reasonable sum of lire, would provide us with a straw bed, and, if we wanted it, bread and wine.

At five o'clock in the afternoon the two mule-drivers arrived, leading minute, extensively upholstered animals. Small dark men, unshaven and scowling, they stood silently about like brigands, flicking their whips. The first part of the journey, a vertical hairpin track cut through the cliff face immediately above Sant'Angelo, is made tricky by loose stones and teeters along the edge of precipices. Every few yards the mules slither, the drivers bolstering them up by pressing their buttocks or breaking their slide. We climbed comparatively quickly through bare scrub, on one side sheer drops over dried-out ravines, on the other the overhanging cliff face. At each turn the flat, white roofs of Sant'Angelo grew smaller and more precise, a romantic village of toy houses lapped by water. The *castello* on its rock looked like an impacted tooth, the sea like brackets emphasising the split nature of the village, its haphazard scatter of boats. From above, the blackness of arched doorways, the black holes of windows, the scaffolding on unfinished villas, made

Sant'Angelo look as if it had been under shell fire. The sky was now like a bloodshot eyelid, a drop of blue in a corner. The heat gone, the sea turning indigo, it would soon be dark.

By the time we reached Serrara, a small inland village high above the road, the mules were looking disenchanted, the drivers even more inscrutable. Mostly grey stone, with an imposing gateway, Serrara has the neat compact appearance of a hamlet on the Yorkshire moors. We pass a boot-maker's shop, a wine shop, a grocery. Groups of people, mostly women and young boys, could be seen coming down with bundles of reeds on their heads, swaying decoratively. Already they would be laying in fuel for the winter, cutting down the overgrowth, the patches of startling, green cane.

The drivers became less reticent. My own mule was called Togliatti, after the Italian Communist leader. His owner declared himself to be a Communist, a rare admission in the south, and he doggedly stuck to the view that only a Communist government could help the landworkers. Mussolini, alone in recent Italian history, did something to improve agricultural conditions, though like all peasants of the south, neither driver seemed to think that they were anything other than put upon. Life south of Rome has always been a struggle against the elements and politicians don't waste much sleep over it.

We reached Fontana just as the sun slipped like a lozenge into the sea. Fontana is the highest point reachable by road; from then on there is only a rough path up the mountain, the continuation of our own. It is steep, arid going, almost unrelieved by trees or vegetation. Occasionally we passed a peasant's disused, crumbling cottage. Halfway up there were remains of a viaduct, after that only a scurfy opening in colourless scrub. It grew perceptibly colder, the air clean and sweet after the coast. There were single lights at various levels, then far below –

Sant'Angelo, like a stationary railway carriage, doubling its lights on the sea.

We began the last stage of the climb in near darkness. The gaunt, ragged outline of Epomeo, its double peak suspended threateningly over us, seemed to come near, then retreat into the night. We had the impression of far greater height than actually existed, for we had climbed from sea level. Already the gulf was like a military table-map. In the distance we could just make out the orange husk of Naples, the cone of Vesuvius. The guides pushed doggedly on ahead of us, their red woollen caps just visible as they turned to shout throatily at the mules who by now had slowed down, churlish and defiant. We began to be glad of our jerseys.

Near the summit the path flattened out, the mountain narrowing above grey scrub into a forked peak. We emerged from the undergrowth on to an open, unfinished-looking stump of rock, with built into it at one end an oblong stone building.

We were greeted by a buffeting wind, suddenly exposed to the elements. A huge door in front of us opened into a labyrinth of dark passages; immediately to its right, lights were burning in a small chapel whose door was open.

As we dismounted, a tonsured, slight figure wearing a brown habit came out of the chapel.

The drivers, having taken cheese, hunks of bread and wine, returned almost immediately to Sant'Angelo, perhaps an hour's descent. We entered the cool, musty passages of the hermitage, shepherded by the peasant caretaker, a lay-brother who enjoyed the courtesy title of "Padre". He had already lived on Epomeo for several years, accompanied by a small retinue, two or three boys, a bedraggled old woman, some goats and chickens. Living during the day as an ordinary peasant, he put on, at the approach of visitors, his long brown habit and rope girdle. Like the hypochondriac in Molière's *Le Malade imaginaire* unable even to hear unless suitably attired – "*Donnez-moi ma robe pour mieux entendre*" – he liked to dress for the rôle he earned his living from. The tenant of a hermitage, he dressed the part of a religious hermit.

The hermitage consisted of two passages cut into the rock. Shaped in a T, six cells have been hollowed out of the cross-section. Originally built by a monk from the mainland, who came to Ischia to find sanctuary from persecution, it had become a traditional refuge for miscreant priests and for those sentenced to special penance. Not for many years used for any serious religious purpose it is only kept going by the caretaker, allowed to occupy it as a home in exchange for simple religious offices.

Inside it was dark, except for a spirit lamp held by the young boy who conducted us. He took us first to the caretaker's own cell, a square room used as bedroom and kitchen. A bunk lay in one corner, in another were several crates of wine. Under the small, round window something was frying on a charcoal fire. A candle burned on a table by the bed, its erratic light flickering over effete religious pictures taken from magazines. A wax effigy of Christ, a sack of vegetables, were propped on the floor.

The old woman, her grey hair like a bird's nest, was peeling potatoes in a corner. Bottles of wine were produced from the crate, a loaf of bread and some cheese brought out of a cupboard. The caretaker himself motioned us to follow him through the other passage, clanking his keys till we reached the end and a wooden door.

Inside was a small cell, its low bed covered with straw, a plain wooden chair and table under a grated window. He lit a lamp for us, then told the boy to put down the bread and wine. From inside a hutch we could hear curious scratches, a squeaking like a concertina bag being slowly depressed. "You will be all right here," he said, then, "Rabbits," and smiled at last, giving the crate a proprietary kick.

He was still young, perhaps thirty-five, his face a little tortured, but shrewd, his manner awkward and self-effacing. We stood for a while looking at one another. Then, after making a slight, abrupt bow, he withdrew.

Later, we went out on to the parapet at the end of the passage. The building – all of it rock-hewn – sloped, so now, at its most extreme height, we emerged on to a small exposed ledge, like the bridge of a ship. We were at the very top, a sheer, impelling drop to Fontana and Sant'Angelo below. From here we could see the whole island, the five villages of Forio, Casamicciola, Lacco Ameno, Porto d'Ischia and Sant'Angelo like coloured paws; the inner necklace of *lampari*, their bow-lights trained on the water; the strip of illuminated coast from Gaeta to Sorrento. The gulf looked magically alive: scintillating, mercurial, full of romantic readiness and hope. In its throb of light there was the expectancy that the Gentleman from San Francisco had experienced, at the same time a sense that there would always be disappointment, that the lights would never quite glitter for us, that they would recede as we approached. As we turned back to our cell we felt an inexplicable sadness, quite unrelated to the situation. Only the island seemed constant, swinging on invisible moorings.

We awoke early to thick oysterish fog, the sky unhealthily pink. Rocks five feet below were invisible, the island no more than an instinct. The hermitage was still quiet, soundless save for the clacking of poultry, the rustle of rabbits in their cage.

We finished the remainder of our grapes, rinsed our mouths

with wine, then waited for the fog to clear. After an hour it was no better. The caretaker seemed uncertain what to expect. Once, he said, when the mist had stayed for a whole week, they had lost two chickens and a rabbit over the top. In the circumstances we decided to set off.

At first seeing only a yard in front, we eventually reached clearer air. At Fontana we dropped into the blue, the gulf scalloped and fresh below, the Sorrentine cliffs rouged with sunrise. The first workers were already out, hacking away with billhooks, their long bundles swaying on their heads. Above us, the summit of Epomeo was still hidden, fog like a tricorne over it. A few years ago, on a similar morning, an aeroplane had hit the mountain, no traces of it ever found.

The descent took less than an hour. The first people we saw in the village were the mule-drivers, rubbing down their mules, polishing and laying out the harness. I felt a proprietary interest in Togliatti who blinked soberly at me from under circuses of flies. He was not a handsome specimen, but, like Stevenson's Modestine, who accompanied him in the Cévennes, "cheap and small and hardy, and of a stolid and peaceful temper . . . not much bigger than a dog, the colour of a mouse, with a kindly eye and a determined under-jaw, yet neat and high-bred with a quakerish elegance".

There was considerable excitement in the village: a large octopus and *dentista* had been caught in the night and half the village had collected to witness the weighing. The fish writhed on the scales, its polished gills working under bloodshot eyes. Suddenly its silver-green back shuddered, it half rose and slid broken to the floor. Bubbles rainbowed with blood burst noiselessly on the maroon stone. Beauty, cruelty, a kind of admiration, collaborated in the audience's enjoyment. What could be eaten was outside the range of pity.

Our room was welcoming, so near and yet so far the night before. The white sand of Maronti beckoned beyond the open shutters. The sea was like sheet metal. We took the dinghy over and were soon taking the first of many bathes.

Porto d'Ischia

BACK; THE ISLAND set like a butterfly in memory. We see it now as a whole, the towns in relation to one another, the proportion of coast to mountain, the character of each community. We see it of course in only one mood, early autumn, under which daily the gulf hardens from blue mist to emerald, then turquoise clarity. In the sun's ruthlessness it has been without subtlety, its tones unmodified.

We came yesterday by motorboat from Sant'Angelo, taking the bleaker south-easterly course. The only signs of occupation above the sheer cliffs are the inland villages of Barano and Succhivo. The sea sucks and squelches round lethal rocks and caves with quiffs of scrub on them. Grottoes drip with saliva. Occasionally a puffin dodders white-stomached on a rock, pompously appraising the sea. The cliffs have the austerity of confessionals.

Off Capo Grosso we paid a line out behind the boat and hooked a large *malamite*. We played it for ten minutes, pulling it along in the wake like a silver-green dart before bringing it in. Jerked over the side, it fell exhausted at our feet at the bottom of the boat. Beautiful to look at, it had – we discovered later – no more taste than any of the other fish we tried.

Testaccio, the Grotta del Mago, the beach of Cartaromano

we chugged slowly past in the lee of the *castello* and its harbour. Soon the pink and blue cubes of Ischia Ponte, precise under a fringe of pines, were on our port beam. The afternoon Naples boat passed us as we turned close inshore along the beaches and through the tiny entrance of the flask-shaped harbour.

For convenience on our last night we've taken a room at the Bel Tramonte, overlooking the harbour. It smells pleasantly of fish. We leave for Procida tomorrow. No island can be left without regret, for who knows whether we will ever return. In the fading light, the water glows, a rich syrup in which boats are becalmed like fruit bottled in alcohol. Summer is already stringing itself up, ships' sirens announcing arrival and farewell. We shall remember their melancholy music and some of their names.

Procida

PROCIDA, AS WE sidle in to its quay, looks pleasantly unpretentious. No dramatic volcanic cone, more an animal on its back with a large head. The prison is its dominant feature. The vaguely oriental waterfront, pink, blue and yellow houses fronted by cafés, is a working place for the repair and painting of boats. Its single cobbled street is overshadowed by the dome of San Giovanni. Narrow alleyways run up off this to a central spine, the other steeper side of which drops to a fishing-boat harbour. There, a white sailors' church holds its own among fortified buildings that have mostly collapsed or slipped into the sea.

Procida's 10,000 population, spread over a length of two

miles, width a mere mile or so, is decreasing, I learn. Four nearly contiguous, unobtrusive craters, with yellow and grey trachytic crusts, carry some scrub and few trees. Sancio Catholico, which gives its name to the place where the boats arrive, is no more than a huddle of houses, boatyards and a jetty, but for all its lack of conventional shelter and facilities seems to do quite well for itself.

Ischia, and the leisurely, meditative life, is behind us now, but we are only here for a few days and then it's back to London, and goodness knows what. The war still seems very close, despite my year in Germany, but now money is coming to an end and I have to get a job. But what job? Going back to Oxford, like Kingsley and others of my contemporaries at St John's have done, doesn't really appeal. I don't think I'm an academic. I could play county cricket for a season but that would only be delaying the inevitable.

These notes I've been making won't probably lead to anything. I have wanted more than anything to write good poems, for which several years in a destroyer gave me a subject, albeit a restricted one. Could one loaf about in the Mediterranean, making a career for oneself as Larry Durrell has done, with such brilliance? I must find something that can become my own, more than anyone else's. Cricket might see me through, if I can learn to be a good journalist, but it is too late now for what my father wanted of me, the colonial or diplomatic service.

This island now is beginning to fill me with melancholy, the closing chapter of a relationship with V. who is going off to make a new life as a model and designer. From the lemon orchard beneath our balcony the scent, soon to be left, adds to my gloom. The elegant, eighteenth-century houses in this street, set back behind high walls and gardens, their windows barred, belong to the past. There were nobility of a kind here once and despite the decay and rubbish it has retained a reclusive, patrician air. The nobility, however, have been replaced by petty officials and better-off tradesmen. Peasants gradually evolve into landowners if they're lucky. Once upon a time the locals were all serfs in the service of foreigners. Now the island belongs to the natives and one wonders what they will make of it. Will Procida go the way of Capri and Ischia, or remain a kind of thriving market garden, sustaining a few fishermen? The Procidans' traditional skills have always been as shipbuilders, but no-one seems to want ships any longer.

Our hotel, consisting of four clean, simple rooms, is the only one on the island, though there must be *pensioni*. Food is provided in the evening, local wine by the jug. At the bottom of the garden there's a small bathing beach, the *castello* above it, and a view of Capri in the distance.

The only interesting character to have come from here, John of Procida, spent hardly any time on the island. Norman Douglas in *Siren Land* describes him as the first man to conceive the possibility of a unified Italy. "The tremors", he wrote, "of his splendid, sanctified hatred were felt from London to Constantinople." Born early in the thirteenth century in Salerno, John was a distinguished doctor, rewarded for public service by being made Lord of Procida. In this capacity he accompanied King Manfred to Palermo in 1262. From then on his life was one long series of political intrigues. In 1266 he launched successive conspiracies against the Angevins, two years later following Corradino di Svevi to Rome, where he was forced to hide in the suburbs to avoid arrest. His properties were confiscated, but in 1270 he combined with Enrico di Isernia, in exile at Prague, to push the claims of Frederick of Thuringia to the throne of Sicily. When, shortly, the Svevi cause began everywhere to fail, he went into exile in Aragon at the court of Jacob. Still unsatisfied, he took up the territorial claims of his new benefactor, in Sicily, and, in fact, landed there as escort to Jacob's daughter-in-law, Constance, in 1283. He was made Chancellor of the Kingdom, but again intrigues made it impossible for him to remain and he left for Rome, where he died in 1298.

John of Procida is best known for his part in the "Sicilian Vespers", a rising against the French which began on 31 March 1282, at the hour of vespers. A rebellion broke out on Easter Monday in the piazza by the church of Santo Spirito in Palermo, caused, it was believed, by the action of a French soldier who, suspecting that the worshippers had hidden weapons in their dress, began searching the women. A massacre followed, and the few French who escaped were driven out of Sicily.

The castle of Procida was for some years used as a political prison, especially under the Fascists. Now a corrective institution for ordinary criminals, its cracked battlements turn their backs on Naples. A crumbling appendage of alleyways and half-tenanted, roofless houses straggles down behind it to the modern village.

Such season as there is being over, the island has an end-of-term feel. We share the hotel with a distinguished Roman art critic who comes here every year, a trumpeter from a Naples night-club, an engineer, and the widow of an Italian airforce pilot. They appear to have a tacit agreement not to recognise each other. Procida seems to encourage *turismo incognito*, useful all round. The bonds are cut. At meal-times, after intervals of bathing or sitting in secluded corners of the garden, the guests arrive at their own tables, set up their books in front of them, or eat in silence. The bathing, off a strip of sand under overhanging greenery, is as good as anywhere we've been, though on the shallow side. Headlands at either end provide shelter. Swimming out and

looking back the skyline reveals a rich green belt scarcely interrupted by houses. The *paysage idéale* of Lamartine's *Graziella,* set
here, remains undefiled, the inspiration for his pantheistic poetry
and that of de Musset, in which the *mal du siècle* is ever-present,
morbidly romantic. I think of Chateaubriand and Mme de Staël,
of Novalis and Tieck and Eichendorff, of those others who were
the subjects of my interrupted reading at Oxford and who seem
to be lingering here. Rilke wrote of growing melancholy in places
that have a picture-book kind of beauty, somewhat scarce here
where beauty has to earn its keep. There is rarely a moment of
the day when the streets and quay are not resounding to the noise
of builders' hammers. Secrecy and silence reclaim the island as
soon as darkness falls.

The beach at Santa Margherita, on the far side of the island, is
only used by fishermen for mending nets. A ridge of scrub separates the sand from the fishing harbour of Chiaiollella, round
which the small village of San Giuseppe is spread. To the west,
across a narrow stretch of water, the island of Vivara, a hump of
closely cultivated rock about a quarter of a mile long, obscures
most of Ischia, only Epomeo and the buff quay of Casamicciola
are visible. Today a heavy sea has been running on this side
of the island. The beach here, the Chiaiollella, unlike the
overhung bay off the Carbogno where we normally bathe, is
completely exposed to the east winds which round the Abruzzi.
In the north, storms have a certain eloquence, a poetic intensity
which produces an elation of its own. In the Mediterranean,
they act as irritants, intrusions between the landscape and
oneself. It is like the break-up of a relationship, disharmony
where there was only harmony. We try not to let it spoil our
natural courtesies. It ought not to, but does affect us.

*

To reach the castle and its attendant abbey, you have to pene-trate the oldest part of the town. Inside a stout containing wall a kind of miniature Aragonese city, predominantly of yellow stone, is cushioned by several acres of vine. The lower end of the citadel is a barracks, above which the planes of further walls, as in a painting by Ghika, intersect to form a fortified semi-circle of battlement. The top, reached through a tunnel, is crowned by the fifteenth-century abbey and its circular tower. The whole area is packed, dank and airless, the network of lanes shaded by the steep, inhospitable buildings, their surfaces only broken by the slits of windows. It cannot have been much fun stationed here, only the sea boiling below as a distraction, but there still seems to be a community of camp followers, the women blinking like moles as they emerge from the semi-darkness into bright sunlight. Two sixteenth-century chapels, now disused, preside over small, refuse-covered squares. A heavy iron gate keeps out intruders. Yet, despite its top-heavy situation on the island, its bleak quarantine air, there are agreeable interludes, surprising in their context: a neat line of palm trees, flowerbeds thick with geraniums, flat roofs laid out with washing of different colours. It is no longer a wholly masculine world.

Prowling round past indifferent guards, we could see men out-lined on the wall and smell the drifting odours of cookhouses. Prisoners carried pails across the bare parade-ground; warders stood chatting to girls at the entrance. It was midday and trolleys, with meals congealing on tin plates, were being wheeled out of the galleys into the barred cells opposite. Gladstone's letters show the appalling conditions in nineteenth-century Italian prisons. Now, in this ordinary civil prison for severe offences, what we were allowed to see of it seemed acceptable. All these islands have a formidable prison tradition, but in Procida an informal kind

Procida from the sea

of relationship seemed to exist between warder and prisoner. The greatest part of the punishment is probably exile, sexual deprivation and removal from family, though only too evidently there are compensations.

From the prison you can see the whole gulf, the mainland from Pozzuoli to Sorrento, Capri's double hump, mauve in the summer mist, the skyline above Naples broken by the goitre of Vesuvius. It was still hot when we left the area through small off-shoots of the old citadel and across dilapidated squares flanked by roofless buildings. It was silent except for chickens squawking and panicking into disused stables. The narrow cobbled streets, flies circling over refuse, wind backwards and forwards, sea like a glass wall at the end of them. We followed narrow turnings as in a maze, pushed back now by cul-de-sacs, now by sheer cliffs. The gulf stretched like blue linen all round us.

In the late afternoon we walked the whole extent of the south-east coastline, a two-hour exercise on a cliff path with the sea on one side and lemon trees and vines on the other. Procida lemons are famous. Gardens reach down on the south to a wall overlooking the Carbogno, a white fringe of water spilling over a copper brow of sand. Further along, towards the wooded cliffs of Punta Solchiaro, the shadows lengthen, the whole eastern coast dark green, ribbed with oyster on the skyline. Villas are few and far between. Steps cut in the rock of a small cove lead to a bath built by Ferdinand II in a miniature enclosure, where the King could enjoy sea-water and the sensation of bathing without the inconvenience or dangers of the open sea. Overlooking the harbour of Chiaiollella are some old houses, the Bourbon relics of larger buildings scattered about the hillside round them.

We hired a boat and sailed to Vivara. With a strong evening breeze and the current against us, the mile up the Canale di Procida took nearly an hour. Vivara is private property, an unsubmerged crater shaped like a crescent, with a height of between 200 and 350 feet above sea level.

There are no beaches or any landing stages on the island, to which the only approach is up steps built into the rock at the north-eastern extremity. The steps lead under a stone archway, up a steep path sheltered by oaks, winding over the back of the rock to where, at the end of beautifully laid-out gardens and surrounded by trees, two seventeenth-century farmhouses stand adjacent to each other. A fringe of cypresses runs round the edge of the island. Now the leaves were russet, the moon already out and where the sea, half an hour earlier, had been stained with sunset, a bar of moonlight polarised Ischia, Vivara and Procida.

Vivara has the smell and feel of an English manor. Olive avenues, vine terraces interspersed with fig trees and oaks over-hanging slender limes, reinforce the formality of the place, a marine estate that seemed left to enjoy its seasons. We saw no-one about, though presumably someone lived there from time to time.

Beyond the cliffs the Castello d'Ischia rose dark and forbidding above the flickering waterfront lights of Ischia Ponte. Epomeo was velvet in the dark, streaked with grey. At our backs, at the far end of the gentle sprawl of Procida, the prison glittered like a casino. Once upon a time Vivara was owned by a retired priest who defended his possession by firing at any boat that approached.

No-one now looked likely to fight over the island. As we prepared to leave, a motorboat arrived at the landing stage. Two men emerged and as we drew near and began to make polite noises they waved them aside, gesturing we were free to go wherever we liked. We took them at their word. Then, the tide and wind at our backs, we needed only fifteen minutes to reach Chiaiollella, sailing in the hard moonlight past the hand-ful of *lampari*, their bow-lights probing the water.

There is a sunken ferry in the harbour, rusting and undigni-fied, lying half out of the water, half aground. I remember such a sight in the harbour at Bastia in Corsica, equally grisly. Why do they allow them to moulder in this way? The ships I saw sunk in the war sank properly, leaving no debris. These are not welcoming objects for visitors, their first sight of the island. Now they are our last sight as our steamer, sirens sounding, pulls away. The waterfront blurs into a muddle of colours, a golden dome among them. We pick up speed and soon only the mud-coloured mound of prison and dove-coloured abbey betrays that there is anything there at all.

Perhaps it is all a mirage, only ourselves and the other passen-gers restlessly moving from place to place at all real. In transit, past and present seem equally unsubstantial, as if at any moment a lapse of memory could dissolve them.

The future, however, is only too real. We sweep gently into the wide arms of the Bay of Naples, private and historic ghosts lingering in its riches: Via Caracciolo, Via Partenope, and behind the Beverello where we finally tie up, the Palazzo Reale and Teatro San Carlo, once places of assignation in a demoralised city. Time for a quick lunch at Bersagliera in Santa Lucia, boats bobbing under the puddingy medieval walls of Castel dell'Ovo and then up the long tree-lined Corso Umberto I to Piazza Garibaldi, host to pimps, whores and drug-sellers. Under the huge glass cavern of Stazione Centrale we steam away from the south back to what Wystan Auden in his poem "Ischia" calls our "soiled productive cities".

Castel dell'Ovo, Naples

Ischia: *Autumn 1998*

Hotel Excelsior, Porto d'Ischia

HALF A CENTURY has passed since I first came here but driving up from the harbour it is I who have changed more than Porto. I look out from our verandah and see nothing but trees, we could be in the middle of a wood. Not far from here is the Regina, which now has "Palace" added to its name and is a grander establishment than the one I knew in 1948. The pines that surrounded it remain, though thinned.

We inhabit a circular room in a villa annexe to the hotel whose lush garden opens on a lane on the far side of which is a private beach. There are fewer horse-drawn carriages than in 1948, more taxis and the road out of the port into the interior now has half a mile of boutiques and cafés. But the flowering trees are still a saving grace, the palms and pinewoods forming defensive cordons to the pink buildings, none of which are any higher than the trees.

Thermal springs have for centuries been the main attraction for visitors, mostly Germans. In his treatise on Ischia's mineral waters Dr Iasolini observed in 1588, "If your eyebrows fall off try the baths at Piaggia Romano. If your complexion is a problem you will find the cure in the waters of Santa Maria del Popolo. If you know anyone going bald or who suffers from elephantiasis or whose wife wishes to get pregnant take them to the Bagno di Vitara, they will bless you." These supposedly all-purpose waters are world-famous and we have our own bathing establishment in the Excelsior's tropical garden. In due course we try it out, rather out of place among a circle of corpulent Germans who roll like porpoises and cling to the walls as if by suction.

Ischia has suffered more than most from invasions and piratical plunderings but a happy consequence of the onslaughts by such as Barbarossa and Dragut has been the construction of round and square defensive towers all over the island. Ischia is rather lacking in antiquities compared to Capri and these structures at least provide some sort of historic context. Far worse than the repeated invasions – not least by English sailors during their occupation of these waters in the early nineteenth century – were the cholera epidemics which in 1648 and 1837 virtually wiped out the population. Casamicciola was reduced to a heap of ruins by an earthquake in 1828 but so far none of the volcanic activities of Vesuvius seems to have affected Ischia. In any case, you don't see many scars on Epomeo or on its slopes, the vegetation having closed in everywhere there are no buildings.

The castle here is a strange anomaly, having been sold off to a lawyer. Once only reached by sea, a tunnel fifty yards long was dug into the rock at the order of Alfonso I of Aragon and joined by a causeway to the rest of the island. At the entrance there's a battery, then more tunnels, an archway, a small chapel. Beyond an old guardroom a spiral staircase leads to a drill ground and an ancient well. The cathedral stands on an open space, a square also holding the Convent of the Clarisse and the Church of the Immacolata. The *ossarium* is here and from it one of the great views, though not much use to the poor nuns waiting to die. Beyond the parapet and in the shadow of the great dome the hexagonal temple of St Peter leads to the prisons, deprived equally of spectacular views of Procida and the gulf.

It is odd that a building where so much romantic, political and literary history has taken place should contain no more than echoes of its past, its politicians, kings, poets, prisoners, generals, nuns accorded neither inscriptions nor restoration.

Yesterday we were in Naples, the city at last showing signs of emerging from decades of neglect. I associate it mostly with 1947 when my wartime boss, holed up in the Excelsior Hotel in Via Partenope, took me under his wing and showed me the ropes. His father had been our Ambassador in Rome and the Rodds still owned a house in Via Giulia. The kind of circles they moved in were a far cry from the life described in John Horne Burns's *The Gallery*, one of the great books of the time. *The Gallery*, a kind of elegy to the black markets and sexual underworld of wartime Naples, was published in the late 1940s. It took thirty-five years for Norman Lewis's *Naples '44* to see the light though Lewis, a British Intelligence officer attached to the American Fifth Army, must have seen Naples at the same time.

What I remember of Naples from that period, apart from the fact that almost every girl appeared to have the dimensions if not quite the beauty of Sophia Loren or Silvana Mangano – tiny waist, full breasts, long legs, succulent bottom – is the kind of suppressed excitement one got from simply walking about: Via Benedetto Croce, Piazza Dante, Piazza dei Martiri, Via Salvator Rosa, Via Toledo, Via Carducci, Piazza Amore – the magical names that no amount of squalor or louche activities could dispel. Norman Lewis hadn't published his diary then but reading it now returned me to post-war Naples with brutal efficiency.

Lewis, a sergeant in the Field Security Service, spent almost exactly a year in Naples and surrounding towns. The F.S.S. was undermanned, unsupervised and unsure of its duties. No-one in authority seemed to know what they were doing there, "We seem to be seen as a sort of watered-down version of the SS.

Yet over and over again we've been told it is not our job to take over the duties of the Italian police."

What they did have to do varied from vetting candidates for marriage with Allied soldiers and job applicants for security risks, settling disputes between *carabinieri* and the Pubblica Sicurezza, advising officers on their sexual involvements, seeking out black marketeers, checking for VD: "the situation now is that as many hospital beds in the Naples area are occupied by sufferers from the pox as from wounds and all the other sicknesses together," and in general trying to mediate and where possible moderate sympathetically in problems arising from a city whose buildings were in ruins and whose inhabitants were starving.

When Lewis arrived on 6 October 1943, a month after an armistice had been signed, the city smelled of charred wood, had no water, and the streets were blocked by abandoned trams. He felt nostalgic for his months in North Africa, "forays into the mountains of Kabylie for meetings with the scheming Caïds and the holy men who controlled the tribes, and the secret discussions in the rose arbour in the Palace Gardens of Tunis". In contrast, Naples "promised to be hard-working, sometimes prosaic and fraught with routines". They inherited the Fascist police files which made their job a lot easier, "most Italians lead political lives of utter neutrality, though prone to sexual adventure".

Luckily the autumnal weather was perfect and Lewis was able to scoot about the streets on his motorbike meeting contacts. Informers and denouncers anxious to curry favour with occupying forces were always in attendance on him in his *palazzo*, from which he could get a tantalising glimpse of the bay. There was continual hazard from delayed-action explosive devices left behind by the Germans and every so often a building collapsed. The Germans continued to bomb the city and there were rumours that when the electricity supply was switched on thousands of mines would explode. The whole town was evacuated to the Vomero, the highest point. "For the first time I realised how un-European, how oriental, it was. Nothing moved but a distant floating confetti of doves. A great silence had fallen and we looked down and awaited the moment of devastation." It never came.

As I found in Germany in 1946, one of the hardest tasks in these situations is to distinguish the genuine war criminals from comparatively innocent citizens. According to the Psychological Warfare Bureau's report, ninety-six per cent of the Italian population collaborated wholeheartedly with the Germans, a figure Lewis was disinclined to believe and which made the task of making arrests, especially of women, particularly unpleasant.

It was a relief to escape decision-making when Lewis was put in charge of security in neighbouring towns, though these turned out to be in the criminal Zona di Camorra and lived by their own laws. Here was organised crime on a large scale and the police were powerless to do anything about it. However, Lewis's duties were slightly enlivened by his meeting with Donna Maria Fidora, a former circus performer who specialised in wrestling with a python. She was the richest landowner in the district, kept a private army to manage her estate and keep order, and became a reliable source of information about the activities of the Camorra.

I thought of Lewis looking out of his office window as we wandered about Santa Lucia yesterday. There is a funicular in Piazza Montesanto which takes you up the Vomero hill and I visualised the million and a half citizens of Naples all gathered up there waiting for annihilation. The Vomero houses the Spanish-built Castel Sant'Elmo, a decaying castle above the slum alleyways of the Quartieri. From the nearby baroque seventeenth-century

Carthusian monastery, the Certosa di San Martino, you can look down on Naples and its bay and see only its beauty.

The day of the Anzio landing, which took place on 21 January, has stayed in my mind because several friends were involved. From my safe place in a patrolling destroyer in the North Sea the fighting seemed a long way away. The Germans were still bombing Naples, especially the poor, heavily populated areas round the port, and then in March Vesuvius erupted. Lewis called it "the most majestic and terrible sight I have ever seen, or ever expect to see". He watched it from Posillipo, where Pliny had described the shape of the eruption that destroyed Pompeii as that of a pine tree, and from where Nelson and Emma Hamilton had stood to observe another eruption.

The ash from Vesuvius spread as far afield as Sorrento, Ischia and Capri, "a slow, grey snowfall" as Lewis describes it. Around now Lewis encountered Padre Pio, "the flying monk" who claims that he soared up into the sky to interrupt an aerial dogfight and bring the wounded Italian pilot down in his arms. "Most of the Neapolitans I know – some of them educated men – are convinced of the truth of the story," Lewis drily observes.

On a welcome excursion to Capri he is surprised to see the "haunted" face of Malaparte among a group of his courtiers, having imagined him to be in an internment camp.

As Whitsun approaches – the Neapolitans give it the lovely name Easter of the Roses – there is great anxiety about whether the blood of San Gennaro will liquefy and so halt the flow of lava from Vesuvius. Apparently, it did, reluctantly.

The old order in Italian politics was breaking up. Lewis records sixty officially recognised political parties, not including secret neo-Fascists, Separatists wedded to the abolition of factories and the motor car, and some Salerno fanatics who claim to have discovered the solution to the problem of perpetual motion.

In Naples the workers are Royalist, but there are powerful groups of Christian Democrats, Social Democrats and old-style Communists, the Communists already divided into dozens of mutually hostile factions.

Some girl acquaintances of Lewis announce that they are going to Ischia for the summer "to deflate". They will remain on the Naples side of the island, which is radioactive and rich in iodine, the combination being good for slimming and the complexion. They will eat only rabbits that are bred in darkness.

In July, having visited every town within thirty miles of Naples on duty, Lewis found himself in Pozzuoli, curiously by-passed by the war. He imagines himself in some drowsy Levantine coastal town, its houses coloured sea-washed pink with green Venetian-style pointed windows, in contrast to the austere greys and sombre reds of Naples. Although Pozzuoli is only two bays west of Naples, the inhabitants speak a different dialect and in Roman times included the richest, most debauched and bloodthirsty members of the community. Here Nero murdered his mother, Agrippina, and experimented with torture on his prisoners.

From the Ischia boat you can see the gracious-looking city lolling under its sunken volcano. Lewis was disappointed by the tiny lakes behind Pozzuoli, reputedly the entrance to the under-world, but enjoyed himself among the Greek ruins at Cumae. "Here the spell remained, and here the sense of the grandeur of the past was overwhelming."

Each time I pass the Baia headland, with Pozzuoli just in its protection, I am reminded of earlier visits to the huge Anfi-teatro Flavio, which used to be filled with water for the mock re-enactment of naval battles. There are underground chambers for the wild animals that were kept there before being loosed into the arena, once capable to 40,000 spectators. It was here that

St Paul landed from the *Castor and Pollux* in AD 61 on his way to Rome, his own ship having gone down off Malta.

Baia, two and a half miles further out, witnessed scenes of even more flagrant behaviour, though of less violence than Pozzuoli. The Emperor Claudius owned a holiday villa here, as did Tiberius, Pompey, Julius Caesar and Cicero. Petronius's *Satyricon* has fun at the expense of the sexual goings-on which included Messalina, wife of Claudius, regularly visiting public brothels, and Agrippina, before being murdered by her son Nero, poisoning her husband.

Reading Lewis's account of his day out in Capri, I think he must have been only too pleased to lose himself among the relics of a society, no matter how decadent, whose main problems were not to do with drugs, venereal disease, starvation and mines. I don't know whether they had smallpox and typhoid there in those days, or malaria, of which Lewis had several bouts, but the continuing stench of death and disease led to people walking the streets with handkerchiefs pressed to their noses.

Lewis mentions a habit I have not noticed. To ward off the evil eye men touch their testicles at the approach of a stranger, a commonplace precaution in the south. Women cover their faces with a scarf in a similar situation.

By the middle of September, which is when I am writing this, the Italians in 1944 are growing sick of their occupiers. "A year ago we liberated them from the Fascist monster and they still sit doing their best to smile politely at us, as hungry as ever, more disease-ridden than ever before, in the ruins of their beautiful city where law and order have ceased to exist. And what is the prize that is to be eventually won? The rebirth of democracy. The glorious prospect of being able one day to choose their rulers from a list of powerful men, most of whose corruptions are generally known, and accepted with

weary resignation. The days of Benito Mussolini must seem like
a lost paradise compared with this?"

For some, perhaps, but not for all.

At the end of October Lewis is suddenly ordered to leave
for Taranto, there to embark on the *Reina del Pacifico* for Port
Said. He is to be responsible for the repatriation of 3000 Russian
soldiers who, having previously fought with the Germans, have
gone over to the Partisans. It is a moment of hasty packings, few
farewells and much sadness. "For the last time I look into the
eyes of the enormous and enigmatic female statues flanking
the entrance to the Calabritto Palace and then into the court-
yard itself, where a small child is pissing into the mouth of a
stone lion."

Naples '44 is a wonderful book and I have learned much from
it, not only about the Italians but about the calm, unsensational
ordering of material. The writing of prose, in fact. And, despite
everything, Lewis writes that if he could be born again he'd
like it to be as an Italian, surely the greatest compliment of all.

In 1948 I walked round most of the island as well as up Monte
Epomeo. I shall not do it again. One of the pleasures in revisiting
places is that the "sights" can be taken for granted. The view of
the *castello*, from whatever angle on land or sea, never fails to
please but I have no desire whatsoever to enter its dank rooms
or claustrophobic tunnels. I am happy to recall that Vittoria
Colonna wrote her poetry there and corresponded soulfully
with Michelangelo, but this time round I prefer to eat at one of
the excellent restaurants like Coco's in Ischia Ponte and admire
the *castello*'s cubist planes and rectangles from below. The seaward
side is green with plant-encrusted rock but elsewhere, apart from
a single dome, the coffee-coloured stone is scraped clean as if
by a palette knife. The bullet-pitted buttresses that seem to hold
the whole structure in place fall sheer into the sea with lovely

symmetry and the boats that frolic in the harbour at its feet are all the colours of the rainbow. The village that has grown up here, behind a rather scruffy beach, is a lively tangle of fishermen's houses, wine-cellars, boatyards, domes, turrets and cafés, inland of which stretches the long main street, Via Luigi Mazzella, with its open-air restaurants, museum, church and small piazzas. We return to these every day at lunch time, for it involves just the right length of walk, part seaside, part through the neglected park which has no defined paths and in which it is easy to get lost.

This, a slightly shabby place, is not the Ischia of visitors, but I like it. From the early post-war period it was to Forio on the other side of the island that the first wave of writers and painters gravitated. I'm not sure why this was, except that Forio's beaches were less municipal, cleaner and larger, and that villas were cheaper to rent. It had a rural rather than a port feel. In 1948 they hadn't arrived as yet, but by the time I began spending part of the summer there in the 1950s and 1960s Alberto Moravia was installed, Wystan Auden was occasionally in residence, William Walton was soon to appropriate the heights above San Francesco beach, and Arthur Koestler, flitting about between various women, buying and selling properties, was moping about the death of the wife whom he had treated so atrociously.

For our first summers we rented villas in the old part of Forio. Eduardo Bargheer, the German painter, would saunter past every noon on his way to the beach in his bathing gown, greeting all and sundry with his hearty *Buongiorno, Buongiorno,* his hand raised in a kind of papal blessing. Moravia never looked other than utterly depressed, despite a young woman tagging along. At this period his great books, *Agostino* and *Disobedience, Conjugal Love, The Time of Indifference, The Conformist* were coming out at yearly intervals in English, though none I think were set in Ischia or Capri, where Moravia later acquired a villa.

He was, however, as much a part of Forian life, and Maria's café, as Wystan Auden became. Although I occasionally met Auden in London, our Ischian periods never coincided. I learn from Thekla Clark's engaging memoir of Auden and Chester Kallman that when she first landed on the island in 1951 they were sufficiently habitués to have their own table at Maria's. She records, on their first meeting, Wystan's advice to her companion, the poet Anthony Hecht, to wean himself off Yeats. She and Wystan eventually became friends, able to discuss equally the local Saint, Restituta, who had landed at Forio during the reign of Valerian and who despite torture had refused to renounce her faith, and the limitations of a priest's authority. "A rather superior butler" was Auden's estimate.

Ischia during those summers of the 1950s was an enchanted place, "indeed blessed", Thekla Clark wrote, though the poverty was evident. "When I think of Ischia I think of Wystan striding along with that dreadful dog of his, swinging a soiled string bag crammed with books and the day's shopping . . ." When I see it in memory I see it as blue and white, the white of the houses and the blue of the sea and the sky. Although known as *isola verde*, the green island, I think blue and white is nearer the mark. The summer of 1957, when I was re-starting Ischian life, was Auden's last. He had tried to live there all the year round and did so once. He was now fifty and had recently won the Italian Lincei Prize worth about £20,000. He wanted a house of his own and to go north. His poem "Good-bye to the Mezzogiorno", the last of a group of poems written in or about his Ischian years, puts his reasons for both going and leaving:

> . . . some believing *amore*
> Is better down south and much cheaper

(Which is doubtful), some persuaded exposure
          To strong sunlight is lethal to germs

(Which is patently false) and others, like me,
          In middle-age hoping to twig from
What we are not what we might be next, a question
          The South seems never to raise.

He writes in the same poem about leaving the "gothic North",
its "beer or whisky / Guilt culture" for a "sunburnt otherwhere /
Of vineyards, baroque, *la bella figura*" but in this south "we
spoil in no time, we grow / Flabby, dingily lecherous, and / Forget
to pay bills".

Go I must, but I go grateful (even
          To a certain *Monte*) and invoking
My sacred meridian names, *Vico, Verga,*
          Pirandello, Bernini, Bellini,

To bless this region, its vendanges, and those
          Who call it home: though one cannot always
Remember exactly why one has been happy,
          There is no forgetting that one was.

Auden and Kallman showed few inhibitions in befriending
local boys, setting some up in shops and generally bettering
them. They invited them into a different social circle, which
inevitably they would have to abandon when their benefactors
left. In the 1960s there were boys knocking about among the
fishing boats of Forio who had enjoyed a brief taste of the good
life, though whether they were damaged by it or pined for a
return to it I have no idea.

The Ischian period was comparatively rich for Auden. In his

Collected Shorter Poems 1927–1957, published in 1966, he includes
nearly fifty poems for the years 1948–57, among them some
of his best. Lines from them hang around in the memory and I
used to copy them out on earlier visits, "Sirocco brings the
minor devils: / A slamming of doors / At four in the morning /
Announces they are back" and a poem called "Under Sirius"
which begins: "Yes, these are the dog-days, Fortunatus". The
poem called "Ischia" offers thanks to the island "to whom a
fair wind has / brought me rejoicing with dear friends / from
soiled productive cities" and continues by inquiring "What
design could have washed / with such delicate yellows / and
pinks and greens your fishing ports / that lean against ample
Epomeo, holding on / to the rigid folds of her skirts? The
boiling springs / which betray her secret fever / make limber
the gout-stiffened joint / and improve the venereal act".

There are poems about visiting sailors, a touching one about
a dead cat "for you the Ischian wave shall weep / When we who
now miss you are American dust, and steep / Epomeo in peace
and war augustly a grave-watch keep." Auden at his best could
entertain, instruct, even move, and lines stick in the mind
whatever the obscurity of their context.

Wystan in due course moved to Austria, never to return.
There had been trouble over boys and money, also with Kallman.
There were other changes in Ischia which Thekla Clark records,
"Signs of growing prosperity and worsening taste – a row of
oleanders planted along the sea walk, flashy new additions to
old houses . . . The promontory above San Francesco sprouted
a series of luxury villas with discreet landscaping that would
have been a welcome addition – anywhere else." I never minded
any of this when I arrived, never quite having experienced the
Forio of horse-droppings and carriages, of a single telephone
and camp gossip.

A litany of beaches: Citara, Cava dell'Isola, Chiaia, San Francesco di Paola, but it was always the last one which we used, separated from the town beach by its headland. But now, visiting Forio again, I am dismayed to find the wide sand beach demolished by huts almost to the water's edge. One summer Terence Rattigan rented William Walton's villa and brought a party of friends – Gielgud and Cuthbert Worsley among them. At noon they would descend to the beach in a troupe, Rattigan bearing snacks and a cocktail shaker. He was correcting a very slim manuscript and when I questioned him about it he indicated that it was a new play. So short, I asked. He showed me a page of sparse dialogue. "There are sixty pages here," he said, "each page represents two minutes on the stage. A two-hour play, there's nothing to it."

Otherwise Forio has not changed unpleasantly. Where there were half a dozen villas on the San Francesco hill there are now nearer fifty, but they are more or less buried in trees. The Chiesa del Soccorso still holds white and lonely vigil on its promontory, so far left unthreatened by building works. There was always a dog asleep on its steps and there is one there now. The mountains rise up bare and magnificent behind, the waves crash on the rocks below. I cannot work out exactly where our villas were, there are so many twisting alleyways and winding steps, and still half-demolished, half-built houses, just as I remember them.

We lunch in Maria's, under the palm trees, though she is no longer there. She never married as far as I know so I suppose one of her numerous nephews or nieces now runs the place. It was much the same, almost empty at midday, but now with Vespas roaring past. I doubt whether the talk at night is quite the same as in Auden's day, or indeed when we ourselves were in occupation, with Cyril Connolly, John Lehmann, Keith Vaughan and assorted others staying. But perhaps for someone else Maria's is providing a similar focal point and animation. I hope so.

Starting to read *The Gallery* again, so on a lovely autumn morning take the *Piero della Francesca* across to Naples for the day. Through the pines last night the faint swish of the sea like a nightclub drummer starting up. Past Procida and Vivara and into the swing of the bay. Lago d'Averno, sulphurous among its pine forests, is no more than a suggestion under the snout of Monte Nuovo, but, menacing and deserted, there all the same. The country of Homer and Virgil, of dark deeds and mysterious, unaccompanied one-way journeys, the underworld beckoning.

The attraction of Naples is that the first dazzling glimpse is not mirage but realisable promise, extravagant castles and palaces on the slopes of a mountain with only a slight hold on permanence.

From the Beverello quay we wind our way through hazardous traffic in Via Acton and round the monumental Palazzo Reale, all gilt and marble, to the Teatro San Carlo, an eighteenth-century opera house that preceded even Milan's La Scala. The lifeblood of the city during its wartime savaging, its cool white and gilt stucco interior was both refuge and temple. The Via Roma, which seems recently to have become the Via Toledo, runs north from here right through the city to Piazza del Gesù. The Archaeological Museum, off Piazza Cavour, whose dusty red brick was once a cavalry barracks, houses one of the great collections.

But not for today its frescoes and mosaics, instead a sentimental journey into the glass-roofed Galleria Umberto opposite the San Carlo, which even when I took my first espresso in it in 1947 was still a hive of mischief – pimps, prostitutes, peddlers of all known substances, black-market meat, cigarettes, medicine, toiletries, scents. Everything then was in short supply but in the Galleria, at a price, you could get it.

Norman Lewis doesn't make much of the Galleria's activities, oddly enough, for it must have been central to his inquiries. Butfor John Horne Burns, an American soldier who had slogged his way across North Africa from Casablanca to Algiers, the Galleria in August 1944 – when Lewis was soon to end his year's detachment – became the centre of life, "the unofficial heart of Naples". "It's a cross between a railroad station and a church," he wrote. "You think you're in a museum till you see the bars and shops. Once this Galleria had a dome of glass, but the bombings of Naples shattered this skylight, and tinkling glass fell like cruel snow to the pavement . . . At night the flags, the columns, the archangels blowing their trumpets on the cornices, the metal grids that held the glass before the bombs broke it heard more than they saw in the daytime. There were the hasty press of kisses and sibilance of urine on the pavement. By moonlight, shadows singly and in airs chased from corner to corner."

It is not quite like that today. We took a ritualistic espresso and a swallow of grappa and watched for a while meetings and negotiations and assignations, but somehow the urgency has gone out of it. Naples is still struggling, even as grand schemes for its regeneration are under way, but the Galleria has become smart, most of the touts long since departed to Piazza Garibaldi and the Stazione Centrale. It would take a brave foreigner or one reckless with lust to enter discussions there.

Naples used to be a good place for strolling about, only jangling trams to be avoided. Now the traffic hurtles at you from all angles, though in Santa Lucia in the shadow of Castel dell'Ovo or along Via Partenope behind the fishing port the surroundings compensate. If you're lucky you may come upon the Via Chiaia, home of Armani and Valentino, a few blocks north from Via Partenope. In the Palazzo Sessa, Nelson courted the

Ambassador's wife Emma, though there is nothing to tell you
so. Once upon a time I used to while away an hour or two
waiting for an unpunctual lady in the Gran' Café Gambrinus,
a stately nineteenth-century coffee house opposite the Opera.
The place seemed full of dandyish Italians doing exactly that. A
Negroni in the soothing bar of the Excelsior revives memories
long buried, half a lifetime away.

The Gallery consists of a series of portraits, not all set in Naples
but all relating to war, its participants and camp followers. Mostly
they have their beginnings in America, develop in North Africa
and end up in Naples in the late summer of 1944. They are GIs,
officers, Red Cross women, chaplains, each finding some sort
of catharsis in the open-fan Bay of Naples, more specifically in
the Galleria. "It was like all outdoors going on inside. He liked
the feeling of being roofed over without any coffin sensation of
claustrophobia." These people, the soldier says to himself, are all
in search of love, and they are all on the verge of breakdown.

Momma's bar in the Galleria Umberto shelters negroes, Italian
prostitutes, South African sergeants, Desert Rats, French sailors,
homosexuals of all races. There are fights sometimes at closing
time, but this was the moment Momma loved best, "a present-
ment of infinite possibilities, of hectic enchantments, of the
fleeting moment that could never be again because it was too
prosperous and frantic and keyed up".

North Africa remains a strong presence in *The Gallery*, a halfway
station with an ineradicable scent. American soldiers become
men there, it seems, and learn about sex and suffer heartbreak.
By the time they arrive in the Galleria Umberto they are on the
way to becoming world weary. "Major Motes saw himself in a
mirror in one of the bars – white-haired, quite stooped, his walk
unsteady, a tic under his left eye."

On 3 October 1943, Naples had fallen to the Fifth Army,

and now it was the Germans, so lately installed, who had taken to shelling and bombing the city. The streets were full of ambulances, the bay crammed with liberty ships and Red Cross vessels. Over the next year the girls of Naples learned ways to survive and to seek an accommodation with their liberators. Some even fell genuinely in love with them, only to be told their lovers were moving on, to the front up north. Some Americans suffered heartbreak, too, not over girls but over the discovery that although their country had more wealth and better plumbing it was spiritually bankrupt. "Our propaganda did everything but tell us Americans the truth – that we had most of the riches of the modern world, but very little of its soul . . . I remember that in Naples, though my heart had broken from one idea, it mended again when I saw how good most human beings are. In love and sunlight and music and humanity, Italy has something that humanity sorely needs." So a GI among the squalor and bartering and venality of 1944 Naples comes to the same conclusion as Norman Lewis.

But these GIs don't get off scot-free. The Galleria Umberto may be the source of much excitement and frivolous entertainment but as well as being the heart of Naples it also conducts a kind of hell. There is a grisly chapter in *The Gallery* called "Queen Penicillin" which describes how one unfortunate soldier, believing he has met the love of his life, discovers he has syphilis. He is shunted off to the Medical Centre at Bagnoli where a bored major tells him, "You're not going to have a good time here. Our whole set-up is guaranteed to make you hate everything about us. We don't want men coming back here, do you see? There's no excuse for getting VD. No excuse whatever."

Luckily for this GI, penicillin treatments had just begun. Instead of six months, the treatment consists of injections every three hours for eight days. "Every needle meant another X on the roster opposite his name and three hours nearer to his release."

Ironically, the Medical Centre had been built on the site of Mussolini's World Fair, nude, muscled statues in helmets everywhere. At last, his treatment over, the soldier returns to the Galleria Umberto. "Though it was noon he seemed to see Marisa standing there with her arms out to him. So he took the ampoule of penicillin out of his pocket and hurled it against the wall where her ghost flickered. The glass smashed, the yellow liquid ran like bright molasses to the pavement."

Life in the Galleria is not over yet; only in wartime it is more intense and more hazardous. *The Gallery* ends as it began: "There is an arcade in Naples that they call the Galleria Umberto. In August, 1944 everyone in Naples sooner or later found his way into this place and became like a picture on the wall of a museum. The Neapolitans came to the Galleria to watch the Americans, to pity them and to prey upon them. The Americans came there to get drunk or to pick up something or to wrestle with the riddle. Everyone was aware of this riddle. It was the riddle of war, of human dignity, of love, of life itself."

There is much philosophising in *The Gallery*, speculation about the nature of goodness, a little about evil. Many of the figures that flit about the Galleria are due to die, to pass from sight into the unknown. The Galleria is only one part of Naples: "And Naples is on the bay, in the Tyrrhenian Sea, on the Mediterranean. This sea is a centre of human life and thought. Wonderful and sad things have come out of Italy. And they came back there in August, 1944. For they were dots in a circle that never stops."

Once you have read *The Gallery* Naples is never the same. I am tempted to return once more, for a last glimpse at its wartime ghosts, but they will have fled. Better let sleeping dogs lie.

John Horne Burns never quite recovered from the amazing success of *The Gallery*. He retired to Florence, became an alcoholic and died there at the age of thirty-seven. He wrote one other novel, *Lucifer with a Book*.

Holed up in Porto during a morning's rain, nothing could be more soothing. The trees drip, the sand on the beach acquires a kind of acne, the sea becomes ironed out. In the late afternoon it clears and we walk through the public gardens, along oleander-bordered lanes. There are hotels, a few *pensioni*, among the umbrella pines. The public beaches are no great shakes but you are soon at the harbour and there one can sit happily until what in India is known as the "hour of the cow dust". Never more than five minutes pass without a ferry or *aliscafo* arriving or leaving, a yacht or fishing boat trying to get out of the way, some poor wretch in a dinghy manoeuvring to find a new perch. There is a smell of fresh paint, a constant hammering.

The harbour's almost closed circle creates a particular kind of intimacy. Few of these classy white steamers, languid yachts, coastguard launches, are going very far, to Naples or Sorrento possibly, or just round the island. The mainland is always in sight, layers of grey-green hills behind a series of bays, with Vesuvius lurking off-centre.

Just behind the port offices, in the grounds of the former royal palace, there is the largest of the island's thermal establishments. Ischia has no shortage of *fumarole* or thermal springs, and wherever you go you come across people hobbling to and fro from baths. The whole island sometimes seems to be bubbling. Inland the hills are studded with small vents exhaling fumes, as if a legion of despised underground smokers were in action.

Although many visitors to Ischia come for cures, they do not come particularly to Porto. Few people here seem on their last legs and the young of both sexes are very pretty.

I want to go again to San Montano, as perfect in its secretive way as Porto. I feared that its crescent of white sand at the mouth of a valley and between two protective, almost joining headlands, might now be built-up and ruined. On the top of the hill between San Montano and Lacco Ameno a new hotel, the elegant San Montano, with several swimming pools and fantastic views from its various terraces, overlooks the bay. Rather than taking the valley path directly to the beach, we had taken the bus into Lacco Ameno and laboured on foot up the steep, winding Via Monte Vico that leads to the hotel. In this way, by seeing the bay from far above, we could cushion any disappointment.

It turned out not too bad. The headlands, as thick in trees as ever, are unmarked, the beach just as flawless. Some sort of small hotel complex, with recreational area and swimming pool, seems to have been established among the trees behind the beach, but so far it has not encroached. Wiser, perhaps, if

San Montano

you can afford it, to look down on it from on high, all the same.

From the San Montano terrace, Forio lies to our left, just out of sight beyond a promontory matted with trees. To the right, under ancient Monte Vico, stretch the rather scrappy streets of Lacco Ameno. The *fungo*, that mushroom-shaped block of rock, gives the harbour area some kind of identity, but otherwise this characterless group of houses bisected by the main road to Forio has a sleepy, desultory feel. A tree-lined piazza, its seats occupied by rickety old men, a parish church, a small museum, is the extent of it, though curiously the Rizzoli publishing group chose nearby cliffs to insert two of Ischia's most luxurious hotels, the summer resort of film stars and playboys, so magazines tell us.

In one of Lawrence Durrell's books he writes about "Islomania", a rare affliction of spirit. He quotes as authority his new friend Gideon, he of "the monocle, the clipped silver hair, the polished boots", first met on a boat embarked in Alexandria and bound for Rhodes. These "Islomanes", Gideon used to remark, were descendants of the Atlanteans, for whose lost city of Atlantis their subconscious continually yearns. Gideon and Durrell developed an interest in the works of the Rev. Fanshaw Tozer, an eccentric nineteenth-century divine whose book *Aegean Islands*, published in 1887, contained the ominous sentence, "There is an element of excitement attending a voyage to Rhodes arising from the uncertainty which exists with regard to reaching that island."

"Islomanes" – do we, I, feel happier cut off from the mainland? I don't know. Despite visits to almost every island in the Mediterranean, and the Caribbean for that matter, I doubt I would want to live on any of them. Perhaps the real Islomane doesn't mind what island it is, so long as he can get off it and find another. Certainly, up here on Monte Vico you could quickly lose all ambition, exercising the body, reading, outside of time.

The hilltop villages of Barano and Serrara Fontana are another world altogether. In this late autumn the sky colours, the foliage, the quality of sunsets behind Monte Epomeo, have begun unostentatiously to alter, the fierce leonine face of the inner island to mellow. Above Maronti beach a few houses are settled on the cliffs, but higher up there are no surfaces on which to build, only hollows, ravines, sheer drops, fissures, all under slimeyish green. Yet, further in still, a small village has amazingly grown up in a kind of hammock of rock. The people in it, so near as the crow flies to sea, probably never venture into it, even by less precipitous routes than the direct one.

From up here on Monte Vico you get a clear view of Capri, resembling a semi-shrouded tanker, its superstructure aft, its bows lean, and beyond it Vesuvius, looking like Mount Fuji, only its peak above cloud. Nothing is flat here, the hills veined and muscular. Nearly 7000 people live in the small pockets of Piedimonte, Testaccio and Buonopane, each one notable for its church, its beautifying spring, or in the case of Buonopane its Greek-style dance, the "Ndvezzata".

The scrub at the foot of Monte Vezzi has turned rusty, the outside world for these villages, mild though the climate is, will soon feel even more remote. As autumn is shed, winter will close them in, specialists in darkness. "And now one more year of knowing nothing has gone by: once more the Pleiads are sinking; the plane tree is bare; the bowstring relaxed." So Palinurus reflected in *The Unquiet Grave.* But if our day is taken up with scratching a living out of barren soil, can we miss what we don't know about or have no time for?

In Barano and Serrara Fontana you are as near to the summit of Epomeo as you can get without making the final ascent. I doubt whether the hermit who was there forty years ago is still in residence but if I'm alive so may he be. The tiny church of St Nicola and its hermitage, hollowed out of volcanic tufa, continues to draw pilgrims to watch the fabulous dawns and sunsets, as good a reason for making the climb as any.

Those evenings at Maria's in the 1950s and in the rented Walton villa on the San Francesco hill seem suddenly not so long ago. The much-lamented Barbara Skelton, once my companion here, wrote of her husband Cyril Connolly's "coolie" legs and with his pointed straw hat on as he padded about the beach, it was hard not to smile at so apt a description. It was often impossible then to tell who looked the more disgruntled, Connolly or Moravia; in Moravia's case I think it was natural gloom, in Cyril's an affliction of the liver. "Liver's lousy", were the last words he spoke to me on his deathbed. Life too often ends, not with dignity, but in wretched circumstances. I think, among my friends, of the suicides of John Minton, of Keith Vaughan and Cuthbert Worsley, all once happy here, of the wretched end of Henry Green. Only Stephen Spender, at a good age, went quietly and suddenly, though still too soon. Gavin Ewart, a soldier here in the war and whose superior knowledge of Latin made the translations from Iasolini later in this book a great deal easier, died in a hospice on Clapham Common with the desire for poetry still strong in him. We were friends for half a century.

The sirens are bleating in the harbour, the grapes ready for gathering. On our way out we shall make a last call on Procida, its sunken freighter of years ago still askew. The least visited of Neapolitan islands its destiny is probably to be by-passed, a place on the way to somewhere else. There are worse fates.

PART II

Ischia and Procida: A Few Facts

(There are certain intimacies in all ladies' lavatories
we just lease to imagination)
FINNEGAN'S WAKE

ISCHIAN HISTORY GOES back to the time when the whole
of Italy was covered by water and what is now known as the
Tyrrhenian Sea was a mountainous continent, of which today
only the peaks of Corsica, Sardinia and Elba survive. During
the late Mesozoic and the Eocene ages this continent gradually
subsided, as the Apennines appeared from the waves. Later, in
the Pleiocene age, much of Italy was reclaimed by the sea and
the Gulf of Naples was formed.

Geologically, the bed of the Gulf of Naples and the subsoil
of Campania Felice are the same. Through the breaks in the
earth's crust, basaltic lava was forced to the surface, a principal
constituent of its rich volcanic soil.

The island of Ischia itself is now thought to be the result of
several eruptions of different types, and not of a single large
volcano.

The first signs of human habitation in Ischia appear in the
neolithic age, rather at the time of transition between the
stone age and the bronze age. There are only a few remains –
tools, fragments of pottery, flint and obsidian – but they are
sufficient to indicate that the island was fairly densely inhabited
at that time (about 3000 BC).

Before this Ischia was still subject to volcanic eruptions and
too hot for occupation. Capri, however, was not yet an island

but part of the Sorrentine peninsula, already inhabited, as the flint instruments and weapons of the late palaeolithic period show. Herr Buchner, writing of Ischia in 1948[1], picturesquely proposes that the eruption of the island from the sea must have been witnessed by the men of the mainland – those men who had as their companions the elephant, the hippopotamus and the prehistoric rhinoceros.[2]

The Ponziane islands were too small and too far from the continent to be inhabited by palaeolithic man, but in the succeeding age one of them, the island of Palmarola, became important as the centre of the export trade in obsidian. During the bronze age there was a village on the hill of Castiglione on Ischia, between Porto d'Ischia and Casamicciola, as excavations show. These remains are characteristic of what has been called "apennine civilisation", which extended from Romagna to Puglia and from Umbria to Lucania. Traces of this culture have also been found in the Grotta delle Felci and in the Grotta Nicolucci at Sorrento.

The Greeks brought with them the arts of civilisation, particularly the art of pottery. The architectural ornaments of terracotta found at Pompeii were made in Pithecusa. Even as late as 1838 ceramics were, next to wine, the most important product of the island. Now, however, only two furnaces remain, at Casamicciola and Porto d'Ischia. It is known that in 160 BC Pithecusan wines

1. *Origine e Passato dell'Isola d'Ischia* – G. Buchner & A. Rittmann (Naples, 1948) – the source of nearly all the geological and historical facts mentioned here.
2. In a prehistoric cave at San Ciro on the Bay of Palermo were found "the bones of two species of hippopotamus . . . With these were associated the remains of *Elephas antiquus*, and bones of the genera *Bos, Cervus, Sus, Ursus, Canis*, and a large *Felis*' – Sir Charles Lyell: *The Geological Evidences of the Antiquity of Man.*

travelled as far afield as Sicily, Taranto and Carthage but, more important still as an export, the characteristic black varnished pottery of this period has been found in the South of France, Spain and North Africa.

Besides Apollo, Demeter, Zeus, Hera and the Dioscuri (Castor and Pollux) the god most worshipped by the islanders seems to have been Aristaeus, an agricultural deity. Fruit and vines profited from the volcanic nature of the soil and the local wine was highly prized. Iasolini in his book on Ischia (1588) gives the name of the popular wines as "il Sorbigno, il Greco, il Latino, il Coda cavallo" (horse's tail).

The modern name of Ischia is derived from the Latin "Insula Major" (Capri was presumably thought of as "insula minor"). This was shortened to "Insula" and then, in local dialect, to "Iscla", which eventually became "Ischia".

Medical Antiquities

(With notes on Iasolini)

STRABO, PLINY, STATIUS and Celius Amelianus all mention the therapeutic virtues of the hot springs of Ischia. They were, however, never exploited during the Roman era, because of the danger of volcanic eruptions and earthquakes. Most of the organised bathing took place at Baiae and Pozzuoli on the mainland.

A few Roman remains still exist near the Terme Regina Isabella and contemporary votive tablets can be seen in the Naples museum; these were discovered near the Nitroli spring in 1757. The dedicatory inscriptions give thanks for successful cures to Apollo and the nymphs of the spring, the Nitrodes or Nitrodiae. The tablets represent Apollo with a lyre and two or three nymphs at his side, carrying conches or vessels from which they pour the healing water.

It is clear from Pliny that the danger from earthquakes and volcanic action was always present and he mentions one occasion when a small town was swallowed up and a lake appeared in its place (*"Pithecussis ... oppidum haustum profundo, alioque motu terrae stagnum emersisse"*). This lake can only have been the Lago del Bagno, which Ferdinand II in 1853 converted into the present harbour of Porto d'Ischia by cutting through the narrow bar of land that separated it from the sea. Pliny's story of the lake was regarded as a traveller's tale until modern geological research vindicated him.

*

The rarest and most interesting book about the medicinal waters of Ischia is by the Neapolitan doctor Iasolini – *De Rimedi Naturali che sono nell' Isola di Pithecusa; Hoggi detta Ischia* ("The Natural Remedies which are to be found in The Island of Pithecusa, Today called Ischia"). It was published in 1588 at Naples and dedicated to the Lady Geronima Colonna, Duchess of Monteleone ("*Illustrissima et Eccellentissima Signora*"). Its extreme rarity and interest make a brief summary necessary.

The book opens with a short passage on the divine nature of fire, with particular reference to the volcanic nature of Ischia, which Iasolini claims is the best island in the world. To prove this he gives a long quotation from Strabo (Book V) containing the classical references to Ischia in Pindar, Homer and Virgil.

This is followed by the Greek story of the Cercopi, two brothers called Candolus and Atlas, rogues and brigands, who ill-treated all the strangers who fell into their hands. At length they even dared to practise their evil arts against Jupiter himself, who as a punishment turned them into monkeys.

Ovid and Boccaccio, according to Iasolini, put Typhoeus under Sicily; Virgil and Lucan, on the other hand, located him correctly under Ischia. He summarises what the learned Giovanio Pontano wrote about Ischia in the second book of his *De Bello Neapolitano*, paying particular attention to the experience of Bartolomeo Pernice, a Genoese merchant travelling to Naples. Passing close to the island Pernice noticed several luminous rocks scattered on the sea shore. This is probably the only eye-witness account of the eruption of 1301.

Iasolini goes on to describe the geographical features of Ischia, its wines and its birds, especially the waterhen, which arrive thin and unfit to eat but become fat and palatable in the winter. This is attributed by some to the fact that they feed on a certain herb, but Iasolini claims that it is due to swimming in the medicinal waters of a volcanic lake.

A description follows of the various baths and hot springs, giving their location and qualities. The hot springs can be used for cooking, while the waters of Barano make women beautiful and give long life to the inhabitants. Iasolini lists eleven fresh-water springs, thirty-five hot springs, one *fango* (mud-bath), various showers, nineteen *sudatorii*[3], five sand-baths.

The next section contains a long disquisition on the relative merits of fire and water. Iasolini gives instances of the praise of water in ancient writers, quoting the sacredness of rivers, the use of the sea for commerce. Water, he concludes, is the superior element; baths are mentioned in the *Odyssey*, were used by the Greeks and Romans, and are recommended by Galen "in whom medicine reached the culmination of perfection". Baths, as used by the ancients, were of two kinds, taken for pleasure or medicinally. Baccio, Iasolini says, lists three types of men who go to the baths – "those despaired of by the doctors, who go, so to speak, to re-forge their bodies, and for the most part suffer harm from it, often wrongly blaming their doctor and the bath. Others, who take good counsel, come back refreshed and, for the most part, cured of their ailments; for it is very true that, among all the powers of medicine, one sees most miracles at the baths (which almost every day we witness, not without the greatest wonder) and especially in the baths of Ischia. The third class are those who take no heed, who rush in with too much haste, and those thrifty ones who, while they think to avoid great expense, do not realise that baths without the advice of a good doctor are more costly than those undertaken on medical advice."

3. Literally "sweat houses".

Iasolini emphasises the proper preparations necessary before taking the baths – "And I have observed that all those who take baths after first having taken sarsaparilla, or lignumvitae or china-root and being purged two or three times first (for the reason that the illness demands the said remedies) have all experienced wonderful effects from the baths, being advised by good doctors and not those who pander to the tastes of the sick man, of whom there is no dearth – but woe to the flatterers and to those who accept flattery, that see it and feel it!"

To illustrate the fact that moderation in bathing is necessary Iasolini quotes the distich found in the ancient baths of Diocletian – "worthy to be carved in gold rather than in marble" –

> *Balnea, vina, venus, corrumpunt corpora sana;*
> *Corpora sana dabunt – balnea, vina, venus.*[4]

The baths vary every year, dry summers and wet springs making them dangerous. A medical writer, Savonarola (not the Fra Girolamo "*che fù impiccato ed arso*" in the Piazza Signoria of Florence) goes so far as to say: "If the daily temperature of the summer is too hot and he who takes the bath stays there too long he will fall into an acute fever . . . dysentery, pain in the eyes, putrefaction of the private parts and other like diseases, especially if he is a person of a hot and dry constitution."

After quoting three pages of Galen, Iasolini gives his own precepts for bathing, emphasising the golden rule – NELLI BAGNI BISOGNA SCHERZARE NE PREVARICARE ("In the baths one should not fool about or go too far").

Great attention must be paid to the quality of the drinking water used by the bather. Water from the spring on Epomeo ("*aqua di Buceto*") or the water called "*di Nitroli*" from near Barano are

4. "Bathing, wine and love corrupt healthy bodies; healthy bodies are produced by – bathing, wine and love."

both to be recommended. The practice of drinking the actual waters of the bath, as some people do, is most harmful.

Of food he writes: "Let the bread that is eaten be well leavened and properly baked, not hot, as it is when freshly taken from the oven, nor in any way tainted or made of badly mixed flour and baked not more than two days ago, or at the most three. Some doctors of the baths prohibit other things and ban all unleavened food and food made of flour, such as 'pastilli' and macaroni, all herbs (and especially when eaten raw), fish, game, buttermilk, butter and all forms of dairy produce, fruits, vegetables, everything bitter, sauces, fried foods and other such things, such as pertain to a more liberal existence. But to tell the truth this is too strict a rule, nor is it commonly observed in the baths. Usually good meat commends itself, fresh eggs and the ordinary everyday condiments, nor is it to be thought or understood that in any way is it prohibited or forbidden to eat (with discretion) both fruit and herbs and other such things which are not so often eaten in the baths. For this reason that, as we have already said above, according to the regulation of the bath no prescription is so important as that everything which is eaten should be chosen with care, and good."

Of wine: "It is all the more necessary diligently to ensure that one chooses good wines, that have no fault, that are of medium body and substance; that give nourishment without straining the digestion, are not 'austere' nor sweet; of which there is great plenty and abundance in Ischia, so that each man may choose wines according to his taste, 'Greci', 'Sorbigni', costly, pure, mixed, clear, 'small', and those that contain only a little water and are stronger, or less strong, as it may be most fitting for the individual. And among all these different sorts of wine I should say that the 'Sorbigni', being light wines, are the best, not the heavy wines mixed with 'Greek' wine, or at least the clear wines and that called 'horse's tail', precisely because they are not very bitter. Because they are wines without fumes and one can drink them without harm, nor do they go to the head, as some do, that send to sleep those who drink them; but they give force and strength to the entrails and limbs of the human body. Those wines that are slightly less austere commend themselves and are better esteemed than those that are light and penetrating."

And of food again: "And to be brief, one must abstain from everything that of its nature corrupts, those things that inflame, that are hot and desiccative. For this reason a drink of fresh eggs, if there is no contra-indication, is very suitable for the beginning of a meal; meats that are temperate, such as chickens, pheasants, partridges, the flesh of sucking calves, of small birds, of little goats, and suchlike foods. One must avoid and abstain from meat that is too fat, heavy and too hot."

Iasolini's Book II advises when and how to bathe, according to the age, sex and physique of the patient. One should not bathe when the weather is too cold or too hot. The spring and the beginning of the summer and of the autumn are the best times of the year. One should wear only white linen trousers "*brevi circa le parti vergognose*" and have the head covered, "so that the vapours from the baths may not fill the head". Slow immersion is to be recommended, and one should not remain too long. A patient who stays too long in a hot bath finds his toes and fingers become wrinkled – a bad sign.

After the bath, "the sick man should have himself well dried by his servants and be well covered with a cloak; he should go to bed but, as he lies there, he should not sleep, as Baccio rightly says in contradiction to Faloppio: let him sweat for an hour more or less and dry himself with a light towel, and do so until he has returned to his former state; let him then rise from his bed, having first completely dried his sweat and, being well wrapped up, let him walk a while and then eat moderately and afterwards sup, all the time avoiding sleep."

Iasolini then gives Francesco Aretino's eighteen rules for bathing, all of them sound common sense and in accordance with what he has already written.

The remainder of the work describes the peculiar virtues of the various baths in Ischia. For example, the Bagno del Gurgitello cures, among other things, sterility – "for certainly among all the diseases of the uterus, sterility is a signal vice; which without doubt has many causes. Foremost among these is a certain hardness, which in many cases the uterus may have naturally but more often from some accident of it being hot or dry or from the discharge to which women are subject known as leucorrhoea or from the excess of menstrual blood; or even the suppression of this. All of which causes have need of particular consideration and require different kinds and regimes of bathing, especially in cases of sterility. To combat the hardness, it is necessary to proceed with softening and moistening agents, as also against the dry and hot distemper. But particularly subject to all three of these causes of sterility are women who are viragos, that have the nature of men, hotness, dryness, and a certain natural heat of the womb, which conditions cannot be cured or made better without continued and copious use of moistening and softening baths." Iasolini later states that he himself knew a lady of quality who was sterile, but after drinking the waters of this bath (not even immersing herself in it) had many fine sons.

There follow forty pages of advice on how to deal with emergencies arising from the use of the baths.

Finally, Iasolini gives a table of diseases of different parts of the body which can be cured by the waters of Ischia, recommending different baths for each disease.

The impressive list, with its comforting contradictions, includes the following:

THE HEAD

Headache – that is, pain in the head that is not longstanding but only beginning.

Cold distemper and wetness of the head.

Vertigo.

Epilepsy or the falling sickness.

Loss of memory.

Frenzy, called phrenitis.

To fortify and comfort the brain.

THE NERVES

For spasms.

For paralysis.

For tremor.

For contraction and retraction of the sinews.

THE EYELIDS

For lack of hair in the eyelids.

For inflammation of the eyes, called ophthalmia.

For ulcers of the eyes.

For squinting.

For cataract or primary suffusions.

To make the vision acute.

THE EARS

For pains in the ears.

For whistling, noises and echoes heard in the ears.

For deafness from hot causes.

For ulcers of the ears.

THE NOSTRILS

For ulcers of the nostrils, called *ozaena*, and other ulcers that are difficult to cure.

For fleshy excrescences, called *sarcomata*, other warts, pimples and polyps.

THE MOUTH, GUMS AND TEETH

For ulcers of the mouth, the gums and the tongue.

For split lips.

For relaxed and softened gums.

For hard projections, tumours and ulcers of the tongue and impediments of speech.

THE TEETH

For toothache and to keep the teeth firm and white.

THE THROAT, THE JAWS AND THE WINDPIPE

For inflammations of the pipe and swollen tonsils and for the *colonnella*, called relaxed uvula.

For distillations of the gullet.

For roughness of the arterial trachea, called the windpipe.

THE LUNGS AND CHEST

To make the voice good and sonorous.

For diseases of the lungs.

For roughness and other diseases of the chest.

For coughs.

For asthma.

For pleurisy or puncture.

THE HEART

To strengthen the heart.

THE BREASTS

For breasts made hard by abundance of milk or scirrhus, but not affected by cancer.

To make the flow of milk copious.

THE STOMACH

For vomiting and nausea.

For wind and flatus.

For hiccoughs.

To induce vomiting.

For rumbling of the stomach.

For acid farting.

For loss of appetite.

THE LIVER

For hardness of the liver.

For the bad habit known as cachexy and to cure and comfort the liver.

For dropsy.

THE SPLEEN

For obstruction of the spleen.

To reduce an enlarged spleen.

THE INTESTINES

For pains in the intestines.

For diseases of the colon.

For dysentery.

For worms.

For colicky pains or iliac disturbances.

THE BOTTOM

For cracks or fissures of the anus.

For ulcers of the podex or of the bottom.

For protuberance of the anus.

THE KIDNEYS

For pain in the loins.

For gravel and stone in the kidneys.

For hot distempers of the kidneys and of other natural parts.

THE BLADDER

For the retention of urine in the bladder.

For diabetes.

For heat of the urine.

To break up and bring out stones from the kidneys and the bladder.

THE PRIVATE PARTS OF MEN

To excite and stimulate the venereal appetite.

To increase the semen.

To extinguish lust and nocturnal pollutions.

For dilated and varicose veins of the testicles.

For gonorrhoea and over-abundance of semen.

For all hard tumours of the testicles.

For warts on the penis.

For twisting of the virile member.

THE PRIVATE PARTS OF WOMEN

To induce menstruation.

For immoderate menses.

For sterility and to aid conception.

For pregnant women.

THE UTERUS

For hardness of the uterus which often prevents conception.

For cold distemper of the uterus accompanied by tumours.

THE EXTREMITIES OF THE BODY

For gout in the feet.

For sciatica.

For gout in the hands.

For arthritic pains.

For stiffness and stones in the joints, however caused.

Visitors

Les images s'entr'ouvrent maintenant sur quelques points; je découvre subitement et par intervalles Portici, Caprée, Ischia, le Pausilippe, la mer parsemée des voiles blanches des pêcheurs et la côte du golfe de Naples, bordée d'orangers: c'est le paradis vu de l'enfer.

CHATEAUBRIAND, *Voyage en Italie* (1804)

Naples, 21 Mars (1817) – Je me sens possédé par ce noir chagrin d'ambition qui me poursuit depuis deux ans. A la manière des Orientaux, il faut agir sur le physique. Je m'embarque, je fais quatre heures de mer, et me voilà à Ischia, avec une lettre de recommandation pour don Fernando.

Il me conte qu'en 1806 il s'est retiré à Ischia, et qu'il n'a pas vu Naples depuis l'usurpation française, qu'il abhorre. Pour se consoler du manque de théâtre, il élève une quantité de rossignols dans les volières superbes. "La musique, cet art sans modèle dans la nature, autre que le chant des oiseaux, est aussi comme lui une suite d'interjections. Or une interjection est un cri de la passion, et jamais de la pensée. La pensée peut produire la passion; mais l'interjection n'est jamais que de l'émotion, et la musique ne saurait exprimer ce qui est sèchement pensé." Cet amateur délicat ajoute: "Mes alouettes ont quelque-fois le matin des falsetti qui me rappellent Marchesi et Pacchiarotti."

Je passe quatre heures fort agréables avec don Fernando, qui nous déteste, et les bons habitants d'Ischia. Ce sont des sauvages africains. Bonhomie de leur patois. Ils vivent de leurs vignes. Presque pas de trace de civilisation, grand avantage quand le

*p ... et ses r ... font toute la civilisation. Un homme du peuple,
à Naples, vous dit froidement: "L'année dernière, au mois d'août,
j'assassinai un homme." Si vous lui proposez de partir un
dimanche à trois heures du matin, pour le Vesuve, il vous dit,
frappé d'horreur: "Moi, manquer la sainte messe!"*

*Des rites s'apprennent par coeur: si vous admettez les bonnes
actions, elles peuvent être plus ou moins bonnes: de là l'examen
personnel, et nous arrivons au protestantisme et à la gaieté d'un
methodiste anglais.*

STENDHAL, *Rome, Naples et Florence* (1817)

Shadowy Aornos darkened o'er the helm
The horizontal aether; Heaven stripped bare
Its depths over Elysium, where the prow
Made the invisible water white as snow;
From that Typhaean mount, Inarime,
    There streamed a sunbright vapour, like the standard
      Of some aethereal host;
      Whilst from all the coast,
    Louder and louder, gathering round, there wandered
Over the oracular woods and divine sea
Prophesyings which grew articulate –
They seize me – I must speak them! – be they fate!

SHELLEY, "Ode to Naples"[5] (1820)

*En parlant ainsi, nous descendions légèrement les rues en pente
de Procida. Nous arrivâmes bientôt sur la marine. C'est ainsi
qu'on appelle la plage, voisine de la rade ou du port dans
l'archipel et sure les côtes d'Italie. La plage était couverte de
barques d'Ischia, de Procida et de Naples, que la tempête de la
veille avait forcées de chercher un abri dans ses eaux. Les*

5. Celebrating the proclamation of a Constitutional Government at Naples.

marins et les pêcheurs dormaient au soleil, au bruit décroissant
des vagues, ou causaient par groupes assis sur le môle. A notre
costume et au bonnet de laine rouge qui recouvrait nos cheveux,
ils nous prirent pour de jeunes matelots de Toscane ou de Gênes
qu'un des bricks qui portent l'huile ou le vin d'Ischia avait
débarqués à Procida.

LAMARTINE, *Les Confidences* (1849)

Quand le soleil baissait, nous faisions de longues courses à
travers l'île. Nous la traversions dans tous les sens. Nous
allions à la ville acheter le pain ou les légumes qui manquaient
au jardin d'Andrea. Quelquefois nous rapportions un peu de
tabac, cet opium *du marin, qui l'anime en mer et qui le console*
à terre. Nous rentrions à la nuit tombante, les poches et les
mains pleines de nos modestes munificences. La famille se
*rassemblait, le soir, sur le toit qu'on appelle à Naples l'*astrico,
au clair de la lune … On y voit la vieille mère filer, le père fumer
sa pipe de terre cuite à la tige de roseau, les jeunes garçons s'ac-
couder sur le rebord et chanter en longues notes tramantes ces
airs marins ou champêtres dont l'ascent prolongé ou vibrant a
quelque chose de la plainte du bois torturé par les vagues ou de
la vibration stridente de la cigale au soleil; les jeunes filles
enfin, avec leurs robes courtes, les pieds nus, leurs sou-brevestes
vertes et galonnées d'or ou de soie, et leurs longs cheveux noirs
flottants sur leurs épaules, enveloppés d'un mouchoir noué sur
la nuque, à gros noeuds, pour préserver leur chevelure de la
poussière.

Elles y dansent souvent seules ou avec leurs soeurs; l'une
tient une guitare, l'autre élève sur sa tête un tambour de basque
entouré de sonnettes de cuivre. Ces deux instruments, l'un
plaintif et léger, l'autre monotone et sourd, s'accordent
merveilleusement pour rendre presque sans art les deux notes

*alternatives du coeur de l'homme: la tristesse et la joie. On les
entend pendant les nuits d'été sur presque tous les toits des îles
ou de la campagne de Naples, même sur les barques; ce concert
aérien, qui poursuit l'oreille de site en site, depuis la mer
jusqu'aux montagnes, ressemble aux bourdonnements d'un
insect de plus, que la chaleur fait naître et bourdonner sous ce
beau ciel. Ce pauvre insecte, c'est l'homme! qui chante quelques
jours devant Dieu sa jeunesse et ses amours, et puis qui se tait
pour l'éternité. Je n'ai jamais pu entendre ces notes répandues
dans l'air, du haut des* astricos, *sans m'arrêter et sans me
sentir le coeur serré, prêt à éclater de joie intérieure ou de
mélancolie plus forte que moi.*

LAMARTINE, *op. cit.*

OF ISCHIA

It is a delightful spot, and the homeliness of its accom-
modations is not without its charms . . . While at Ischia,
we ascended the Monte di Vico, and Monte d'Epomeo,
which command the most enchanting views imaginable.
A hermit resides in a cave at the summit of the latter; and
did the honours of his rude dwelling with much urbanity
and intelligence. The ascent is exceeding abrupt; and the
latter part of it we were compelled to accomplish on
foot, leaving our mules behind us. From the hermitage,
the island is looked down on, with its vines and figs,
presenting a mass of brilliant verdure, only broken by the
stone terraces that crown nearly all the flat-roofed houses;
many of them surrounded with rustic trellis-work, over-
grown by flowering plants, or vines. The blue and sparkling sea is spread out as if to serve as a mirror to the azure
sky that canopies it; and the white sails that float on it
resemble swans gliding over some vast and tranquil lake.

The hermit seemed gratified with our lively admiration of the prospect from his dwelling; and assured us that use had not palled the pleasure it afforded him.

"I know not whether it appears more lovely," said he, "when sparkling in the bright beams of the morning; or when the sun sinks into the sea, casting its red light over the scene."

On returning, our guide led us by a still more abrupt path than the one by which we had ascended; and the mode by which the muleteers got their mules down some of the worst parts of the route surprised me. A few of them went below, while others forced the animal head-foremost to the edge of the summit of the steep; and, holding it by the tail, to prevent it from falling, let it gradually descend, until the men beneath, who had clambered up a portion of the ascent to encounter it, were enabled to grasp it, and assist it to the bottom. The loud neighing of the mules, and the cries, exclamations, and curses of the muleteers, formed a chorus by no means harmonious; and when the feat was accomplished, the laughter in which the men indulged, as they imitated the kicking and neighing of the mules, was irresistibly comic.

THE COUNTESS OF BLESSINGTON,
The Idler in Italy (1839)

During our *séjour* at Ischia, we were much gratified by the music heard nightly in the little hamlets, as we returned from our evening rides: groups of three and four persons, with guitars, were seen seated on a terrace, or on a bench before their houses, singing Neapolitan airs, and barcaroles, in a style that would not have offended the ears of Rossini himself; while, in another quarter might be found a party dancing the merry tarantella, to the sound of a guitar and tambourine, to which their voices, as well as their feet, kept perfect measure. Rarely did we pass two hundred yards without meeting such groups; and when we paused to listen to their songs, or see the dancing, they invariably offered us seats, and then continued, without any embarrassment.

The fête-dress of the female inhabitants of Ischia is very picturesque and becoming, and totally unlike that of the Neapolitan women; the men wear scarlet caps, of the Phrygian shape, and are a fine-looking and hardy race. The females are much handsomer than those of Naples; and have very expressive countenances, and gentle manners. The mud, sand, and mineral baths at Ischia are considered very beneficial in rheumatic and cutaneous diseases, and are much frequented.

On our return we stopped to see the island of Procida, which, though much inferior to Ischia, is well worthy of being visited. Here wine, bread, grapes and figs, of the most delicious quality, were offered to us by the women; and one or two of the houses which we entered, though homely to the last degree, were so clean, that the fruit presented to us in them might be eaten without the smallest apprehension or dread.

THE COUNTESS OF BLESSINGTON, *op. cit.*

OF EPOMEO

> Et nous aux penchants de ses verts Elysées
> Sur ses bords où l'Amour eût caché son Eden
> Au murmure plaintif des vagues apaisées
> Aux rayons endormis de l'astre élyséen,

Sous ce ciel où la vie ou le bonheur abonde.
Sur ces rives que l'oeil se plait à parcourir,
Nous avons respiré cet air d'un autre monde.
Elise! et cependant on dit qu'il faut mourir.

LAMARTINE[6]

Yesterday we dined on Mount Vesuvius; today we were to have dined on its victim, Pompeii; but "by the grace of God, which passeth all understanding", since Bartolomeo himself, that weather soothsayer, did not foresee this British weather, we are prevented. In the meantime, all this week and the next is replete with projects to Istria,[7] Procite, etc etc, so God only knows when I can worship again my Diana of Ephesus.

SIR WILLIAM HAMILTON
in a letter to his wife Lady Emma Hamilton (*c.*1798)

Their as been a prince paying us a visit. He is sixty years of age, one of the first families, and as allways lived at Naples; and when I told him I had been at Caprea, he asked me if I went there by land. Only think what ignorance! I stared at him, and asked him who was his tutor.

LADY HAMILTON in a letter to Greville (*c.*1798)

"O God," says she, "your *eccellenza* is very ungrateful! He as been so good as to make your face the same as he made the face of the Blessed Virgin's, and you don't esteem it a favour!" "Why," says I, "did you ever see the Virgin?" "O yes," says she, "you are like every picture

---

6. As quoted by D'Ascia, in *Storia d'Ischia*, who calls him the "Bard of Bordeaux".
7. Presumably Ischia?

that there is of her, and you know the people at Iscea
fel down on their knees to you, and beg'd you to grant
them favours in her name."

Dialogue between LADY HAMILTON *and her Italian
maid, in a letter to Greville (c.*1798)

*C'était la saison où les pêcheurs du Pausilippe, qui suspendent
leur cabane à ses rochers et qui étendent leurs filets sur ses petites
plages de sable fin, s'éloignent de la terre avec confiance et vont
pêcher la nuit à deux ou trois lieues en mer, jusque sous les
falaises de Capri, de Procida, d'Ischia, et au milieu du golfe de
Gaëte.*

*Quelques-uns portent avec eux des torches de resine, qu'ils
allument pour tromper le poisson. Le poisson monte à la lueur,
croyant que c'est le crépuscule du jour. Un enfant, accroupi sur
la proue de la barque, penche en silence la torche inclinée sur la
vague, pendant que le pêcheur, plongeant de l'oeil au fond de
l'eau, cherche à apercevoir sa proie et à l'envelopper de son filet. Ces
feux, rouges comme des foyers de fournaise, se reflètent en longs
sillons ondoyants sur la nappe de la mer, comme les longues traînées
de lueurs qu'y projette le globe de la lune. L'ondoiement des vagues
les fait osciller et en prolonge l'éblouissement de lame en lame aussi
loin que la première vague la reflète aux vagues qui la suivent.*[8]

LAMARTINE, *op. cit.*

*Il y a tant de puces à Naples que c'est, je crois, ce que la Vénus
Callipyge y cherche.*

SAINTE-BEUVE, *Voyage en Italie* (1839)[9]

8. Night fishing is still carried on by these methods on the Tyrrhenian and
Adriatic coasts.
9. A notebook unpublished during Sainte-Beuve's lifetime.

*Vu Ischia, songé à Farcy, à Lamartine; impression triste, quant
à moi. Ischia me paraît aride; le volcan éteint, l'Epomée, a
jadis crevé par la base et a recouvert la plage d'informes
et hideuses scories; c'est laid. Ce volcan était en train de devenir
quelque chose, il a manqué sa fortune de volcan; il a fait long
feu.*

*A Ischia. Les lieux les plus vantés de la terre sont tristes et
désenchantés lorsqu'on n'y porte plus ses espérances. Tout golfe
de Baia y devient* il mare morto.

*Est-ce parce que j'ai été parricide pour Lamartine (tu
quoque fili – moi aussi, helas!) que ce golfe de Baia, si doux
pour lui, m'a paru amer? Combien j'éprouve le contraire de ce
que j'y voyais d'avance sur la foi de Lamartine! Cette côte est
déserte, aride, bouleversée, frappée de mort; la vie s'est déplacée,
elle est vis-à-vis sur l'autre plage, à Sorrento. A Baia, c'est la
ruine, l'abandon; la Jérusalem et la Sodome du golfe de Naples;
un air de désolation s'étend sur cette petite Babylone, les délices
du monde romain.*

SAINTE-BEUVE, *op. cit.*

*Ce soir, 31 mai, en descendant du Vésuve, à cinq heures et demie,
admirable vue du golfe: fines projections des îles sur une mer
blanche, sous un ciel un peu voilé; ineffable beauté! Découpures
élégantes: Capri sévère, Ischia prolongée, les bizarres et gracieux
chaînons de Procida; le cap Misène isolé avec sa langue de terre
mince et jolie, le château de l'Oeuf en petit l'imitant, le Pausilippe
entre eux doucement jeté; en tout un grand paysage de lointain
dessiné par Raphael – Oh! vivre là, y aimer quelqu'un et puis
mourir!*

SAINTE-BEUVE, *op. cit.*

There was an Old Person of Ischia,
Whose conduct grew friskier and friskier;
He danced hornpipes and jigs, and ate thousands of figs,
That lively Old Person of Ischia

EDWARD LEAR, *A Book of Nonsense* (1846)

When I left Naples, in February, the Baron Porcari was confined in the Maschio of Ischia. He was accused of a share in the Calabrian insurrection and was awaiting his trial. This Maschio is a dungeon without light, and 24 feet or palms (I am not sure which) below the level of the sea. He is never allowed to quit it day or night, and no one is permitted to visit him there, except his wife – once a fortnight.

GLADSTONE (source unknown)

Going on deck at sun-rise, I found the felucca contending with a head wind, but luckily in a smooth water. On our right lay high dark mountains thrown into picturesque forms, with shore lined with hamlets and towns. This was Ischia. Ahead was another island, of the same character, resembling a gigantic sea-wall thrown before the bay. This was Capri. On our left lay a small, low, level island, teeming with life; and to the north and east of us opened the glorious Bay of Naples . . .

J. FENIMORE COOPER, *Excursions in Italy* (1838)

I look, through a vista of five large rooms, by means of doors, directly at the panorama presented by Naples, which town lies directly across the bay, at the reputed distance of eighteen miles; though I see St Elmo so distinctly, that it appears not half so far. Of course, when

seated on the terrace, the view is infinitely more extended.
The sea limits it to the West. Ischia, dark, broken, and
volcanic, but softened by vegetation and the tints of this
luxurious atmosphere comes next; then Procida, low,
verdant and peopled. The misty abrupt bluff of Mycenum
is the first land on the continent, with the Elysian fields,
the port of the Roman galleys, and the "Hundred
Chambers". The site of delicious Baiae is pointed out by
the huge pile of castle that lies on the hill-side, and by
the ruined condition of all the neighbouring objects of
curiosity, such as the Sibyl's cave, the lake of Avernus, the
bridge or mole of Agrippa. Behind a little island called
Nisida, the bark of St Paul must have sailed when he
landed at Puteoli, on his way to Rome. The palace of
Queen Joan, the grotto of Pausilippo, the teeming city
and the bay dotted with sails, follow . . . and a pile of
dingy earth, or ashes, just marks the position of Pompeii.

J. FENIMORE COOPER, *op. cit.*

We hauled up to windward of Procida, sailing through
an element so limpid that we saw every rush and stone
on the bottom in five-fathom water. Having opened the
channel between the two islands, we bore up for the
town of Ischia, where we arrived a little before sunset.
Here a scene presented itself which more resembled a
fairy picture than one of the realities of this everyday
world of ours. I think it was the most ravishing thing, in
its way, eye of mine ever looked upon. We had the black
volcanic peaks of the island for a background, with
the ravine-like valleys and mountain-faces, covered with
country-houses and groves, in front. The town is near
the southern extremity of the land, and lies along the

shore for more than a mile on a bit of level formation; but, after passing a sort of bridge or terrace, which I took to be a public promenade, the rocks rose suddenly, and terminated in two or three lofty, fantastic, broken fragment-like crags, which make the south-eastern end of the island. On these rocks were perched some old castles, so beautifully wild and picturesque, that they seemed placed there for no other purpose than to adorn the landscape. By a curvature of the land, these rocks sheltered the roadstead, and the quaint old structures were brought almost to impend over our heads . . . Until that moment I was not fully sensible of the vast superiority of the Italian landscapes over all others. Switzerland astonishes, and it even often delights, by its union of the pastoral with the sublime; but Italian nature wins upon you until you come to love it like a friend . . . The effect is to pour a flood of sensations on the mind that are as distinct from the commoner feelings of wonder that are excited by vastness and magnificence, as the ideas awakened by an exquisite landscape by Claude are different from those we entertain in looking at a Salvator Rosa . . .

Our "attempts" to obtain lodgings at the town of Ischia were unsuccessful and we shaped our course for a villa on the coast two or three miles distant, where we were received. Our *coucher* was a little unsophisticated, most of the party using mattresses on the floor; but we had brought tea with us, and made a good supper.

Arrangements for the night were soon made . . . The idea of putting two people in the same bed, even if married, scarcely ever comes into the heads of the Europeans of the Continent, nearly every bedroom of

Moorish buildings, Porto d'Ischia

the least pretension, if intended for the use of two, having its two beds. I have seen double-beds in Italy, it is true; but they were as large as small houses. That peculiar sentiment of the Western American, who "wondered that any man should be such a hog as to wish a bed all to himself," appears never to have suggested itself to a people so destitute of "energy".

J. FENIMORE COOPER, op. cit.

On a summer evening in 1867, while he was at work on *Peer Gynt*, which is certainly the most Norwegian of all that he has written, he stood looking out upon the Italian island of Ischia. Suddenly he said: "Look at that fine hop-garden!" A Danish friend who was with him made the remark: "But it is not hops; it is grapes," and Ibsen corrected himself. "Yes, you are right! Now and then I have to pull my own ears to realise that I am not in Norway."

HALVDAN KOHT, The Life of Ibsen, 1931

FROM POZZUOLI

Nisida, Ischia dans le lointain, le cap Misène, ne ressemblent point à des êtres réels, mais à des ombres nobles sur le point d'arriver à la vie.

TAINE, Voyage en Italie (1866)

Here is an enchanting scene – the vision of the superlatively pretty towering city and island of Procida, resplendent in its flourishing verdure, scented in spring by the orange blossom, with its overhanging vines, from which comes a wine like a liqueur, with its famous channel dotted with white sails and furrowed by muscular oarsmen, presents itself, as the poet Gioviano Pontano has depicted it, like a Nymph who used as a mirror the calm waves of the sea. Three eminences raise it from its flatness as it lies softly extended and from these it took as its emblem three towers,[10] that is to say the Terra Murata, the Mozzo and the Cottino.

The seafront, that is divided into two long arms, one to the East and the other to the West, and affords the inhabitants pleasant walks during the summer months, and the abundance of houses of antique construction, partly rebuilt and restored, present a more pleasing picture than one might have formed on one's arrival for the first time. Especially at the times when the passenger steamers come and go, for they leave the port and return here in the evening hours, does it wear an imposing aspect, when it is full of passengers disembarking, of relatives, friends, customs officials and *finanzieri*,[11] the curious and the idle onlooker. The sea is very fertile in fish and all kinds of these are found off the shores of the island. There is abundance of fruit, the grapes are exceptionally sweet and the figs excellent, ripening remarkably soon; there is no lack of greenery and there are thistles, big artichokes and fennel, very palatable to eat. Its coastline, seven miles in circumference, with most delightful inlets and promontories because of which it seems here to advance and distend itself into the sea and there to flirt with the sea and retire, coupled with the salubriousness of its air, led Celestino Guicciardini, in his *Mercurio Campano*, to call it a well-formed garden. Procida is two

10. The crest of John of Procida.
11. Officials, similar to our coast guards.

miles from the continent and two from the island of Ischia, eight from Pozzuoli and fourteen from Naples. Both the poet Juvenal and Virgil pronounced it to be the most beautiful, the first preferring it to the city of Rome itself, the second saying that it was next to no other country.

M. PARASCANDOLA,
Procida dalle Origine ai Tempi Nostri (1893)

The lack of work has forced a whole colony of sailors to emigrate to Marseilles, Alexandria, Port Said, Buenos Aires, and it is my opinion that there is no part of the world where the Procidans have not pitched their tents in the quest for employment.

M. PARASCANDOLA, *op. cit.*

The town of Procida stretches up the slopes of the castle-hill from the seashore in the form of an amphitheatre, backed and interspersed with vineyards, orange groves, and fruit gardens. The houses, with their flat terraced roofs and external staircases, resemble the buildings of modern Greece . . . The island is richly cultivated with vineyards, and fruit gardens, which supply the markets of the Capital, and constitute a source of the prosperity of the inhabitants. The red wines are of a superior quality, but the chief industry is shipbuilding, some of the principal shipowners of S. Italy being natives of Procida. On Michaelmas Day and on the 8th of May the women dress up in Greek costume and dance the tarantella.

A Handbook for Travellers in Southern Italy and Sicily
Published by John Murray (1892)

Although the last flowers – purple asters – are faded,

clematis hangs blossoming over a wall, sun lies on the sea, and behind the sun, just opposite me, the outline of Capri can be seen beside the foothills of Sorrento . . . There is the bay, the occasional silhouette of oarsmen in lovely concentrated movement, and just that something which gives a boat its being; in the distance, sailing ships. Then the curve towards Posilippo, the whole margin looking as though it had just been flung out, and to the left the projecting castle, as if wrapped in a cloak or set in front of the sun like one of Rembrandt's figures. And strange the noises: the rapid trotting of little horses, the chattering of primitive wheels, the little bells on the horses' necks reproducing their trotting in miniature, cries in between, shouts, music, children's voices and cracking whips – everything strange even to the popping of the acorns under my feet in the little garden. If only it could go on, this being known by no-one.

RAINER MARIA RILKE,
Selected Letters 1902–26 (trans. R. F. C. Hull)

Returning home through Italy, we stopped four days at Naples. In her picturesque setting of the happiest combination of sea and mountain scenery, the inspirer of generations of poets and artists is also the Naples of the *lazzaroni*, the Eldorado of beggars, and as it struck us, of armies of well-fed priests.

MRS R. C. MORGAN,
Glimpses of Four Continents (1911)

Lucky the mortal who arrives on the summit of San Costanzo during one of those bewitching moments when the atmosphere is permeated with a glittering haze of floating particles, like powdered gold-dust. The view over the Gulf of Naples, at such times, with its contours framed in a luminous aureole rather than limned, is not easily forgotten. They are rare, and their glory of brief duration. On other occasions this fairy-like effect is atoned for by the clarity; not only Siren land, but half Campania, lies at our feet. Far away, the sinuous outlines of Tyrrhenian shores with the headland of Circe and the Ponza islets that call up grim memories of Roman banishments; the complex and serrated Apennines whose peaks are visible into the far Abruzzi country; nearer at hand, Elysian Fields, Tartarus and Cimmerian gloom, and the smoking head of Vesuvius decked with a coral necklace of towns and villages. Not an inch of all this landscape but has its associations. Capua and Hannibal; the Caudine Forks; Misenum and Virgil; Nisida, the retreat of a true Siren-worshipper, Lucullus; the venerable acropolis of Cumae; Pompeii; yonder Puteoli, where the apostle of the gentiles touched land; here the Amalfitan coast, Paestum, and the Calabrian hills.

And everywhere the unharvested sea. The sea, with its intense restfulness, is the dominant note of Siren land. There is no escaping from it. Incessant gleams of light flash from that mirror-like expanse; even when unperceived by the senses, among squalid tenements or leafy uplands, they will find you out and follow, like some all-pervading, inevitable melody. How the *Odyssey* throbs with those luminous vibrations! Forest voices are the music of Bach; we seem to wander in cool wooded glades with sunlight pouring through leaves overhead, to breathe the fragrance of dew-spangled moss and fern, to hear the caress of light winds playing among the crowns and the rustling of branches and streamlets and all those elfish woodland notes which the master himself, in his solitary wanderings, had heard and thenceforth imprisoned everlastingly – coaxing their echoes into those numbers whose enchantment none but chosen spirits, little less than angels, can unseal. Some are of multiple voice, like that god-gifted Tchaikovsky, whose melancholy is flecked by exotic passions such as Mozart or Beethoven never sang – for how shall that come out of a man which was never in him? – lilting, supersensuous measures from old Samarkand where they loved with the love of daemons; muffled pulsations, oft-repeated, doom-enforcing; or an ominous metallic quaver – the wail of the myriad Tartars, who fell by the blood-stained waters of Tengis, or, it may be, some premonitory cry of his own tormented soul that fled from earth, all too soon.

Others may reflect the camp or court. But Homer voices the sea . . .

NORMAN DOUGLAS, *Siren Land* (1911)

Try also that [the wine] of Ischia. As a *vino da pasto*, it is surpassed by none south of Rome; indeed, it is drunk all the world over (under other names), and a pretty sight it is to see the many-shaped craft from foreign ports jostling each other in the little circular harbour, one of the few pleasing mementoes of Bourbonism. Try it, therefore, through every degree of latitude on the island, from the golden torrents of thousand-vatted Forio up to the pale primrose-hued ichor, a drink for the gods, that oozes in unwilling drops out of the dwarfed mountain grapes.

Large heart in small grape.

Try also the red kinds.

Try them all, over and over again. Such, at least, was
the advice of a Flemish gentleman whom I met, in bygone
years, at Casamicciola. Like most of his countrymen,
mynheer had little *chiaroscuro* in his composition; he
was prone to call a spade a spade; but his "rational view
of life", as he preferred to define it, was transfigured and
irradiated by a childlike love of nature. "Where there is
no landscape", he used to say, "there I sit (i.e. drink)
without pleasure. Only beasts sit indoors." Every morning
he went in search of new farmhouses in which to *sit*
during the afternoon and evening. And every night,
with tremendous din, he was carried to bed. He never
apologized for this disturbance; it was his yearly holiday,
he explained. He must have possessed an enviable
digestion, for he was up with the lark and I used to hear
him at his toilette, singing strange ditties of Meuse or
Scheldt. Breakfast over, he would sally forth on his daily
quest, thirsty and sentimental as ever. One day, I remember,
he discovered a cottage more seductive than all the
rest – "with a view over Vesuvius and the coastline – a view,
I assure you, of entrancing loveliness!" That evening he
never came home at all.

NORMAN DOUGLAS, *op. cit.*

A few years ago I witnessed on Ischia a case more pathetic
than this one . . . Coming back with Norman [Douglas]
from a bathe at San Montana beach, we entered the
village of Lacco Ameno – not by the main road but by one
of the little alleys that branch off to the left of it, at the
back of the church. At this point are some fairly big
houses, shattered in the earthquake of 1883 and since

then not repaired. There, in a niche in one of them – a niche that had presumably contained the statue of some saint – sat a very old woman, all huddled up. The niche was higher than our heads, and there was just room for her inside it. A terrifying apparition: the nearest approach to a witch that ever I hope to see! She was dressed in black; white hair came tumbling over her tawny and wrinkled face, and her eyes at once fixed themselves upon us. Her right hand was held to her ear as if she listened to something. What was she listening to? She might have been waiting to hear what she heard in 1883 – the music of the Singing Stone, which heralded that particular earthquake as it had heralded others, and about which a Danish writer, Bergsoe, has written a short story. The *Pietra Cantante* legend, now perhaps forgotten, was an article of faith among the common people in that year and earlier days. They believed that if a certain pinnacle of rock, visible from Casamicciola, gave forth its sad and long-drawn wail, an earthquake was at hand.

There was a fisherman about fifty yards further on . . . I went to him for information. "Was she in the earthquake?" "That old woman? Yes; and they pulled her out alive, but her husband was killed. They had just been married. Then she went mad. You see her, up there? That's where she likes to be. She is so old, we have to humour her. And she always sleeps out of doors; she won't trust any house, not even the new huts of wood. *Povera vecchia*; she won't last much longer. And the worst of it is, when the wind blows hard, she thinks it is something else, and begins screaming furiously and frightening everybody in the place."

G. ORIOLI, *Moving Along* (1934)

Ischia in 1944

On March the 19th Vesuvius erupted
And they pulled in the guns from the neighbouring
　　airfields.
The GOR was at Torre Annunziata
When a cloud of purplish dust settled over everything
(The lava at night was the sight of the century
But could not be mentioned in letters because of
　　security)
Drifting south to Salerno and Sicily,
Sticking in the hair, gritty on the teeth
Inches thick on the ground – and the Major
Was given a rocket by a REME inspectorate
Because of the filthy state of the transport.

I was given leave in the middle of April –
Brigade had two vacancies for a hotel on Ischia –
For 48 hours. I went with the Signals Officer.
Sunlight on the water and the Porto d'Ischia,
Gay with the Air Sea Rescue launches.
We could easily hear the guns on the mainland,
As the Allies waited to cross the river,
Like dogs barking but afraid of the water
(Too many rivers on the way up Italy).

It was quiet and hot on a hillside of fireflies
Under Epomeo. We had Army rations
Which the hotel cooked disdainfully –

Too poor to afford the supplementary lobsters
The Americans ordered at a dollar a time.
However, we were merry on white wine from Epomeo,
The Signals Officer not being used to drinking.
Later we went down to the town, where the locals
Had barred their doors against drunkenness of the
    troops.
Some ORs were wearing Service Dress hats of straw
Made by the inhabitants, like ridiculous boaters.

After bathing and climbing the ruins of the fortress
Next day, we decided to return to Naples.
Our food was running out and our lack of money
Lowering our prestige in the eyes of the Italians,
Who gave farewell roses to the American nurses.

From the steamer landing, the vicious life of Naples
Seemed infinitely promising, Ischia more fruitful
Terrain for a mistress or a serious honeymoon.

GAVIN EWART (1944)

Please visit the Harvill Press website at

www.harvill.com